Memory Reconsolidation in Psychotherapy

THE NEUROPSYCHOTHERAPIST
SPECIAL ISSUE

Edited by Matthew Dahlitz & Geoff Hall

Chapters in this edition have previously been published in *The Neuropsychotherapist*.

For information about content reproduction write to: Permissions, The Neuropsychotherapist, PO Box 1030, Park Ridge, QLD, 4125, Australia.
Alternatively email editor@neuropsychotherapist.com

Editor-in-Chief: Matthew Dahlitz
Associate Editor: Geoff Hall

Cover image: ktsdesign/Bigstockphoto.com

Title: Memory Reconsolidation in Psychotherapy: The Neuropsychotherapist Special Issue.

ISBN-13: 978-1506004341 (paperback)
ISBN-10: 1506004342

1. Psychotherapy. 2. Memory Reconsolidation. 3. Neuroscience. 4. Brain-based therapy. 5. Neuropsychotherapy.

Printed in the United States of America

NEUROPSYCHOTHERAPIST.COM

Preface

How often can we say therapy has been a categorical success? Welcome to our special issue on memory reconsolidation (MR)—a foundational process with the potential, if properly understood, to consistently bring about the kind of transformational change that we look for in the lives of clients. Featured in this issue is Bruce Ecker, one of the foremost experts in applying techniques that fulfil the neurobiological requirements to achieve MR in clinical practice. In fact all of the authors in this issue are experts in their respective fields, demonstrating the unifying nature of MR in such diverse therapies as the Alexander technique, energy psychology, neuro-linguistic programming, and progressive counting. Understanding the biological basis of our memory and how it can be modified is the key to effective therapeutic change, especially when emotional memories are driving unwanted symptoms.

In putting together this special issue I would like to acknowledge Bruce Ecker for his decades of study, observation, and subsequent articulation of what is behind our clients' pathology—or rather, their adaptive schemata that are no longer so adaptive—and what we, as therapists, can do about it in a definitive way. Equipped with academic rigour and experience from his first career as a research physicist, Bruce has been able to tease out, from densely technical accounts of neuroscientific studies, the essence of memory reconsolidation for psychotherapy. Not only has he crystalised this theory for psychotherapy but he has applied it himself over many years of clinical practice to develop what he calls coherence therapy. This therapeutic approach, co-developed with Laurel Hulley, clearly demonstrates the tranformationally powerful effects of memory reconsolidation and paves the way for many different modalities to realise a common mechanism of change during therapy. It is my hope that this special issue will inspire you to explore your own ways of recognising and capitalising on the process of memory reconsolidation for transformational change in your clients.

Matthew Dahlitz
Brisbane
January 2015

Contents

A PRIMER ON MEMORY RECONSOLIDATION AND ITS PSYCHOTHERAPEUTIC USE AS A CORE PROCESS OF PROFOUND CHANGE

by Bruce Ecker, Robin Ticic, and Laurel Hulley

Emotional learnings underlie and drive the vast majority of unwanted behaviors, emotions, thoughts and somatization addressed in psychotherapy. For example, consider a man in his early 40s suffering from pervasive social anxiety, who seeks relief in therapy. He is guided by the therapist to bring attention into what he is actually experiencing emotionally and somatically when among people, and for the first time in his life he becomes explicitly aware of expecting harsh rejection from others if he were to "say or do anything wrong." This previously non-conscious but fear-generating expectation had wordlessly defined the world of people for as long as he could remember. His emotional brain had learned this implicit model of how human beings respond from many, many frightening interactions with his explosively angry, rejecting father in childhood, plus a few sizable reinforcements by two schoolteachers, male and female.

His autobiographical memory and conscious narratives contained much about suffering his father's anger, but nothing about the generalized model that he carried into all social situations, so his social anxiety had been for him a mysterious affliction. With the shift from implicit to explicit knowing of what he had learned to expect, his anxiety now made deep sense to him as the emotion that naturally accompanied his living knowledge of how people respond. These learned constructs had never appeared in his conscious experience of anxiety. Such implicit constructs and models formed in emotional learning are well-defined, yet rarely show up in conscious experience themselves, much as a colored lens just in front of the eye is not itself visible.

A vast range of miseries is maintained by non-conscious emotional learnings, such as depression that is really the deeply forlorn state of having learned from cold, critical parents that one is unworthy of love. Being completely unaware of one's own most life-shaping learnings is remarkably commonplace. Unfading across the decades, emotional learnings display an inherent tenacity that is the bane of psychotherapists and their clients, yet this extraordinary durability appears

Adapted for *The Neuropsychotherapist* from **Unlocking the Emotional Brain: Eliminating Symptoms at Their Roots Using Memory Reconsolidation** by Bruce Ecker, Robin Ticic and Laurel Hulley. Routledge, 2012 to be a survival-positive result of natural selection, which crafted the brain such that any learning that occurs in the presence of strong emotion—such as core beliefs, constructs and coping tactics formed in the midst of childhood suffering— becomes locked into subcortical implicit memory circuits by special synapses (see for example LeDoux, Romanski & Xagoraris, 1989; McGaugh, 1989; McGaugh & Roozendaal, 2002; Roozendaal, McEwen, & Chattarji, 2009).

And it appeared that natural selection had not created a key for that synaptic lock. After more than 60 years of research on the extinction of acquired responses in animals and humans, neuroscientists had concluded by 1989 that the *consolidation* of a learning in emotional memory was a one-way street, making consolidated learnings indelible, unerasable, for the lifetime of the individual. Acquired emotional responses could certainly be suppressed temporarily in various ways, such as when an exposure procedure suppresses fear learnings through the process of extinction, or through methods of affective regulation (for example, teaching relaxation techniques to counteract anxiety or building up resources and positive thoughts to counteract depression). However, the research had shown that such counteractive measures do not actually dissolve or erase the original, problematic emotional learning (Bouton, 2004; Foa & McNally, 1996; Milner, Squire, & Kandel, 1998; Phelps, Delgado, Nearing, & LeDoux, 2004). Rather, they only create a second, preferred learning that competes against and can regulate or override an unwanted response under ideal conditions, but usually not for long under real-life conditions. Relapses are almost inevitable, particularly in new or stressful situations. No wonder therapists and clients often feel they are struggling against some unrelenting but invisible force.

Indelibility implied that despite their limitations, counteractive methods were the only possible psychotherapeutic strategy for reducing symptoms based in emotional memory. Their extreme durability makes negative emotional learnings one of the biggest causes of suffering in human life, and it seemed we were forever stuck with them.

The Reconsolidation Breakthrough

From 1997 to 2000, however, a major breakthrough occurred in our understanding of how emotional memory works. Several studies by neuroscientists showed that the brain does come equipped with a key to those locked synapses after all (Nader, Schafe, & LeDoux, 2000; Przybyslawski, Roullet, & Sara, 1999; Przybyslawski & Sara, 1997; Roullet & Sara, 1998; Sara, 2000; Sekiguchi, Yamada, & Suzuki, 1997). Working with animals, researchers had reactivated a target emotional learning and then found that its locked neural circuit had temporarily shifted back into an unlocked, de-consolidated, labile, destabilized or plastic state, which allowed the learning to be completely nullified, along with behavioral responses it had been driving. The labile circuit soon consolidates once again, returning it to a locked condition, which is why researchers named this newly discovered type of neuroplasticity *memory reconsolidation*. (The term "reconsolidation" is used by neuroscientists in two ways, however. It can denote the relocking of synapses in the final step of the natural process of synaptic unlocking and relocking, but it can also refer to the overall process of unlocking, revising and then relocking the synapses encoding a specific memory. The intended meaning is usually clear from the context.)

The pivotal research that guides use of reconsolidation in psychotherapy came when Argentinian neuroscientists Pedreira, Pérez-Cuesta and Maldonado (2004) showed that memory reactivation alone was not sufficient for unlocking the synapses encoding a target learning. They identified a critical experience, described below, that is required in addition to the experience of reactivation in order to unlock a target learning. This full map of the brain's built-in process for unlocking an emotional learning, allowing new learning to fundamentally unlearn, rewrite and eliminate it during the labile period, is of momentous significance for the psychotherapy field.

It's now clear that the consolidation of emotional memory is not, as had been believed for a century, a one-time, final process, and that emotional learnings are not indelible. Rather, neural circuits encoding an emotional learning can be returned to a de-consolidated state, allowing erasure by new learnings before a relocking—or reconsolidation—takes place. Counteracting and regulating unwanted acquired responses is *not* the best one can do because emotional learnings can be dissolved, not just suppressed. (There are, however, certain clinical situations, including severe crises and emergencies, in which use of counteractive methods remains primary.)

Neuroscientists have also shown that after a learned emotional response has been eliminated through the reconsolidation process, the individual still remembers the experiences in which the response was acquired—as well as the fact of having had the response—but the emotional response itself is no longer re-evoked by remembering those experiences. This finding that *autobiographical* memory is not impaired by erasure of a piece of emotional memory reflects the well established anatomical separateness of different types of memory, which allows erasure of a specific emotional learning stored in an emotional implicit memory network without affecting the contents of autobiographical, narrative memory stored in a neocortical, explicit memory network.

The critical sequence of experiences identified by Pedreira et al. was subsequently confirmed by many other studies (see listing in Ecker, Ticic & Hulley, 2012). The use of this sequence with human subjects can be seen in controlled studies that eliminated operant conditioning in infants (Galluccio, 2005), classical fear conditioning (Schiller, Monfils, Raio, Johnson, LeDoux & Phelps, 2010), and cue-triggered heroin cravings (Xue et al., 2012).

Psychotherapists in the early 1990's had identified the same sequence of critical experiences, culling it from many observations of profound change events in therapy, that is, events resulting in permanent cessation of a longstanding emotional response and associated symptoms (Ecker & Hulley, 1996, 2000a, 2000b). Ecker and Hulley developed the sequence into a therapeutic methodology (now known as Coherence Therapy, formerly Depth Oriented Brief Therapy) and have observed its effectiveness for dispelling a wide range of symptoms and problems at their emotional roots (see Table 1). That this methodology was capable of dissolving acquired, implicit emotional schemas was later fortuitously corroborated by reconsolidation research.

It is clear, though, that no single school of psychotherapy "owns" the process that induces memory reconsolidation because it is a universal process, inherent in the brain. We believe this process is often carried out in quite a few psychotherapies of transformational change (see Table 2), even though in most of these the steps of

Table 1
Symptoms observed dispelled by the reconsolidation process as carried out in Coherence Therapy*

Symptoms Dispelled	
Aggressive behavior	Food/eating/weight problems
Agoraphobia	Grief and bereavement problems
Alcohol abuse	Guilt
Anger and rage	Hallucinations
Anxiety	Inaction
Attachment-pattern behaviors & distress	Indecision
Attention deficit problems	Low self-worth
Codependency	Panic attacks
Complex trauma symptomology	Perfectionism
Compulsive behaviors of many kinds	Post-traumatic symptoms
Couples' problems of conflict/communication/closeness	Procrastination
	Psychogenic/psychosomatic pain
Depression	Sexual problems
Family and child problems	Underachieving
Fidgeting	Voice and speaking problems

*An online bibliography of published case examples indexed by symptom is available at http://www.coherencetherapy.org/files/ct-case-index.pdf

Table 2
Some of the focused, experiential, in-depth psychotherapies that are congenial to fulfilling the therapeutic reconsolidation process
Psychotherapy
Accelerated Experiential Dynamic Psychotherapy (AEDP)
Coherence Therapy* (formerly Depth Oriented Brief Therapy*)
Eye Movement Desensitization and Reprocessing (EMDR)*
Emotion-Focused Therapy (EFT)*
Focusing-Oriented Psychotherapy
Gestalt Therapy
Hakomi
Internal Family Systems Therapy (IFS)
Interpersonal Neurobiology (IPNB)*
Neuro-Linguistic Programming (NLP)
Traumatic Incident Reduction (TIR)
* Therapies for which reconsolidation has been cited as mechanism of change in publications by founders or leading exponents (see text)

the reconsolidation process are not explicitly identified within the therapy system's own set of concepts, terms and methods. However, carrying out the steps of the process *knowingly* can significantly increase a practitioner's frequency of achieving powerful therapeutic results, as we have seen in the course of many years of training work.

Memory reconsolidation is the only known form of neuroplasticity capable of deleting an emotional learning, so we may infer that the requisite steps must have taken place whenever therapy of any kind yields a lasting disappearance of a long-standing response pattern. With clear knowledge of the brain's own rules for deleting emotional learnings through memory reconsolidation, therapists no longer have to rely largely on speculative theory, intuition or luck for facilitating powerful, liberating shifts.

Neuroscientists verify erasure of an emotional learning by observing these distinctive markers of change:

- *Non-reactivation:* A specific emotional reaction abruptly and lastingly can no longer be reactivated by cues and triggers that formerly did so or by other stressful situations.

- *Symptom cessation:* Symptoms of behavior, emotion, somatics or thought that were expressions of that emotional reaction also disappear permanently.

- *Effortless permanence:* Non-recurrence of the emotional reaction and symptoms continues without counteractive or preventative measures of any kind.

In therapy too, these are the all-important markers of transformational change—the ideal result of therapy—as distinct from incremental change through counteractive methods that compete against, but do not actually eliminate, the emotional roots of the person's symptoms. (For more extensive discussion of counteractive versus transformational change, see Toomey & Ecker, 2009.) According to current neuroscience, whenever these markers are observed and firmly established in clinical work, erasure via reconsolidation is a valid inference. On the basis of that logic, proponents of several psychotherapies of transformational change have inferred that reconsolidation must be the neurobiological mechanism of change induced by their methods: Coherence Therapy (Ecker, 2006, 2008; Ecker & Hulley, 2011; Ecker & Toomey, 2008), Emotion-Focused Therapy or EFT (Greenberg, 2010, 2012), exposure with acupoint tapping (Feinstein, 2010), Eye Movement Desensitization and Reprocessing or EMDR (Solomon & Shapiro, 2008), Interpersonal Neurobiology or IPNB (Badenoch, 2011), and psychoanalytic therapy (Gorman & Roose, 2011). In addition, the demonstrated effectiveness of an imaginal reenactment protocol for dispelling post-traumatic symptoms has been attributed to reconsolidation (Högberg, Nardo, Hällström & Pagani, 2011).

How Reconsolidation Works

Reconsolidation has been demonstrated with nematodes, honeybees, snails, sea slugs, fish, crabs, chicks, mice, rats and humans, for a wide range of different types of emotional learning and memory as well as for non-emotional memory, such as motor memory and semantic (factual) memory, corresponding to memory networks in many different anatomical regions of the brain (reviewed in Nader & Einarsson, 2010). For clinical purposes, however, we are concerned mainly with emotional memory, so our discussion of reconsolidation is focused in that area. Happily, it isn't necessary for therapists to consider details of brain anatomy because the sequence of experiences that launches reconsolidation is the same for all regions and types of memory studied.

Requirements for de-consolidation: reactivation plus mismatch. As noted above, researchers' early inference that memory reactivation alone destabilizes a memory's neural circuits was overturned in 2004 by the demonstration, in an animal study, that in order for de-consolidation to occur, a critical additional experience must take place while the memory is still reactivated (Pedreira et al., 2004). This second experience consists of perceptions that vividly mismatch—that is, deviate saliently from—what the reactivated target memory expects and predicts about how the world functions. Many subsequent studies also have demonstrated this requirement of mismatch for inducing de-consolidation (summarized by Ecker et al., 2012). Interestingly, the mismatch can be either a full contradiction and disconfirmation of the target memory or a novel, salient variation relative to the target memory.

If the target memory is reactivated by familiar cues but not concurrently mismatched, synapses do not unlock and reconsolidation is not induced (e.g., Cammarota, Bevilaqua, Medina & Izquierdo, 2004; Hernandez & Kelley, 2004; Mileusnic, Lancashire & Rose, 2005).

In an article reviewing the research, Lee (2009, p. 417) wrote, "It is not simply that memory reactivation must differ in some manner to conditioning.... Instead, reconsolidation is triggered by a violation of expectation based upon prior learning, whether such a violation is qualitative (the outcome not occurring at all) or quantitative (the magnitude of the outcome not being fully predicted)." Lee proposed that "the existence of a prediction error signal [from some brain region] might be a crucial pre-requisite for reconsolidation to be triggered" (p. 419).

Despite the many demonstrations that reactivation alone does not induce reconsolidation, the early, premature conclusion that an emotional memory unlocks with every reactivation continues to be promulgated by science journalists and even some neuroscientists. They appear to be unaware of the well-established mismatch requirement, which may reflect the not uncommon time lag for widespread recognition of all findings in any rapidly emerging, complex field.

Reconsolidation window. After a target learning has been reactivated and mismatched, its neural circuits remain in a de-consolidated or labile state for about five hours, as demonstrated by a variety of animal and human studies (Duvarci & Nader, 2004; Pedreira, Pérez-Cuesta & Maldonado, 2002; Pedreira & Maldonado, 2003; Schiller et al., 2010; Walker, Brakefield, Hobson & Stickgold, 2003). It is during this "reconsolidation window" that the target learning is directly revisable by new learning and can be radically unlearned and, as a result, no longer exist in emotional memory (without impairing autobiographical memory). After five hours the labile neural circuits naturally reconsolidate and can no longer be altered by new learning, until reactivation and mismatch experiences are again created.

Precision of erasure. When a de-consolidated memory is unlearned and erased, erasure is limited to precisely the reactivated target learning, without impairing other closely linked emotional learnings that have not been directly reactivated. This was shown both in an animal study using chemically induced erasure (Debiec, Doyère, Nader, & LeDoux, 2006) and in a human study using endogenous, behavioral erasure (Schiller et al., 2010). Likewise, Kindt, Soeter, and Vervliet (2009) demonstrated in a human study that erasure of a learned fear did not impair autobiographical memory of the experiences in which subjects had acquired the conditioned fear response.

Reconsolidation versus extinction. Researchers have shown that reconsolidation and extinction are neurologically distinct processes (Duvarci & Nader, 2004; Duvarci, Mamou, & Nader, 2006) and that they can occur either entirely independently of each other or simultaneously with a complex interaction. As noted earlier, it's well established that extinction training forms a separate learning in a physically separate memory system from that of the target learning, and that the extinction learning competes against, but does not unlearn or replace, the target learning. In contrast, reconsolidation allows a new learning to act upon the target learning directly, erasing it if the new learning contradicts and disconfirms the original learning.

Some studies have used a protocol identical to extinction training during the reconsolidation window to create the new learning that contradicts and erases the target learning (e.g., Monfils, Cowansage, Klan & LeDoux, 2009; Quirk et al., 2010; Schiller et al., 2010; Xue et al., 2012). Robust, long-lasting erasure is observed to result, so it is apparent that the *neurological* effect created by this special use of "extinction training" is not extinction (the creation of a separate, competing learning) but rather erasure via reconsolidation (the updating of the target learning by the contradictory learning). If, however, the same protocol is applied after the window has closed, only extinction results. Thus a particular behavioral learning procedure can have quite different neurological effects and behavioral consequences depending on whether or not it is carried out during the reconsolidation window. "Reconsolidation cannot be reduced down to facilitated extinction" was the conclusion of the study by Duvarci and Nader (2004, p. 9269). When the procedure traditionally termed "extinction training" is applied during the reconsolidation window and the result is unambiguously not extinction, the procedure in that instance could more appropriately be labeled "memory update training" rather than "extinction training" to avoid conceptual errors and confusion. Indeed, the beauty of the reconsolidation window is that during that window, to unlearn is to erase.

However, the century-old, deeply familiar label of "extinction" has tenaciously stuck with this protocol even in the situation just described where it does not produce extinction. Researchers (and science journalists) typically refer to this procedure as, for example, "extinction-induced erasure," "extinction training during reconsolidation," the "memory retrieval-extinction procedure," and "erasing fear memories with extinction training." We describe this potentially misleading situation here so that our readers may be spared some unnecessary confusion. The extinction training protocol is well suited to research requirements because of its simple, well-defined structured, but it is only one of a potentially unlimited number of forms in which new learning may occur during the reconsolidation window.

Utilizing Memory Reconsolidation in Psychotherapy

Summarizing the discussion above, we now know, from both reconsolidation research and clinical observations, that the behavioral process of transformational change of an existing emotional learning—following the brain's rules for unlearning and erasing a target learning—consists of these three steps:

1. **Reactivate.** Re-trigger/re-evoke the target knowledge by presenting salient cues or contexts from the original learning.

2. **Mismatch/unlock.** With reactivation occurring, create an experience that is significantly at variance with the target learning's model and expectations of how the world functions. This step unlocks synapses and renders memory circuits labile, i.e., susceptible to being updated by new learning.

3. **Erase or revise via new learning.** During a window of about five hours before synapses have relocked, create a new learning experience that contradicts (for erasing) or supplements (for revising) the labile target knowledge. (This new learning experience may be the same as or different from the experience used for mismatch in step 2; if it is the same, step 3 consists of repetitions of step 2.)

4. After this three-step sequence, researchers also conduct an erasure verification step consisting of behavioral tests that determine whether the markers of erasure, listed above, are observed. We refer to this as step V (for verification) and carry it out in therapy also.

Steps 1-2-3 above, which we call the *transformation sequence*, appears to have the potential for a significant enhancement of the practice of psychotherapy, because it is the brain's built-in core process for transformational change of acquired responses. Importantly, this sequence is a series of experiences defined without reference to specific techniques for bringing about those experiences. This means that in its application to psychotherapy, it can be carried out by therapists using their own choices of experiential techniques from a range of possibilities that may well be limited only by the inventiveness of therapists. The erasure sequence is a theory-independent, universal meta-process, and as such it can richly foster integration within the psychotherapy field. In *Unlocking the Emotional Brain* we examine case studies from five different experiential psychotherapies with methods that differ greatly from one another—AEDP, Coherence Therapy, EMDR, EFT and IPNB—

and we show that all three steps of the transformation sequence are detectable in the implementation of each therapy and appear to be responsible for the effectiveness of each in bringing about transformational change (Ecker et al., 2012). This sequence, therefore, may serve as a cross-platform map and shared language with which practitioners, researchers and clinical teachers and trainers can understand and communicate about diverse psychotherapies in a unified, meaningful manner.

Dwell with us for a moment on the "new learning" that serves to rewrite and erase the target learning in step 3 above. Quite differing forms of new learning have been used in the many research studies of endogenous reconsolidation. For clinical use, what is clear is that the new learning must feel decisively *real* to the person based on his or her own living experience. In other words, it must be experiential learning as distinct from conceptual, intellectual learning, though it may be accompanied by the latter. It is often extremely useful to guide new learning experiences in imagination, taking advantage of the fact that the emotional brain hardly distinguishes between imaginally and physically enacted experiences (as demonstrated empirically by, for example, Kreiman, Koch & Fried, 2000).

Carrying out each step of the transformation sequence requires detailed knowledge of the target emotional learning, but a psychotherapist is of course initially completely in the dark about that with each new client. Neuroscientists, in contrast, know all details of the target learning because in a reconsolidation study they first create the emotional learning to be erased. Instilling that learning in subjects occurs on day 1 of any given lab study. Then, on day 2, they make use of their knowledge of the target learning in every step of the three-step process of erasure—reactivation of the target learning; creation of an experience of mismatch of the target learning; and creation of an experience of new learning that contradicts and rewrites (and thereby erases the content of) the target learning. Researchers could not carry out these crucial three steps for erasure if they did not know the specific content of the target learning.

It follows, then, that in therapy some preparational steps are necessary in order to gain access to the ingredients needed for following the recipe of the transformation sequence. The ingredients that have to be gathered by the therapist from the client are accurate knowledge of (A) the specific symptoms to be dispelled, (B) the specific emotional learnings generating those symptoms, and (C) experiences that vividly contradict those emotional learnings. As soon as those three items are in hand, the transformation sequence is then carried out.

As a rule, the emotional learnings maintaining a therapy client's symptoms are not conscious at the start of therapy, and they are areas of deep vulnerability and some complexity. *Retrieving* them into explicit awareness for step B typically constitutes the majority of the therapeutic work. Various psychotherapies (see Table 2)

Table 3 Steps of Process for Clinical Application of Memory Reconsolidation	
Therapeutic Reconsolidation Process	
I. Accessing sequence (preparation)	A. Symptom identification B. Retrieval of target learning (symptom-requiring schema) C. Identification of disconfirming knowledge
II. Transformation sequence	1. Reactivation of symptom-requiring schema (B) 2. Activation of disconfirming knowledge (C), mismatching symptom-requiring schema (B) 3. Repetitions of (B)-(C) pairing
III. Verification	V. Observations of: --Emotional non-reactivation --Symptom cessation --Effortless permanence

have developed specialized, focused methods for this in-depth retrieval work, and often it can be carried out in just a few sessions—and sometimes in only one or two sessions—though of course the number of sessions increases commensurate with the complexity and severity of the case.

On the basis of knowing the specific makeup of the client's retrieved, underlying learning, the therapist then begins step C, the task of *finding* a vivid, contradictory experience to be used both for mismatch in step 2 of the transformation sequence and for new learning in step 3. Finding mismatch material means finding living knowledge from the client's own experience or creating a new experience that contradicts the target learning. Either can serve as knowledge that contradicts, rewrites and eradicates the target learning.

Thus in the clinical situation, a preparatory process consisting of the following three steps is needed initially in order to carry out the transformation sequence identified in reconsolidation research:

A. Symptom identification. Actively clarify with the client *what* to regard as the presenting symptom(s)—the specific behaviors, somatics, emotions, and/or thoughts that the client wants to eliminate—and *when* they happen, that is, the percepts and contexts that evoke or intensify them. This information is needed for embarking upon step B efficiently.

B. Retrieval of target learning. Retrieve into explicit awareness, as a visceral emotional experience, the details of the emotional learning or schema underlying and driving the presenting symptom. Knowledge of this material in turn allows the therapist to carry out step C, identification of disconfirming knowledge.

C. Identification of disconfirming knowledge. Identify a vivid experience (past or present) that can serve as living knowledge that is fundamentally incompatible with the model of reality in the target emotional learning retrieved in step B, such that both cannot possibly be true. The disconfirming material may or may not be appealing to the client as being more "positive" or preferred; what matters is that it be mutually exclusive, ontologically, with the target learning. It may be already part of the client's personal knowledge or may be created by a new experience. It will be used to carry out step 2 of the erasure sequence—the mismatch that destabilizes the target learning.

By systematically seeing to the fulfillment of the seven steps, A-B-C-1-2-3-V, therapists can bring about liberating therapeutic shifts with optimum efficiency and consistency. We refer to the full seven-step sequence as the *therapeutic reconsolidation process* (see Table 3).

Case Illustration

Our example of the man with social anxiety can illustrate how the process unfolds, though here only a brief sketch is possible. (For detailed case studies, see Ecker et al., 2012.) The therapist in this case was a practitioner of Coherence Therapy, which has a methodology that explicitly guides steps A-B-C-1-2-3-V (Ecker & Hulley, 2011).

The man initially described his problem as feeling tense, anxious, tight and held-back whenever he was among people, with a long list of unhappy results in his life. This was enough of step A, symptom identification, to begin step B, the retrieval of the coherent emotional learnings that were necessitating his anxiety around people. Revisiting a specific recent instance, the therapist said, "Some part of you seems to know something about how it isn't safe around people. You're aware of feeling tightly held back from expressing yourself, so see if you can let this part of you that knows and feels the jeopardy finish this sentence, without pre-thinking it: 'I better not just say whatever's on my mind here, because if I did—.'" What arose spontaneously to finish the sentence wasn't words; it was the image of his father spewing anger. The therapist asked, "Was it with him that you learned it wasn't safe to express yourself?" He then described a childhood riddled with bullets of harsh, piercing anger from his father. Dad would bellow, for example, "How can you be so *stupid!*" over even the smallest of mistakes. By the end of his first session, with the therapist's facilitation the client was lucidly feeling and verbalizing his previously non-conscious knowledge that "If my own dad hates me and rejects me for doing or saying anything wrong, then everyone else will too, because I'm too stupid to be accepted or loved, and that's terrifying for me, and my only safety is in holding everything back and staying as unnoticed and invisible as I possibly can."

Once retrieved from implicit to explicit knowing, this material may seem obvious, but it was very new and emotional for this man to face and feel it. The therapist wrote those words on an index card and handed it to him for daily reading between sessions—a task of integration of this newly discovered emotional schema, or what is called the *emotional truth of the symptom* in Coherence Therapy, into everyday, conscious awareness.

Emotional learning consists of much more than stored memory of the "raw data" of what one's senses were registering and what emotions one was experiencing during an original experience. Also learned—in implicit memory—is a constructed *mental model*, or schema, of how the world functions, which is the individual's abstracting and generalizing of the raw data of perception and emotion (Held, Vosgerau & Knauff, 2006; Siegel, 1999). This model is created and stored with no awareness of doing so. It does not exist in words, but is no less well-defined or coherent for that. The emotional brain thereafter actively uses this model or schema for self-protectively *anticipating* similar experiences in the future and recognizing them instantly when, according to the model or schema, they appear to be occurring. Emotional memory converts the past into an expectation of the future, without our awareness, and that is both a blessing and a curse. It is a blessing because we rely daily on emotional implicit memory to navigate deftly through all sorts of situations without having to go through the slow, labor-intensive process of figuring out, conceptually and verbally, what to do; we simply know what to do and we know it quickly. It is easy to take for granted the efficiency and speed with which we access and are guided by a vast library of implicit knowings. Yet our emotional implicit memory is also a curse because it makes the worst experiences in our past persist as felt emotional realities in the present.

The therapist, familiar now with the specific make-up of the client's symptom-generating emotional learning, could begin step C next, the search for contradictory, disconfirming knowledge. This man's implicit learning with Dad had generalized to all other people, as is often the case. So, early in the second session, the therapist said, "I wonder if we could find any experiences you've had where you made a mistake that was visible to the other person, but he or she *didn't* respond in an angry, rejecting way like Dad would do. Which of those experiences really stand out, in your life?" The man remembered a few and mentioned them in a detached, off-hand manner. With that information completing the A-B-C preparatory work, the therapist could now carry out the 1-2-3 process of reconsolidation and transformational change, as follows.

The therapist began, "Let's review now, for a few minutes, the whole range of your experiences with making mistakes—and it would be good if you could allow the *feelings* of what we'll revisit, along with the ideas." With a somewhat softer, slower voice the therapist then led step 1, the reactivation of the target learning, by saying, "On one side is all those many times when dad became so angry and rejecting over some mistake you made, and that was so painful and so scary for you, and you really expected, ever after, that most everyone else would also reject you harshly for any mistake, as though it was apparent to everyone that you are too stupid to be accepted or loved. Can you feel that expectation in your body?" The man, who was gazing at the floor as he allowed the experience being guided, simply nodded.

The therapist then rolled seamlessly into step 2, the mismatch by contradictory living knowledge, by saying, with a slight pause after each sentence, "Ok. And on the other side, what you actually have experienced is all sorts of people who remain *friendly and relaxed* when they see that you've made a mistake. The *store clerk* was friendly and relaxed when you returned the book because you'd bought the wrong one. Your *co-worker* was friendly and relaxed just last week about your mistake of sending him the May figures when he had asked for the April figures. Your *twelfth grade teacher* was friendly and relaxed about the mistake you made about the structure of the final paper. Your *college advisor* was friendly and relaxed about your mistake over the materials he needed from you. All these people have been so *different* from Dad."

This completed step 2, the mismatch that juxtaposed his expectation of harsh rejection side-by-side with his clear experiences of non-rejection for making a mistake. He had never before held those experiences next to each other, in the same field of awareness. According to reconsolidation research, that juxtaposition, with each of the two experiences feeling very real while also feeling that both cannot possibly be true, is what accomplishes the neurological marvel of unlocking the synapses of the target learning.

The therapist now asked, "What are you feeling?" The man said he was feeling "sort of surprised, and sort of relieved." This was an initial indication that he had experienced the juxtaposition in the intended manner.

For step 3—the new learning that will rewrite and replace the target learning—Coherence Therapy simply repeats the same juxtaposition experience from step 2 several more times during the rest of the session. This can be done as a structured technique of reguiding or in a more naturalistic manner by simply expressing empathy for or interest in the juxtaposition experience itself—for example, by saying, "I'm wondering, how is it for you to be in touch with both sides like this—your deep old expectation that most everyone will react harshly like Dad to any mistake, and your own observations again and again that most people *don't* react like Dad to a mistake you've made, and instead they stay friendly and relaxed? How is it for you to be in touch with both?" That natural query guides the client once again to bring attention to and to feel both at once, for a repetition of the juxtaposition experience. Then, in the course of continuing to debrief the experience, the therapist can easily find more opportunities to yet again guide the client's attention to resample the juxtaposition. After some three or four repetitions, the 1-2-3 transformation sequence is complete.

The therapist again prepared an index card for daily reading, this time with words that would keep recreating the juxtaposition experience: "I really expect that my saying or doing something wrong will mean to *everybody* what it always meant to Dad—that I deserve angry rejection for being so stupid—and yet, look at all these people who stayed friendly and kind and *didn't* react like Dad."

The next session began with the therapist asking how it had been to stay in touch with what was on the card and how his anxiety had been. He explained that in both his weekly group meeting at work and at a friend's birthday party he had felt only a "mild edginess that's maybe about normal" and was able to participate, if somewhat awkwardly, in conversation, instead of being silenced by anxiety. The absence of his symptoms in these two situations that formerly triggered them were key markers that began to accomplish step V, verification of erasure of the target learning, his generalization to all people of Dad's responses.

Dissolution of the target learning isn't always the end of the therapeutic process, however, because the unlearning of a model in one area can have direct ripple effects on models in other important areas of personal meaning, with emotional consequences that need to be resolved. This kind of process was indicated when the client added, "But it wasn't exactly a walk in the park like I thought at first it would be because, well, if everybody *isn't* like Dad—if most people *aren't* like that—now Dad looks really mean. Now I feel like I have this cruel father, and I've been pretty agitated about that." The next several sessions moved through the man's feelings of anger, a need for accountability from his father, and grieving, all of which arose from his shifted perception of his father.

Clinical experience has shown us that when significant emotional issues emerge in response to erasure, it is the resolution of these emotional issues that allows erasure to hold. In other words, in the domain of the complex emotional learnings created by humans, an existing model of reality is allowed to dissolve, or not, depending on whether the emotional results feel tolerable to the person both consciously and unconsciously. Successful erasure is not purely a bottom-up, mechanistic or neurological process, but rather is governed in a more top-down manner by the personal meanings and feelings involved.

As a short, basic illustration, our case example was free of various types of complication that develop with some clients at any of the steps A-B-C-1-2-3-V. (For more complex case studies showing such complications, see Ecker et al. (2012).) Yet even this simple vignette indicates how the therapeutic reconsolidation process differs in some fundamental ways from how therapy is usually done. Throughout the process, the therapist guided the client to be as fully as possible *in touch* with the underlying material causing all the trouble, rather than to oppose it, get away from it, interrupt it, override it. The therapist also empathized equally with both sides of the juxtaposition and did not indicate one side as being more valid than the other—because for the therapist to take sides would be to foreclose the emotional brain's own process of determining what to regard as false, and would set up a counteractive process that only suppresses the target learning rather than a transformational process that dissolves it.

The Emotional Coherence Framework

The convergence of neurobiological and clinical knowledge described above allows us to assemble a unified account of:

- *Emotional learning and memory*, with emphasis on its adaptive, coherent nature and the specific content and structure of symptom-generating emotional implicit learnings

- *The unlearning and deletion of emotional implicit knowledge* through the sequence of experiences required by the brain for memory reconsolidation

- *The therapeutic reconsolidation process*, which is the entire set of steps needed for putting into practice the required sequence of experiences in psychotherapy sessions

We call this unified body of knowledge the Emotional Coherence Framework, and in our own clinical practices we have seen its value for facilitating liberating therapeutic breakthroughs consistently.

New learning always creates new neural circuits, but transformational change occurs only when new learning radically unlearns, unwires and replaces an existing learning, rather than merely forming alongside existing learning and competitively regulating it. The use of new learning to erase an existing, unwanted learning is precisely what the therapeutic reconsolidation process achieves. It consists of steps that guide therapy yet allow an extremely broad range of techniques to be used for guiding the key experiences, so a therapist's individual style of working continues to have great scope of expression. It involves richly experiential work that utilizes a therapist's skills of emotional attunement and focuses the placement of empathy so as to cooperate closely with the brain's rules for accessing and dissolving the emotional learnings at the root of the clients' presenting symptoms. Major, long-standing symptoms, entrenched negative reactions, insecure attachment patterns, unconscious core schemas, and emotional wounds can cease as soon as their very basis—a cluster of particular emotional learnings—no longer exists.

When a person in therapy retrieves his or her emotional learnings into awareness experientially, these learnings are always found to be both specific and completely coherent: they fully make sense in light of actual life experiences and are adaptive in how they embody the individual's efforts to avoid harm and ensure well-being. In the clinical field there is already much recognition of the importance of coherence in an individual's conscious narratives of life experience. That, however, is neocortical coherence. The emphasis in the Emotional Coherence Framework is on the coherence of the emotional brain—subcortical and right-brain coherence, the coherence that is intrinsic to implicit emotional learnings and, when retrieved into conscious awareness, creates new autobiographical coherence most meaningfully and authentically.

The emotional brain's implicit yet highly specific meaning-making and modeling of the world is innate and begins very early in life. For example, infants three months old form expectational models of contingency and respond according to these models (DeCasper & Carstens, 1981), and 18-month-old children can form mental models of other people as wanting things that differ from what they themselves want and will give the other what he or she wants (Repacholi & Gopnik, 1997), and can form models that distinguish between intentional and accidental actions (Olineck & Poulin-Dubois, 2005).

The timeless persistence of underlying, symptom-generating learnings across decades of life, long after the original circumstances that induced their formation have ceased to exist, is often taken as meaning that they are "maladaptive" and that the symptoms they produce signify a "dysregulation" of emotional brain networks. The emotional brain—particularly the subcortical emotional brain or limbic system—is likewise often described as "primitive" and "irrational." However, these pathologizing and pejorative terms prove to be fundamentally at odds with what research has revealed about the inherent durability of emotional learning and its astute, experience-driven modeling (discussed at length in Toomey & Ecker, 2007).

The faithful retriggering of one's early learnings is, in fact, exactly what natural selection crafted the brain's emotional learning centers to do, not a faulty condition of disorder or dysregulation—unless one is prepared to say that it is a dysregulation of evolution itself, not of the individual.

Memory research and clinical observations thus support a non-pathologizing, coherence-focused, top-down model of symptom production in the wide range of cases where symptoms are generated by emotional implicit memory. This is the central perspective of the Emotional Coherence Framework. Some symptoms have causes other than learning and memory, of course, such as the genomic causes of autism spectrum conditions or the biochemical causes of hypothyroidism-induced depression. Viewing symptom production as dysregulation may be accurate in such cases.

The tenet that a person's unwanted moods, behaviors, thoughts or somatization may be generated by unconscious emotional learnings or conditioning has figured in many forms of psychotherapy since Freud's day, but the approach within the Emotional Coherence Framework is new, firstly, in guiding swift and accurate retrieval of those emotional learnings, bringing them experientially into direct awareness, and, secondly, in its non-theoretically-based, research-corroborated methodology for prompt dissolution of those retrieved learnings at their emotional and neural roots through memory reconsolidation.

Conclusion

Reconsolidation research has revealed—for perhaps the first time in human history—the process that commutes the life sentence of problematic emotional learning. The seven-step therapeutic reconsolidation process represents the direct translation of this research to psychotherapy in technique-independent and theory-independent terms. It is a map of the facilitation of the brain's built-in process for dissolving existing, operative emotional learnings, and it stands outside of all particular systems and schools of psychotherapy. Beyond enhancing the effectiveness of individual therapists, the therapeutic reconsolidation process has rich ramifications for the psychotherapy field that include a unified understanding of diverse therapies of transformational change, clarification of when insecure attachment learnings are, or are not, involved in a given client's problem, and a serious challenge to nonspecific common factors theory by identifying the role of specific factors in transformational change (see Ecker et al., 2012). What fertile ground for the emerging field of neuropsychotherapy!

Bruce Ecker and Laurel Hulley are the originators of Coherence Therapy (coherencetherapy.org) and coauthors of *Depth Oriented Brief Therapy: How to Be Brief When You Were Trained to Be Deep—and Vice Versa* and the *Coherence Therapy Practice Manual and Training Guide*. Ecker is codirector of the Coherence Psychology Institute, has taught for many years in graduate programs, has been in private practice near San Francisco since 1986, and is on the Panel of Experts of *The Neuropsychotherapist* website and magazine. Hulley is director of education and paradigm development of the Coherence Psychology Institute and co-founder of the Julia Morgan Middle School for Girls in Oakland, California.

Robin Ticic is director of training and development of the Coherence Psychology Institute and is in private practice near Cologne, Germany, specializing in trauma therapy and clinical supervision of trauma therapists. She has served as a psychologist for the Psychotraumatology Institute of the University of Cologne for many years, provides a low-fee counseling service for parents, and is author of the parenting guide *How to Connect with Your Child*, published in English and German.

References

Badenoch, B. (2011). *The brain-savvy therapist's workbook*. New York: W. W. Norton & Co.

Bouton, M. E. (2004). Context and behavioral processes in extinction. *Learning and Memory*, 11, 485–494.

Cammarota, M., Bevilaqua, L. R. M., Medina, J. H., & Izquierdo, I. (2004). Retrieval does not induce reconsolidation of inhibitory avoidance memory. *Learning & Memory*, 11, 572–578. doi: 10.1101/lm.76804

Debiec, J., Doyère, V., Nader, K., & LeDoux, J. E. (2006). Directly reactivated, but not indirectly reactivated, memories undergo reconsolidation in the amygdala. *Proceedings of the National Academy of Sciences*, 103, 3428–3433. doi: 10.1073/pnas.0507168103

DeCasper, A. J., & Carstens, A. A. (1981). Contingencies of stimulation: Effects on learning and emotion in neonates. *Infant Behavior and Development*, 4, 19–35. doi:10.1016/S0163-6383(81)80004-5

Duvarci, S., & Nader, K. (2004). Characterization of fear memory reconsolidation. *Journal of Neuroscience*, 24, 9269–9275. doi: 10.1523/JNEUROSCI.2971-04.2004

Duvarci, S., Mamou, C. S., & Nader, K. (2006). Extinction is not a sufficient condition to prevent fear memories from undergoing reconsolidation in the basolateral amygdala. *European Journal of Neuroscience*, 24, 249–260. doi: 10.1111/j.1460-9568.2006.04907.x

Ecker, B. (2006). The effectiveness of psychotherapy. Keynote address, 12th Biennial Conference of the Constructivist Psychology Network, University of California, San Marcos, California.

Ecker, B. (2008). Unlocking the emotional brain: Finding the neural key to transformation. *Psychotherapy Networker*, 32 (5), 42–47, 60.

Ecker, B., & Hulley, L. (1996). *Depth oriented brief therapy.* San Francisco: Jossey-Bass.

Ecker, B., & Hulley, L. (2000a). Depth-oriented brief therapy: Accelerated accessing of the coherent unconscious. In J. Carlson and L. Sperry (Eds.), *Brief therapy with individuals and couples* (pp. 161-190). Phoenix: Zeig, Tucker and Theisen.

Ecker, B., & Hulley, L. (2000b). The order in clinical "disorder": Symptom coherence in depth oriented brief therapy. In R. A. Neimeyer & J. D. Raskin (Eds.), *Constructions of disorder: Meaning-making frameworks for psychotherapy* (pp. 63-89). Washington, DC: American Psychological Association Press.

Ecker, B., & Hulley, L. (2011). *Coherence therapy practice manual and training guide.* Oakland, CA: Coherence Psychology Institute. Online: http://www.coherencetherapy.org/resources/manual.htm

Ecker, B., Ticic, R., & Hulley, L. (2012). *Unlocking the emotional brain: Eliminating symptoms at their roots using memory reconsolidation.* New York: Routledge,.

Ecker, B., & Toomey, B. (2008). Depotentiation of symptom-producing implicit memory in coherence therapy. *Journal of Constructivist Psychology*, 21, 87–150. doi: 10.1080/10720530701853685

Feinstein, D. (2010). Rapid treatment of PTSD: Why psychological exposure with acupoint tapping may be effective. *Psychotherapy: Theory, Research, Practice, Training.* 47, 385–402. doi:10.1037/a0021171

Foa, E. B., & McNally, R. J. (1996). Mechanisms of change in exposure therapy. In R. M. Rapee (Ed.), *Current controversies in the anxiety disorders* (pp. 329–343). New York: Guilford Press.

Galluccio, L. (2005). Updating reactivated memories in infancy: I. Passive- and active-exposure effects. *Developmental Psychobiology*, 47, 1–17. doi: 10.1002/dev.20073

Gorman, J. M., & Roose, S. P. (2011). The neurobiology of fear memory reconsolidation and psychoanalytic theory. *Journal of the American Psychoanalytic Association*, 59, 1201–1219.

Greenberg, L. S. (2010). Emotion-focused therapy: A clinical synthesis. Focus, 8, 32–42. Online: http://focus.psychiatryonline.org/cgi/reprint/8/1/32

Greenberg, L. (2012). Emotions, the great captains of our lives: Their role in the process of change in psychotherapy. *American Psychologist, 67,* 697-707. doi: 10.1037/a0029858

Held, C., Vosgerau, G., & Knauff, M. (Eds.) (2006). *Mental models and the mind: Current developments in cognitive psychology, neuroscience and philosophy of mind.* Amsterdam: North-Holland Publishing.

Hernandez. P. J., & Kelley, A. E. (2004). Long-term memory for instrumental responses does not undergo protein synthesis-dependent reconsolidation upon retrieval. *Learning & Memory, 11,* 748–754. doi: 10.1101/lm.84904

Högberg, G., Nardo, D., Hällström, T., & Pagani, M. (2011). Affective psychotherapy in post-traumatic reactions guided by affective neuroscience: memory reconsolidation and play. *Psychology Research and Behavior Management, 4,* 87–96. doi: 10.2147/PRBM.S10380

Kindt, M., Soeter, M., & Vervliet, B. (2009). Beyond extinction: Erasing human fear responses and preventing the return of fear. *Nature Neuroscience, 12,* 256–258. doi:10.1038/nn.2271

Kreiman, G., Koch, C. and Fried, I. (2000). Imagery neurons in the human brain. *Nature, 408,* 357-361. doi: 10.1038/35042575

LeDoux, J. E., Romanski, L., & Xagoraris, A. (1989). Indelibility of subcortical emotional memories. *Journal of Cognitive Neuroscience, 1,* 238–243. doi: 10.1162/jocn.1989.1.3.238

Lee, J. L. (2009). Reconsolidation: Maintaining memory relevance. *Trends in Neuroscience, 32,* 413–420. doi:10.1016/j.tins.2009.05.002

McGaugh, J. L. (1989). Involvement of hormonal and neuromodulatory systems in the regulation of memory storage. *Annual Review of Neuroscience, 2,* 255–287. doi: 10.1146/annurev.ne.12.030189.001351

McGaugh, J. L., & Roozendaal, B. (2002). Role of adrenal stress hormones in forming lasting memories in the brain. *Current Opinions in Neurobiology, 12,* 205–210. PMID: 12015238

Mileusnic, R., Lancashire, C. L., & Rose, S. P. R. (2005). Recalling an aversive experience by day-old chicks is not dependent on somatic protein synthesis. *Learning & Memory, 12,* 615–619. doi: 10.1101/lm.38005

Milner, B., Squire, L. R., & Kandel, E. R. (1998). Cognitive neuroscience and the study of memory. *Neuron, 20,* 445–468. PMID: 9539121

Monfils, M.-H., Cowansage, K. K., Klann, E., & LeDoux, J. E. (2009). Extinction-reconsolidation boundaries: key to persistent attenuation of fear memories. *Science, 324,* 951–955. doi: 10.1126/science.1167975

Nader, K., & Einarsson, E. O. (2010). Memory reconsolidation: an update. *Annals of the New York Academy of Sciences*, 1191, 27–41. doi: 10.1111/j.1749-6632.2010.05443.x

Nader, K., Schafe, G. E., & LeDoux, J. E. (2000). Fear memories require protein synthesis in the amygdala for reconsolidation after retrieval. *Nature*, 406, 722–726. PMID: 10963596

Olineck, K. M., & Poulin-Dubois, D. (2005). Infants' ability to distinguish between intentional and accidental actions and its relation to internal state language. *Infancy*, 8, 91–100. doi: 10.1207/s15327078in0801_6

Pedreira, M. E., & Maldonado, H. (2003). Protein synthesis subserves reconsolidation or extinction depending on reminder duration. *Neuron*, 38, 863–869. doi: 10.1016/S0896-6273(03)00352-0

Pedreira, M. E., Pérez-Cuesta, L. M., & Maldonado, H. (2002). Reactivation and reconsolidation of long-term memory in the crab *Chasmagnathus*: Protein synthesis requirement and mediation by NMDA-type glutamatergic receptors. *Journal of Neuroscience*, 22, 8305–8311. PMID: 12223585

Pedreira, M. E., Pérez-Cuesta, L. M., & Maldonado, H. (2004). Mismatch between what is expected and what actually occurs triggers memory reconsolidation or extinction. *Learning & Memory*, 11, 579–585. doi: 10.1101/lm.76904

Phelps, E. A., Delgado, M. R., Nearing, K. I., & LeDoux, J. E. (2004). Extinction learning in humans: Role of the amygdala and vmPFC. *Neuron*, 43, 897–905. doi: 10.1016/j.neuron.2004.08.042

Przybyslawski, J., & Sara, S. J. (1997). Reconsolidation of memory after its reactivation. *Behavior and Brain Research*, 84, 241–246. doi: 10.1016/S0166-4328(96)00153-2

Przybyslawski, J., Roullet, P., & Sara, S. J. (1999). Attenuation of emotional and nonemotional memories after their reactivation: Role of beta adrenergic receptors. *Journal of Neuroscience*, 19, 6623–6628. PMID: 10414990

Quirk, G. J., Paré, D., Richardson, R., Herry, C., Monfils, M. H., Schiller, D., & Vicentic, A. (2010). Erasing fear memories with extinction training. *Journal of Neuroscience*, 30, 14993–14997. doi: 10.1523/JNEUROSCI.4268-10.2010

Repacholi, B., & Gopnik, A. (1997). Early understanding of desires: Evidence from 14 and 18-month-olds. *Developmental Psychology*, 33, 1, 12-21. PMID: 9050386

Roozendaal, B., McEwen, B. S., & Chattarji, S. (2009). Stress, memory and the amygdala. *Nature Reviews Neuroscience*, 10, 423-433. doi: 10.1038/nrn2651

Roullet, P., & Sara, S. J. (1998). Consolidation of memory after its reactivation: Involvement of beta noradrenergic receptors in the late phase. *Neural Plasticity*, 6,

63-68. PMID: 9920683

Sara, S. J. (2000). Retrieval and reconsolidation: Toward a neurobiology of remembering. *Learning & Memory*, 7, 73-84. doi: 10.1101/lm.7.2.73

Schiller, D., Monfils, M.-H., Raio, C. M., Johnson, D. C., LeDoux, J. E., & Phelps, E. A. (2010). Preventing the return of fear in humans using reconsolidation update mechanisms. *Nature*, 463, 49–53. doi: 10.1038/nature08637

Sekiguchi, T., Yamada, A., & Suzuki, H. (1997). Reactivation-dependent changes in memory states in the terrestrial slug Limax flavus. *Learning & Memory*, 4, 356–364. PMID: 10706372

Siegel, D. J. (1999). *The developing mind: Toward a neurobiology of interpersonal experience.* New York, NY: Guilford Press.

Solomon, R. W., & Shapiro, F. (2008). EMDR and the adaptive information processing model: Potential mechanisms of change. *Journal of EMDR Practice and Research*, 2, 315–325. doi: 10.1891/1933-3196.2.4.315

Toomey, B., & Ecker, B. (2007). Of neurons and knowings: Constructivism, coherence psychology and their neurodynamic substrates. *Journal of Constructivist Psychology*, 20, 201–245. doi: 10.1080/10720530701347860

Toomey, B., & Ecker, B. (2009). Competing visions of the implications of neuroscience for psychotherapy. *Journal of Constructivist Psychology*, 22, 95–140. doi: 10.1080/10720530802675748

Walker, M. P., Brakefield, T., Hobson, J. A., & Stickgold, R. (2003). Dissociable stages of human memory consolidation and reconsolidation. *Nature*, 425, 616–620. PMID: 14534587

Xue, Y.-X., Luo, Y.-X., Wu, P., Shi, H.-S., Xue, L.-F., Chen, C., et al. (2012). A memory retrieval-extinction procedure to prevent drug craving and relapse. *Science*, 336, 241–245. doi: 10.1126/science.1215070

DEEP RELEASE FOR BODY AND SOUL:

MEMORY RECONSOLIDATION AND THE ALEXANDER TECHNIQUE

Robin Ticic & Elise Kushner

Victoria*, a robust and optimistic woman in her late twenties, had just quit her job in Manhattan in anticipation of moving to California in two weeks' time. Her aunt and uncle there had offered her an interesting position in their family business, and Victoria was ripe for a new adventure.

She lived in a 5-story apartment building typical of the residential neighborhood in which she had spent the last several years. The neighbors were mostly middle-class, white-collar workers who were out at the office during the day, as she herself had been until recently. Now, somewhat oddly, she was home during the day, packing and sorting, carrying huge plastic bags full of old belongings down to the garbage bins, going in and out to shop—an entirely unaccustomed rhythm.

Returning home from a short errand around lunchtime, Victoria sensed someone behind her as she approached the entrance to the building. She glanced over her shoulder, having been well trained in matters of safety and security. She saw a young man, probably in his early twenties, dressed in dark jeans and a red T-shirt. He was of an ethnic minority atypical of the neighborhood. Her instinct told her he was up to no good, but her life-long liberal training overruled the feeling, saying that it wasn't right of her to stamp him as evil just because he looked different. Rather than make an effort to shut the door quickly behind her, Victoria allowed him to follow her into the building. The man murmured that he was there to visit his brother, and he stopped outside a door on the second floor, as she continued up to her apartment on the third floor.

Once in her apartment, she felt the rumbling in her subconscious that was trying to tell her that she had never seen a tenant of that ethnic appearance in the building and that the man most likely wasn't visiting his brother. But again her learned habit of "bending over backwards" on issues of racial tolerance squelched the inner voices.

A half-hour later, Victoria went out again on an errand in the neighborhood.

Victoria is a pseudonym. The client is not recognizable from the text and has given her informed consent.

Walking homeward at an atypically slow pace, she felt burdened by a sense of doom. But her irrepressibly positive nature refused to deal with it.

She entered her building and climbed the first one-and-a-half flights of stairs. Waiting there at the top was the man who had followed her in earlier that day. She tried to turn back toward the downstairs door, but he grabbed her wrist and dragged her the rest of the way up to the landing. He had figured out which apartment was hers and shoved her toward the door.

"Open the door!" he commanded. Some instinct told Victoria to be passive and not react. He punched her in the face and knocked her glasses off. "Open it, I said!" he repeated.

"I can't! I can't see anything," she answered. He gripped her from behind, using his left arm as a vise around her neck. With his right arm he reached down, as if to pull something out of his sock.

"I have a knife. Open the door now," he said. He squeezed harder around her neck as she tried to make some sounds, and he punched her with the other hand. She didn't actually see the knife, but she could imagine it clearly.

Victoria let herself become very heavy and uncontrolled, so that the man had quite an effort to hold her upright. The more she tried to scream, the harder he squeezed against her throat.

"Give me the keys!" he said. She handed him her key ring, which, luckily, contained at least fifteen keys: for her own apartment, her brother's apartment, the apartment of a neighbor, the cellar where the garbage cans were, a dance rehearsal room, her parents' country house . . . While the attacker was wrestling with the keys and simultaneously trying to keep Victoria upright, she took the opportunity to collapse in a helpless heap on the floor. At that moment, voices from farther upstairs became audible. There *was* someone at home during the day—someone who was not responding to her screams!

After what seemed like an interminable number of minutes, which Victoria was convinced were her very last, she suddenly sensed he might be losing patience and giving up. She shoved her purse at him and said, "Just take the money and go!" That is what he did.

She listened for the slamming of the downstairs door before picking herself up gingerly and creeping soundlessly up the stairs. She rang at every apartment until finally an old woman opened her door, let Victoria in, and called the police on her behalf.

Later at the police station, having described the man and her stolen purse, Victoria was led to a patrol car and driven around the neighborhood, on the chance that the man might still be nearby. At one point she believed she saw the culprit disappearing between two buildings but was unsure of herself. Back at the police station, she was asked to look through mug shots, which she found to be an extremely depressing experience. It felt to her as if all the evil men in New York City were looking out at her as if they wanted to harm her. These chilling photos were having an emotional impact of their own. She now feared she might never again be safe in this city. One photograph in particular triggered a feeling of horror in her, but she wasn't sure if it was her attacker, since she had hardly seen him from the front. She read that that one was wanted for many crimes, but had never been convicted.

Victoria was no longer able to go into her building or be in her apartment alone during the two weeks remaining before her move. A friend of her brother was between jobs and offered to be her bodyguard until she moved. During these two weeks she spent tortuous hours and days berating herself for having brought the situation on herself by stupidly letting the man into the building. At the same time, she was overjoyed just to be alive!

The nightmares began immediately, and it was always the same. She was walking through her Manhattan neighborhood when she noticed that she was being followed by a man who looked like her attacker, and who was wearing a red shirt. She tried to go more quickly, but her legs were too slow, as if she were trying to run in a swimming pool full of molasses. She felt incapable and hopeless. She panicked and screamed, which woke her up.

She was sure that her fear was specific to that man, and that it would be gone once she had moved from Manhattan, but that was not the case. The nightmares continued, although she was living near her relatives in a small town in California, where she felt quite safe.

For the next 10 years, Victoria enjoyed her new life, new job, and new friends, and was happy on an everyday basis. A few things had changed permanently for her, however: she studiously avoided unsafe neighborhoods and tried not to go out alone after dark, she could not stand to have anyone touch her neck playfully in a mock-aggressive way, she began to listen more consciously and respectfully to what her instincts were telling her about people, and she had a newfound appreciation of the fragility of life and swore to make every minute count. Nonetheless, the Manhattan nightmare continued, night after night. Often she didn't remember in the morning that she had dreamed the horrible dream, but on some level she knew that it was a nightly visitor.

During this time, Victoria's beloved cousin Belle, who lived near her in California, had trained as an instructor of the Alexander Technique (Jain, Janssen, & DeCelle, 2004; Munden & Harer, 2009). This softbodywork approach emphasizes feeling at ease in one's movements, and Belle was a natural talent at it, so Victoria offered herself from time to time for Belle to practice with her.

One day, Victoria asked Belle to do a few minutes of hands-on work with her for a stiff neck, very sure it would help her release some tension. While one of Belle's warm hands was cupping her chin and the other was at the back of her neck, gently swiveling her head, Victoria suddenly remembered that she had the same nightmare every night. She told Belle about it and said it had been happening nightly for the last ten years. At that moment, Victoria felt a rush of muscular release in her neck, as if she could breathe freely again, though she hadn't been aware of not being able to breathe freely. She felt utterly safe in her cousin's hands.

The recurring nightmare stopped immediately, that very night. After a few weeks Victoria started trusting that it was really gone. Only once, many years later, did it return, after an intense recounting of the original traumatic event.

✳✳✳

What took place in Victoria's body and mind during those pivotal moments to cause that rapid, profound shift? It proves instructive to examine the change that occurred through the lens of *memory reconsolidation*, which is the only type of neuroplasticity known to be capable of unlocking and modifying an emotional learning at its neural roots.

The brain requires a particular set of experiences in order to launch the process of memory reconsolidation: the target learning or "knowing" must be reactivated by the presence of salient cues from the original learning. While that learning is reactivated, an experience must take place that significantly mismatches what is expected and predicted by the target learning. In response to this mismatch, the synapses that encode and store the target learning shift into an unlocked, labile state in which they are open to being updated by new learning, allowing prior learning to be nullified and erased (for research reviews, see Agren, 2014; Reichelt & Lee, 2013; for the utilization of memory reconsolidation in psychotherapy, see Ecker, Ticic, & Hulley, 2012, 2013a,b). The liberating shift that Victoria experienced can be understood in terms of that process, as follows.

What learnings had Victoria formed during her traumatic experience in Manhattan, 10 years earlier? As verified by Victoria herself, these nonverbal, implicit learnings can be verbalized as follows:

- Danger lurks everywhere, so I must remain vigilant at all times.
- I can't rely on help in a life-threatening situation.
- When alone I am particularly unsafe.
- When sleeping I cannot be vigilant, cannot protect myself, and am therefore vulnerable to the utmost extent.

- If I ignore my instincts, I endanger myself.

- What happened to me is my own fault, because I didn't heed my own feeling of danger.

- Someone touching my neck means that person intends to put my life in jeopardy.

- I must protect my neck by always holding it firmly under my control.

- Manhattan is full of horrible, mean men who want to do terrible things to me.

- Parts of this experience are too horrible and destabilizing to allow entirely into my conscious awareness.

During the Alexander session, Belle's hands were on Victoria's neck. As she focused on those sensations and the feeling of moving her neck, all at once the body memory of feeling strangled became activated and entered Victoria's conscious awareness. And yet she felt utterly safe in Belle's loving hands, and felt absolutely safe in letting down her guard. On the nonverbal level of body knowledge and emotional meaning, this was a vivid mismatch of Victoria's learnings and expectations that "Someone touching my neck means that person intends to put my life in jeopardy" and "I must protect my neck by always holding it firmly under my control." At that moment of disconfirmation, those learnings lost their chokehold on Victoria, literally as well as figuratively.

Why, then, did the nightmares cease immediately, as well? Victoria's sense of complete safety and loving, empathic accompaniment by Belle enabled her to reveal to Belle—and, even more importantly, to herself—certain previously unspoken, suppressed aspects of the ordeal that she had known "on some level" all along, as she said, including the nightly reliving of life-threatening danger. Opening up to the full experience in this way and yet *not* being destabilized by doing so constituted an additional mismatch, in this case with her established learning that "Parts of this experience are too horrible and destabilizing to allow entirely into my conscious awareness." Victoria's awareness of the experience in Manhattan was now sufficiently de-suppressed that there no longer existed intense, out-of-awareness memory that could intrude while her guard was down during sleep.

Looking back on these dramatic, decisive shifts, Victoria felt that a particular *portion* of her learning that "Danger lurks everywhere, so I must remain vigilant at all times" and a particular *portion* of her knowings about how unsafe it was to be alone—especially alone and *sleeping*—no longer held any emotional validity or realness after that one Alexander session. She could now assess, with awareness and mindfulness, the degree of risk in a given situation, and protect herself accordingly, without feeling that danger lurked everywhere. She observed with regret, however, that she lived in a society in which one could not assume that neighbors would respond with support in time of need.

What enabled these additional shifts to occur? In hindsight, Victoria recognized that the activation of the memory by Belle's hands on her neck included the reactivation of other component learnings listed above. (As a rule, the activation of portions of a schema—in other words, some subset of the knowings formed during a particular experience—activates the entire schema.) And yet Victoria possessed the everyday knowledge that danger is *not* necessarily omnipresent and that she is indeed capable of taking measures to protect herself to a significant extent. This everyday knowledge came into direct juxtaposition with the learned omnipresence of danger that Victoria had formed during her ordeal, serving as yet another mismatch and disconfirmation.

Interestingly, Victoria's learning that "If I ignore my instincts, I endanger myself" did not shift at all. On every level of her being, she chose to retain that new knowledge because it felt completely valid and survival-positive. This type of shift in one's way of being and worldview is a frequent outcome of traumatic experience, even after that experience has been fully processed and integrated into the fabric of one's personal history. Victoria's sense that "What happened to me is my own fault, because I didn't heed my own feeling of danger" softened into "Yes, it was my responsibility to honor my inner voices, and I didn't do that. I learned the hard way, and now I'm more alert to my invaluable inner promptings. I'm better able to protect myself."

Victoria described the final time her nightmare occurred, many years after it had otherwise ceased totally, as a kind of recognition that "Oh, that's right—all of that *did*, in fact, happen to me. And it was really horrible!"

What a fascinating cascade of neurological and subjectively experienced changes was made possible by a single session of work with the Alexander Technique! Awareness of the process of memory reconsolidation and the experiential steps necessary to set that process in motion enables us to begin to understand what is actually happening when such meaningful shifts occur implicitly—as they did for Victoria.

Robin Ticic *is Director of Training for the Coherence Psychology Institute. She is a trauma therapist in private practice near Cologne, Germany, clinical supervisor for Coherence Therapy, and co-author of* Unlocking the Emotional Brain: Eliminating Symptoms at Their Roots Using Memory Reconsolidation.

Elise Kushner *is Assistant Director of Development for the Coherence Psychology Institute. She is a certified coach and trainer in Cologne, Germany, specializing in adult education, interpersonal communication, and coaching competencies for leaders.*

References

Agren, T. (2014). Human reconsolidation: A reactivation and update. *Brain Research Bulletin, 105,* 70–82. doi:10.1016/j.brainresbull.2013.12.010

Ecker, B., Ticic, R., & Hulley, L. (2012). *Unlocking the emotional brain: Eliminating symptoms at their roots using memory reconsolidation.* New York, NY: Routledge.

Ecker, B., Ticic, R., & Hulley, L. (2013a). A primer on memory reconsolidation and its psychotherapeutic use as a core process of profound change. *The Neuropsychotherapist, 1,* 82–99. doi:10.12744/tnpt(1)082-099

Ecker, B., Ticic, R., & Hulley, L. (2013b). Unlocking the emotional brain: Is memory reconsolidation the key to transformation? *Psychotherapy Networker, 37*(4), 18–25, 46–47.

Jain, S., Janssen, K., & DeCelle, S. (2004). Alexander technique and Feldenkrais method: A critical overview. *Physical Medicine & Rehabilitation Clinics of North America, 15*(4), 811–825. doi:10.1016/j.pmr.2004.04.00

Munden, J. B., & Harer, S. (2009). *The Alexander technique resource book: A reference guide.* Lanham, MD: Scarecrow Press.

Reichelt, A. C., & Lee, J. L. C. (2013). Memory reconsolidation in aversive and appetitive settings. *Frontiers in Behavioral Neuroscience, 7,* 1–18. doi:10.3389/fnbeh.2013.00118

NONSPECIFIC COMMON FACTORS THEORY MEETS MEMORY RECONSOLIDATION: A GAME-CHANGING ENCOUNTER?

Bruce Ecker

Nonspecific common factors theory asserts, based on 75 years of randomized controlled trials of different types of psychotherapy, that specific processes and procedures cannot contribute powerfully to therapeutic change. This assertion derives from finding essentially the same rather modest level of efficacy for all of the many therapies studied using randomized controlled trials, or RCTs. Advocacy of nonspecific common factors theory has been especially strong in the last decade (e.g., Duncan, Miller, Wampold & Hubble, 2009).

The fact that the efficacy measured by RCTs doesn't change from therapy to therapy appears to imply that efficacy is due not to the specific methods and procedures used—which researchers call *specific factors*—but rather is due to the qualities of the client, the therapist, and the client-therapist relationship—which researchers call the *nonspecific common factors*, and which include qualities of trust, empathy, and therapeutic alliance, among other things.

According to the statistical data from RCTs, only about 15% of the efficacy of therapy is attributable to specific factors, whereas 85% of the efficacy is due to the nonspecific common factors.

For the last couple of decades, nonspecific common factors theory has come to be accepted as final truth among many clinical psychologists and researchers. It has such a strong following that in some circles, to question it is heretical.

A critical minority has nevertheless continued to challenge its validity (e.g., Coughlin, 2012). That challenge is now entering a new phase with the discovery of memory reconsolidation, a specific process shown by neuroscientists to induce potent change. In this column, I'll describe this situation and offer my speculation about its outcome.

Even before memory reconsolidation entered the picture, various clinicians and researchers were pointing out that nonspecific common factors theory was on thin ice because of how RCTs analyze therapy outcome data: They measure the average outcome of large groups of therapy cases.

This means that buried in those averages are those exceptional individual cases in which profound change occurred—a transformational shift and lasting therapeutic breakthrough. These ultra-effective "outlier" sessions are never closely studied in RCTs to identify possible specific factors associated with such strongly effective results in those sessions.

In short, the RCT is a measurement method that by design heavily obscures the effects of specific factors and generates data that are insensitive to specific factors. That's why some of us think it's illogical and even unscientific to conclude from RCTs, as nonspecific common factors theory does, that specific factors are fundamentally weak.

Another indication of thin ice prior to memory reconsolidation came from psychotherapy process research, which in a controlled manner does examine specific factors and measure their influence on outcome. Each of the cases in a process study is scrutinized individually in order to identify the role of specific ingredients.

Process studies such as those listed in the table have consistently found a specific factor that correlates more strongly with successful therapy outcome than do the nonspecific common factors. The specific factor that surpasses the nonspecific factors most decisively is the *facilitation of an emotional experience that was previously blocked, combined with conscious reflection on the emotional meanings that have emerged.*

For example, the meta-analysis by Weinberger (1995) found that one of the most widely emphasized common factors, the therapeutic alliance, accounted for 11 percent of the variance in therapy outcomes, whereas 40 percent of variance was due to the specific factor of guiding clients to face and feel what they had been avoiding. Such findings directly contradict the central prediction of nonspecific common factors theory.

I'll speculate here that if these considerations somehow haven't been enough to bring about a revision in nonspecific common factors theory, the decisive disconfirmation coming from memory reconsolidation research findings could and should finally tip the scales.

Since 2000, neuroscience researchers studying memory reconsolidation have amassed evidence showing it to be a specific process, innate to the brain, that causes profound change of a kind previously believed impossible: A target emotional learning or conditioning is unlearned so thoroughly that it is erased. What's erased is both the target learning's neural circuitry and the subjective and behavioral response it had been generating. (For a summary of research findings, see Ecker, Ticic & Hulley, 2012, 2013.)

The counter-training process of extinction, extensively researched throughout

---

Table 1

Some Psychotherapy Process Studies

Demonstrating Specific Factor Dominance

Baikie, K. A., & Wilhelm, K. (2005). Emotional and physical health benefits of expressive writing. *Advances in Psychiatric Treatment, 11,* 338-346.

Elliott, R., Greenberg, L., & Lietaer, G. (2003). Research on experiential psychotherapy. In M. Lambert (Ed.), *Bergin & Garfield's handbook of psychotherapy & behavior change* (pp. 493-539). New York: John Wiley.

Greenberg, L. S., Warwar, S. H., & Malcolm, W. M. (2008). Differential effects of emotion-focused therapy and psychoeducation in facilitating forgiveness and letting go of emotional injuries. *Journal of Counseling Psychology, 55,* 185-196.

McCarthy, K. S. (2009). *Specific, common, and unintended factors in psychotherapy: Descriptive and correlational approaches to what creates change.* Doctoral dissertation, University of Pennsylvania. Available online: http://repository.upenn.edu/edissertations/62

Missirlian, T. M., Toukmanian, S. G., Warwar, S. H., & Greenberg, L. S. (2005). Emotional arousal, client perceptual processing, and the working alliance in experiential psychotherapy for depression. *Journal of Consulting and Clinical Psychology, 73,* 861-871.

Oei, T. P. S., & Shuttlewood, G. J. (1996). Specific and nonspecific factors in psychotherapy: A case of cognitive therapy for depression. *Clinical Psychology Review, 16,* 83-103.

Oei, T. P. S., & Shuttlewood, G. J. (1997). Comparison of specific and nonspecific factors in a group cognitive therapy for depression. *Journal of Behavior Therapy and Experimental Psychiatry, 28,* 221-231.

Pennebaker, J. W. (1997). *Opening up: The healing power of expressing emotion.* New York: Guilford Press.

Weinberger, J. (1995). Common factors aren't so common: The common factors dilemma. *Clinical Psychology: Science and Practice, 2,* 45-69.

---

the 20th century, always yielded only temporary suppression, never erasure, of the target learning. So the discovery of memory reconsolidation was a major development.

Controlled studies with human subjects have demonstrated such erasure for learned fear (Oyarzún et al., 2012; Schiller et al., 2010), heroin craving triggered by seeing items associated with heroin use (Xue et al., 2012), and pleasure-seeking operant learning (Galluccio, 2005).

In clinical work, my colleagues and I have applied the specific steps of the memory reconsolidation process to a wide range of symptoms and have observed the same markers of profound change that neuroscientists regard as the distinctive signature of erasure (Ecker, Ticic & Hulley, 2012). The steps of the process have also been identified as being fulfilled in several different psychotherapy systems that yield transformational change (Ecker, Ticic & Hulley, 2012).

Erasure of emotional learnings causes no loss of autobiographical memory of events in one's life. What is nullified are acquired emotional schemas and responses, not memories of events. Erasure of the emotional learning underlying a therapy client's presenting symptom is the ideal form of liberating therapeutic breakthrough, and we now know from reconsolidation research that it results from a specific procedure.

These developments indicate that specific factors can make psychotherapy be far more effective than the modest efficacy ceiling measured when the nonspecific common factors dominate the statistics in RCTs. What RCTs might really be showing is that typically only about 15% of the therapists in the studies have been applying highly effective specific factors. Perhaps the updated message of nonspecific common factors theory II will be that more therapists need to recognize and master the critical specific factors.

Of course, the client-therapist relationship remains indispensably important for good psychotherapy. This is not an either/or situation. It now seems clear that in the most effective psychotherapy, an environment of good nonspecific common factors supports facilitation of the specific factors of emotional accessing and memory reconsolidation.

References

Coughlin, P. A. (2012). The case for specific factors in psychotherapy outcome. Retrieved May 30, 2013 from http://www.youtube.com/watch?v=UJlVCzKM_gA

Duncan, B. L., Miller, S. D., Wampold, B. E., & Hubble, M. A. (Eds.) (2009). *The heart and soul of change: Delivering what works in therapy* (2nd ed.). Washington, DC: American Psychological Association Press.

Ecker, B., Ticic, R., & Hulley, L. (2012). *Unlocking the emotional brain: Eliminating symptoms at their roots using memory reconsolidation.* New York: Routledge.

Ecker, B., Ticic, R., & Hulley, L. (2013). A primer on memory reconsolidation and its psychotherapeutic use as a core process of profound change. *The Neuropsychotherapist, 1,* 82-99. DOI: 10.12744/tnpt(1)082-099

Galluccio, L. (2005). Updating reactivated memories in infancy: I. Passive- and active-exposure effects. *Developmental Psychobiology, 47,* 1–17. doi: 10.1002/dev.20073

Oyarzún, J. P., Lopez-Barroso, D., Fuentemilla, L., Cucurell, D., Pedraza, C., et al. (2012). Updating fearful memories with extinction training during reconsolidation: A human study using auditory aversive stimuli. *PLoS ONE* 7(6): e38849. DOI:10.1371/journal.pone.0038849

Schiller, D., Monfils, M.-H., Raio, C. M., Johnson, D. C., LeDoux, J. E., & Phelps, E. A. (2010). Preventing the return of fear in humans using reconsolidation update mechanisms. *Nature, 463,* 49–53. DOI: 10.1038/nature08637

Xue, Y.-X., Luo, Y.-X., Wu, P., Shi, H.-S., Xue, L.-F., Chen, C., et al. (2012). A memory retrieval-extinction procedure to prevent drug craving and relapse. *Science, 336,* 241–245. DOI: 10.1126/science.1215070

Bruce Ecker, MA, LMFT, is co-originator of Coherence Therapy, co-director of the Coherence Psychology Institute, and coauthor of *Unlocking the Emotional Brain: Eliminating Symptoms at Their Roots Using Memory Reconsolidation*; the *Coherence Therapy Practice Manual and Training Guide*; and *Depth Oriented Brief Therapy*. He is in private practice in Oakland, California, gives clinical trainings internationally, and has taught graduate courses for many years. Clarifying how lasting, transformational change takes place has been the theme of Bruce Ecker's clinical career. He has contributed extensive innovations in concepts and methods of experiential psychotherapy, and has driven the clinical field's recognition of memory reconsolidation research and how it translates into new capabilities of consistent therapeutic effectiveness and psychotherapy integration. For more information, visit www.CoherenceInstitute.org.

PROGRESSIVE COUNTING FACILITATES MEMORY RECONSOLIDATION

Kymberly A. Lasser & Ricky Greenwald

Progressive counting (PC) is a new trauma resolution procedure that has so far been found to be about as effective as EMDR (Greenwald, McClintock, & Bailey, 2013; Greenwald, McClintock, Jarecki, & Monaco, in press), at least as well tolerated, and more efficient (Greenwald, McClintock, Jarecki, & Monaco, in press). In brief, the PC procedure requires the client to watch a movie in their mind of the targeted trauma memory, from beginning to end, while the therapist counts out loud, first from 1 to 10, then to 20, then to 30, and so on, until no further memory-related distress remains (Greenwald, 2013a).

Memory reconsolidation, a neurological process that allows existing emotional learning or conditioning to be erased, technically requires: 1) activating the target learning, 2) destabilizing the activated learning with a disconfirming experience that renders the target learning erasable, and 3) carrying out erasure by guiding a few more disconfirming experiences within a 5-hr window (Ecker, Ticic, & Hulley, 2012). This sequence of activities occurs within PC proper. If therapy clients were to just walk in already prepared to engage in memory reconsolidation work, the practice of therapy would be far simpler. However, in order for that process to take place reliably, it needs to be preceded by: (a) symptom identification; (b) retrieval of target learning (i.e., the symptom-requiring schema); and (c) identification of disconfirming knowledge—steps that are accomplished in quite different ways in different forms of psychotherapy, as shown by Ecker et al. How PC carries them out is illustrated by the case example below.

The PC treatment model implicates unresolved trauma and loss memories (broadly defined), and associated mental models, as the primary underlying basis for most clients' presenting problems. Thus, consistent with Ecker and colleagues' meta-model of therapy approaches that facilitate memory reconsolidation (Ecker et al., 2012), it is a generic or trans-diagnostic treatment approach that allows clinicians to address a wide range of presenting problems (Greenwald, 2013a).

Although the model is routinely used within the traditional hour per week therapy format, in our clinic we provide therapy in an intensive format, in which the client works with the therapist for many hours per day, typically for consecutive days, until the work is done. This allows for greater treatment efficiency, reduces the risk that therapy will be disrupted by life events, and yields rapid results (Greenwald, 2013b). Within the intensive format, certain phases of treatment are performed out of their usual order because most clients are not returning to their home environments each day after treatment. So, for example, strategies to cope with everyday challenges would normally be addressed relatively early in treatment, but in the intensive format these are postponed until near the end, when the client is getting ready to return home.

Here we present a (disguised) case of the first author's (KL) to illustrate how the process of memory reconsolidation unfolds using PC within a phase model of trauma-informed treatment—including evaluation, motivational work, psychoeducation, emotional stabilization, coping skills, trauma resolution, and anticipating future challenges—which is the context within which PC is most likely to be provided (Greenwald, 2013a).

Case Example

"Sara", a self-referred 30-year-old recently married female, traveled cross-country to meet with KL for three consecutive days. When asked what brought her to treatment, Sara described her feelings of loneliness and longing for more quality time with her husband, Matt; this had gradually been getting worse during the last several months of his 70+-hr working weeks.

Sara described a recent situation with Matt in which "we planned to watch a movie together when he got home from work, but he came home late and said he was too tired to watch a movie, and he needed to get to sleep". Then, instead of Matt apologizing or comforting her, "he went off about how stressful his life is right now and then went on talking about a project he was doing at work". In this way the conversation had shifted from a focus on Sara's needs to Matt's needs, and Sara "just listened to what he had to say". Sara became increasingly irritated with Matt towards the end of the night and finally decided that she needed some space, opting to sleep on the living room couch; however, "Matt wouldn't give me my space and insisted we sleep together". Sara also mentioned that Matt had seemed worried that he had done something wrong and insisted on making it right. Sara did not provide him with an explanation, and the night ended with Matt retreating to the bedroom and Sara falling asleep in the bathroom after having locked the bathroom door to get away from him.

Sara went on to explain how emotionally overwhelmed she felt about the relationship and expressed ambivalence about how best to address this. She explained, "I am not sure if I want to stay with him and work on the relationship, or if I should leave him". Sara felt that she had tried so hard to make the relationship work (e.g., she had convinced Matt to attend couples therapy, which they had been attending weekly for six months) that she couldn't imagine giving up on it yet. On the other hand, she also felt, "I can't keep going the way things are. It is exhausting". Thus Sara had come to the realization that she was really stuck, and she said, "I was hoping that by coming here I would be able to figure out which choice I need to make".

KL learned that Sara had experienced chronic childhood emotional and physical abuse, inflicted by her father, while mother was "emotionally absent". Further details of the abuse and its relationship to Sara's current level of functioning in her marriage were ascertained as treatment unfolded.

When asked about her long-term goals, Sara said:

Ideally, I would have a better and more intimate relationship with Matt. There would be less conflict because Matt would be spending less time at work and more time with me. When I suggest something that would be helpful for our relationship, he would actually listen and follow through with it.

Sara did not yet appear to recognize her own role in her problem or the solution, so she was asked to identify any of her own behaviors that could get in the way of her goals. Sara acknowledged:

It is not just him that needs to change. I know that I play a part in this too. I keep asking Matt to make changes that will help our relationship, and when he doesn't follow through, I still keep thinking that eventually he will, and I continue to ask him over and over. I hold on to an unrealistic expectation that he will change in certain ways, and even when he doesn't change I convince myself that he eventually will.

Sara also acknowledged that she was a highly sensitive person, and that sometimes she responded to Matt in ways that provoked him or discouraged him from making changes "because of his fear that screwing up might cause me to become really distressed and irritable". Sara explained:

When Matt disappoints me or upsets me by dismissing something I am feeling or saying, I can't really tolerate it, so I just bottle things up inside and try to push these feelings away by focusing on Matt's needs instead. Then I become really overwhelmed, and then sometimes I just try to isolate myself, or I just explode at the most unexpected times.

This contributed to step a, symptom identification.

Sara was then asked to identify any behaviors that could move her towards her goals. Sara said that she would like to be able to:

> . . . stick up for myself and let Matt know how his words have hurt me. I wouldn't accept his treatment towards me as it has been for a while. Things would have to change; and if Matt didn't change, I would stop holding on to unrealistic hopes, and I would have to move on with my life without him.

Through this discussion, Sara had begun to approach the symptom-requiring schema (step b) underlying her current behavior/symptom of bottling things up inside and responding to Matt's needs in response to an emotional invalidation. The schema involved beliefs, likely rooted in earlier childhood experiences with Sara's father, which discouraged Sara from confronting Matt directly about his behavior, along with an expectation of getting her husband to change. While we might speculate that Sara believed something like, "If I want to be safe, loved, and accepted, I have to prioritize the other person's needs over my own", this treatment approach does not require the client's problematic mental model(s) to be made explicit as this point. Rather, both step b, the explicit accessing of target learnings, and step c, the accessing of vivid contradictory knowledge, develop organically throughout the unfolding PC process, as shown below.

A trauma/loss history was obtained from Sara. For each memory that Sara identified, she also reported the age at which each event occurred and gave a current subjective units of distress scale (SUDS; Wolpe, 1990) 0-10 rating, in which 10 is the highest possible distress and 0 is none at all. Sara identified several memories, which appeared to be thematically related regarding experiences of invalidation, where another person (usually Sara's father) either expected more of Sara than she could provide, or dismissed Sara, or misinterpreted Sara's cues that were indicative of distress. Sara did not yet appear to be aware of this underlying theme that had been woven into her interpersonal relationships.

Then the case formulation was presented. This is the culmination of the evaluation phase of treatment, in which the therapist teaches the client how their trauma/loss history contributes to the presenting problem (Greenwald, 2013a). Sara's strengths and resources were first highlighted, and then her trauma/loss experiences were acknowledged. The therapist then explained:

> Other people who have experienced events like those have said that they learned to believe bad things about themselves that aren't actually true, but which feel true sometimes; things like, "I'm not important; I'm powerless; I'm not safe". Other people have also said that when things like that happened,

there were strong feelings like anger, shame, sadness, or fear. Those feelings can pile up inside and can be like a sore spot. Now, whenever someone dismisses your own needs or perspective I can't help but wonder if it might be hitting that sore spot. Like the other night when Matt answered you by talking about himself. Nobody likes to be disregarded; it would bother anyone at least a little. But if it hits the sore spot, the reaction could be much stronger. Most people have trouble with such strong emotions and will try to get rid of them. You pushed your feelings out of the way, listened to Matt, and then locked yourself in the bathroom. Do you think this might be what's happening with you? Have people ever told you that you react more strongly than they think you should?

Sara responded:

A lot of people, including Matt, think my responses are off sometimes. I even think that I react too strongly sometimes. This does make sense . . . I can see how my childhood experiences set me up for this.

This constituted the completion of step a, symptom identification, and a limited degree of step b, retrieval of target learning.

Based on the case formulation, the therapist recommended trauma resolution work as well as directly addressing certain challenging life situations in support of Sara's goals. Sara agreed to this and subsequently began trauma resolution work via PC.

The first cluster of memories to be targeted involved Sara's father. Sara was asked to focus on the earliest one first, an age 3 memory in which Sara's father spanked her to the point that she had an open sore on her buttocks. Prior to starting PC, this memory was rated as a 10 on the SUDS scale. Sara was guided to come up with a beginning picture before the bad part started and an ending picture after the bad part was over. Sara was then instructed to watch the whole movie in her mind from beginning to end, while KL counted out loud.

The first movie was to a count of 10, after which the therapist asked how bad the worst moment felt on the 0-10 SUDS scale. Sara reported a SUDS of 2, because the movie was so quick that Sara "could not experience the movie fully; vividly". The next movie was to a count of 20, and had a SUDS of 8. Sara become flushed, with tears running down her face, and said, "How could he do this to me? Why would my mom let him do this to me? I was so young and so helpless". Thus, step 1 was accomplished, in that the memory appeared to be activated and, along with it, core beliefs and models formed on the basis of the experience being revisited.

Several movies later, Sara reported a SUDS of 5 and, in tears, exclaimed:

He was always so controlling. I was always expected to eat my dinner a certain way, wear clothes that he liked, engage in sports activities that he wanted me to do, and to behave like a perfect child. And I could never really speak my mind with my father without getting punished for it. If I did anything to go against his hidden rules, because he did have special rules for me that my other siblings didn't have, then he would punish me, but this time was really bad and I didn't deserve it. He was not like other fathers. All the fathers I have known have never punished their children as severely as he punished me. I just didn't know then what I know now. At least he can't control me anymore.

This indicated the introduction of contradictory information (e.g., "my father was the problem, not me" and "he can't control me anymore"); thus step 2 was accomplished, destabilizing the target learnings that were being disconfirmed.

Note that within PC the contradictory and corrective information is typically spontaneously generated by the client. However, the identification of the beginning and ending picture for the movie can sometimes also serve as corrective information, insofar as conveying that the bad part is over might get this done. In this case, for example, Sara said, "At least he can't control me anymore".

In the next movie, Sara reported a SUDS of 1. Sara then spoke of the relationship she had developed with a close uncle:

He taught me about relationships in a different way than my father. He always cared about what I had to say, and often asked for my opinion on things. We had a pretty strong relationship, which really developed out of that first time I sat on his knee when I was six, and he encouraged me to talk about what was upsetting me. Not all relationships are just about pleasing the other person. It feels good to give, but it also feels good to receive, and that's okay. He taught me that.

This was one instance of step 3, in which further corrective information was introduced (i.e., loving people care about your needs and value your thoughts and opinions; healthy relationships are built on both giving and receiving). Instances of step 3 continue, either with the same insight or new ones, during consecutive movies, though the client is not required to articulate each realization.

Four movies later, Sara reported a SUDS of 0, and she said, "I don't know if I am doing something wrong, but the memory just feels distant now. Like I am detached from it or something". The therapist reassured Sara that her brain knew exactly what to do. Sara displayed signs of emotional non-reaction to the traumatic memory itself (e.g., the memory felt distant; she felt detached from it). This began fulfilling the final step of verification of erasure defined by Ecker et al. (2012), which consisted of observing key markers of transformational change: former cues no longer trigger reactivation, symptoms cease completely, and these changes persist effortlessly.

Even at a SUDS of 0, PC continued for two more movies until Sara reported no further changes, indicating that the trauma resolution work for that memory had been completed. Sara appeared curious about the ways that her unresolved issues with her father tied into her present level of distress in her current relationship, but she preferred to keep moving forward with more PC at that moment.

Sara was then guided to work on the worst memory of the father cluster (the sequencing of memories to be treated as per Greenwald, 2013a):

I was complaining over several weeks about having some back pain, and then one day, after I told him that I couldn't do my chores because it hurt so bad, he snapped. He forced me to carry a bag stuffed with 45 pounds of weight, wherever I went, for an entire Saturday. By the next morning, my back pain became so severe that I had to go to the hospital. It turned out to be an untreated injury from when I got hurt in gymnastics, which was then (finally) treated with non-invasive surgery. My back pain went away within several days following surgery.

Sara rated the memory as a SUDS of 7. The first and second PC movies each had a SUDS of 2, and then the third movie had a SUDS of 5. Sara, again flushed, reported:

My father wanted me to suffer like he suffered as a child. It was just him unknowingly recreating his own childhood through me. I get that now. But the fact that my back pain could have been easily addressed and treated, and my father chose to dismiss it, is still difficult to wrap my head around. It is easier to watch the movie now, but it still hurts.

The PC continued for several more movies until Sara got to a SUDS of 0 with no more changes. Sara said:

> You know, I have spent the last thirty years seeing the world through this distorted filter thanks to my dad. I feel like this is the first time I am actually seeing the world through my own eyes with no filter. I realize now that my responses to Matt are actually based in fear, in the same way that they were based in fear when I was a child responding to my father. And somehow this fear has caused me to push my needs aside by stuffing them deep within and focusing on the other person's needs instead. I am always trying so hard to take care of and accommodate other people, even at a cost to myself. Now I get why. It's like I am trying to protect myself from some unknown danger. Despite all this, and as weird as it may seem, I really think I can forgive him now; and that feels quite liberating.

In Sara's comments are indications of how the retrieval of target emotional learnings (step b) continues through the PC process along with accompanying emergence of disconfirming knowledge (step c), resulting in steps 1, 2, and 3 occurring and dissolving the target learnings in a natural manner.

Sara continued to make further connections between her relationship with her father and her relationship with Matt. Sara began thinking about her "desire to please Matt and make him happy". She said:

> I take care of all the household responsibilities—preparing meals, doing the dishes, laundry, and caring for our dog—and all this even while maintaining a full-time job, albeit 30 hours less a week then Matt's 70-hr week. And I do all this because it is how I learned to be in a relationship. Until now, it was all I knew. But I realize that it is just me recreating my relationship with my father, in this endless quest to secure his love and affection.

After all of Sara's key memories with her father were processed with PC, the other memories that had been identified on Sara's trauma/loss list were each processed as well. These took a much shorter amount of time than had been required for the memories of her father, likely because the core issues had already been worked out (consistent with Ecker et al., 2012, as well as Greenwald, McClintock, Bailey, & Seubert, 2014). Interestingly, when it came time to process the three memories involving Matt, Sara's SUDS ratings had decreased significantly compared to the initial ratings (also consistent with Greenwald et al.). For example, Sara's earliest upsetting memory of Matt (involving him publicly embarrassing her) was a SUDS of 10 when completing the trauma/loss history; however, just prior to treating this memory, the SUDS was already down to a 2.

By the afternoon of the third day of therapy, all identified distressing memories had been treated to resolution. The final task was to identify some anticipated challenging moments and practice the desired coping strategies in imagination. Therapy was completed by the end of the third day, with plans to check in by phone two weeks later.

At the telephone follow up, Sara was asked about her emotional reactions to the previously identified trigger situations. Sara said:

Now that I am finally seeing the world through my own eyes without any distortion, I realize that I used to attract the wrong kind of people into my life, and because of this I was always in distress. I attracted people who were never able to give me the love, affection, and validation I so desperately desired. I would lose myself in the relationship, even dismissing my own thoughts and feelings in order to focus on pleasing them. It makes me so sad to think that I never felt my thoughts and feelings were important enough to discuss in my relationships. But it wasn't just that my thoughts and feelings were not important, it was that I was used to being punished for expressing them, and this fear has never escaped me until now. My enduring efforts to please others while dismissing my own needs eventually led to me feeling really burnt out and unable to tolerate those situations with Matt any longer, which is why I think I ended up pursuing treatment.

With some further prompting for specific examples, Sara replied:

Well, I don't have to try so hard to please Matt, or anyone, for that matter. A perfect example is the other night when Matt came home late from work. Instead of doing the usual cleaning routine, or spending hours making Matt's favorite dinner, I decided to go out for dinner and a movie with some of my friends. When I returned home, Matt was sitting in the living room all pissed off and immediately started laying into me about dinner. I told him that I had brought him home leftovers, so that he would know that I was at least thinking about him. But, you know what? Matt was actually disappointed that I had not slaved in the kitchen for him. I was not in the least bit surprised by his response and, honestly, it did not ruffle my feathers in the least bit. Instead of appeasing him, I just let Matt know that I felt that he had taken me for granted. When Matt tried to make the conversation about his needs, which is so typical, I just calmly said to Matt that his needs are important to me, but so are mine. The conversation ended with Matt storming off to another room and me letting Matt know that I still love him, even though I was unhappy with his behavior.

Sara continued:

I realize that it was the old me who picked Matt as a partner. Although being with Matt has always been difficult, the difficulty was familiar to me and easy to accept at the beginning. I got stuck in this pattern of giving everything and then being accepting of not receiving anything in return. Somewhere deep in my unconscious, I guess I thought that this is what love was about. Now I am able to consider myself more. I have a better idea about what constitutes a healthy relationship vs. a destructive relationship, and I can more easily avoid or remove myself from the destructive ones. I have devoted more energy to taking care of myself and less energy trying to please others who take me for granted. Because of all this, I feel really good, and am noticing how much healthier and less stressed I feel. A big weight has been lifted.

The memory reconsolidation process can be considered successful based on the verification of schema nullification in which Sara demonstrated emotional non-reactivity in response to trigger situations that previously activated the schema. For example, she said, "It did not ruffle my feathers in the least bit". Symptom cessation was indicated with, "Instead of appeasing him, I just let Matt know that I felt like he had taken me for granted". Effortless permanence of Sara's symptom cessation and emotional non-reactivity was indicated with, "I feel really good, and am noticing how much healthier and less stressed I feel. A big weight has been lifted".

Discussion

This case illustrated how PC, within the phase model of trauma-informed treatment, accomplished the memory reconsolidation process described by Ecker and colleagues (2012). The preparatory portion of this treatment helped the client to identify her symptoms and to be willing and able to engage in the trauma resolution work itself. The structure and process of PC guided the client to activate her memory of specific traumatic events and then, by attending to her experience in those events repeatedly through the movie viewing process, to become progressively aware of mental models and attributed meanings that she had formed in those events and that were still governing her perceptions and responses in the present. This in turn induced spontaneous recognition of her own vivid, contradictory knowledge, which disconfirmed and erased the longstanding schemas maintaining her emotional and behavioral symptoms. Although Sara was able to articulate these mental processes, we have seen many other PC clients who were not so articulate, yet experienced equivalent outcomes.

PC does not require the client to be insight-oriented or to be able to articulate the mental models that they may wish to change. As long as the preparatory portions of the treatment approach are sufficient to move the client forward, memory reconsolidation occurs within the PC process regardless of whether the client is focused primarily on insight, emotional processing, or some other mental activity (Greenwald, 2012). Thus, while PC works well for insight-oriented therapy clients, it is also suitable for those who are not so inclined.

References

Ecker, B., Ticic, R., & Hulley, L. (2012). *Unlocking the emotional brain: Eliminating symptoms at their roots using memory reconsolidation.* New York, NY: Routledge.

Greenwald, R. (2012). Progressive counting: Asking recipients what makes it work. *Traumatology, 18*(3), 59–63.

Greenwald, R. (2013a). *Progressive counting within a phase model of trauma-informed treatment.* New York, NY: Routledge.

Greenwald, R. (2013b, November 4). Get better faster! (for real) [Web log post]. Retrieved from http://www.childtrauma.com/blog/get-better-faster/

Greenwald, R., McClintock, S. D., & Bailey, T. D. (2013). A controlled comparison of eye movement desensitization and reprocessing and progressive counting. *Journal of Aggression, Maltreatment, & Trauma, 22,* 981–996.

Greenwald, R., McClintock, S. D., Bailey, T. D., & Seubert, A. (2014). *Treating early trauma memories reduces the distress of later related memories.* Manuscript submitted for publication.

Greenwald, R., McClintock, S. D., Jarecki, K., & Monaco, A. J. (in press). A comparison of eye movement desensitization and reprocessing and progressive counting among therapists in training. *Traumatology.*

Wolpe, J. (1990). *The practice of behaviour therapy* (4th ed.). New York, NY: Pergamon.

Kymberly Lasser, MA, is a program developer, researcher, and trauma therapist at the Trauma Institute & Child Trauma Institute in Northampton, Massachusetts. She provides intensive trauma therapy retreats for children, pre/adolescents, teens, adults, families, and couples. She utilises a trauma informed approach known as The Fairy Tale Model.

Ricky Greenwald, PsyD, is the founder and executive director of Trauma Institute & Child Trauma Institute. He was previously on the faculty of the Mt. Sinai School of Medicine, is an Affiliate Professor at the SUNY Buffalo School of Social Work, and is a Fellow of the American Psychological Association. He is the author of numerous professional articles as well as several books. His work has been translated into over a dozen languages. Dr. Greenwald developed many techniques used by EMDR child therapists, and his comprehensive EMDR training model has been emulated internationally. He also developed the MASTR protocol for treating problem behaviors, Progressive Counting, and the Fairy Tale phase model of trauma treatment.

HOW ENERGY PSYCHOLOGY CHANGES DEEP EMOTIONAL LEARNINGS

David Feinstein

The stimulation of acupuncture points (acupoints) by tapping on them—used in conjunction with more conventional psychological interventions—has been shown to be effective in the treatment of a spectrum of psychological disorders (Benor, 2014). Known as "energy psychology" (Gallo, 1998), a variety of protocols have been developed, with Emotional Freedom Techniques (EFT; Craig, 2010) and Thought Field Therapy (TFT; Callahan & Callahan, 1996) being the best known and most widely practiced. Outcome investigations suggest that including the somatic elements of the approach can resolve a range of clinical symptoms with greater speed, power, and precision than psychological interventions alone (see reviews in Church, 2013; Church, Feinstein, Palmer-Hoffman, Stein, & Tranguch, 2014; Feinstein, 2012).

The Treatment Sequence

The early phases of energy psychology treatments generally parallel other therapeutic approaches in that the focus is on establishing rapport, discussing the clinical framework, and identifying the presenting problem(s). The clinician remains particularly alert for emotional, cognitive, and behavioral responses implicated in each presenting problem and the cues, contexts, or memories that trigger them.

Once a salient trigger–response pair has been identified for the initial round of tapping, typically in collaboration with the client, the amount of distress the client experiences when bringing that trigger–response pair to mind is given a 0 to 10 rating on a Subjective Units of Distress (SUD) scale (after Wolpe, 1958). An "acceptance statement" is then formulated (e.g., "Even though I have all this anger toward my father, I deeply love and accept myself"). It is repeated several times while tapping or massaging certain acupoints or other prescribed energy spots on the surface of the skin that are believed to facilitate a somatic implanting of the affirmation.

The first tapping sequence involves between 4 and 14 predetermined acupoints. The tapping is usually self-administered by the client, who firmly taps each point with the forefinger and middle finger while stating a "reminder phrase" that keeps the emotional response active. (The therapist may also shift the wording during this process to target different aspects of the problem.) After going through the tapping points, an "integration sequence" is often used which involves a variety of physical procedures, all believed to integrate left- and right-hemisphere activity while help-ing process the emotions activated by the treatment. This is followed by another tapping sequence using the same points as previously. The steps from the initial acceptance statement to this second tapping sequence are sometimes referred to as a "round".

After each round, another SUD rating is taken, often followed by discussion. The therapist may pose questions such as "How do you know it is still at an 8?" or "What sensations are you aware of when you bring the situation to mind?" The therapist also stays alert for internal objections to overcoming the distress (called "psychological reversals") or for pertinent aspects of the problem that have not been addressed. Any of this may shift the focus of what is targeted for mental acti-vation during the next round. The process is repeated until the SUD rating is down to 0 or near 0. At that point, another dimension of the presenting problem may be addressed.

First-Take Skepticism

On first witnessing a demonstration of these strange-looking procedures some 15 years ago, I wondered what tapping on the skin could possibly have to do with psychotherapy and why anyone would be claiming that it is more effective than es-tablished therapies which enjoy strong empirical support. At the time, no peer-re-viewed efficacy research had been published, only passionate claims from a small number of fringe therapists who were enthusiastically promulgating the method. Watching a demonstration of the new "tapping therapy", I was surprised to be cat-apulted into some serious cognitive dissonance.

I had been invited as a guest to a monthly meeting of local psychologists while visiting their city. The program that evening featured a member of the group who had recently introduced energy psychology into his practice. He was going to do a demonstration of the method with a woman being treated for claustrophobia by another of the group's members. Having done research on "new psychotherapies" while at the Johns Hopkins Department of Psychiatry early in my career, I was keenly attuned to the influences on therapeutic outcomes exerted by factors such as placebo, allegiance, charisma, the contagion of a therapist's belief in a method, and the suggestive power that any clinical intervention may wield.

My skepticism only mounted as I watched the treatment unfold. While what occurred during the first few minutes was familiar and comfortable for me—taking a brief history of the problem (which had not responded to treatments from several therapists) and having the client imagine being in an elevator and giving it a rating of 10 on the 0–10 SUD scale—the next part seemed laughable. The client followed the therapist's lead in tapping on about a dozen points on the skin while saying out loud, "fear of elevators". This was followed by a brief "integration sequence" that included a set of odd physical procedures and then another round of tapping. When the client next rated being in an elevator, her SUD had diminished, from a 10 to a 7. She said her heart wasn't pounding as fast. I was surprised to see any decrease in her sense of distress. I was at the time using systematic desensitization for such cases, while this new procedure did not utilize any relaxation methods and required only two or three minutes from the first rating to the second. Perhaps the woman had developed some affection or loyalty to the therapist and didn't want to embarrass him in front of his colleagues.

Another round of the procedure brought the SUD down to a 5. After another round, however, it was back up to a 7. I was thinking, "See, just superficial fluctuations caused by the set and setting. I knew it wouldn't work!" When the therapist inquired, the woman reported that a memory had come to her of being about eight and playing with her brother and some of his friends. They had created a fort out of a cardboard appliance box. When she was in it, the boys closed the box and pushed the opening end against a wall so she was trapped in the box. They then left her there amidst laughter and jeering. She didn't know how long it was until she was found and freed, but in her mind it was a very long time, as she had been screaming till exhausted. She had not recalled this incident for years, and she rated the memory as a 10.

I thought, "Okay, so something was accomplished! A formative event has been identified that some good psychodynamic therapy will be able to resolve over a series of sessions. However strange the method, it has led to an important discovery that will give the treating therapist a new direction. It has been a useful case consultation." But that's not where it ended. The therapist doing the demonstration started having the woman tap using phrases related to the earlier experience. Within 15 minutes, she was able to recall the incident with no subjective sense of distress (SUD at 0). They then returned to elevators and quickly had that down to 0 as well. I looked on with my skepticism fighting what my eyes and ears were registering.

One of the group members suggested that it would be easy to test this, and the woman agreed to step into a hallway coat closet and shut the door. The therapist was careful to make it clear to her that she was to open the door at any point she felt even slightly uncomfortable. The door closed. We waited. And waited. And waited. After about three long minutes, the therapist knocked and asked if she was okay. She opened the door and triumphantly announced that for the first time since childhood, she was comfortable in a small enclosed space. Meanwhile, I was thinking, "Okay, I'm onto them now! This is a social psychology experiment. We are about to be informed that we have been subjects in a study of how gullible therapists can be!" That announcement never came.

Searching for an Explanation

That demonstration was persuasive enough to cause me to look further into energy psychology and then to go through a certification program in the method. I was finding that the protocol gave a tremendous boost to my clinical outcomes. The physical procedures did not resemble anything I had learned in my clinical training, but when I experimented, I found that without them the psychological procedures were not nearly as effective. As research began to accumulate that corroborated what I was observing with my own clients, and what was being reported by colleagues who were using the method, the question that became most prominent in my mind was, "Okay, if it works, how does it work?"

The first compelling clue came when I learned about an ongoing research program at Harvard Medical School. The investigators were using imaging equipment to document the physiological effects of simulating specific acupuncture points. For instance, the needling of a particular acupoint on the hand (Large Intestine 4) produced prominent decreases of fMRI-registered activation in the amygdala, hippocampus, and other brain areas associated with fear and pain (Hui et al., 2000). Subsequent studies by the same team led to the conclusion that "functional MRI and PET studies on acupuncture at commonly used acupuncture points have demonstrated significant modulatory effects on the limbic system, paralimbic, and subcortical gray structures" (Hui et al., 2005, p. 496). Further investigation provided "additional evidence in support of previous reports" that acupuncture is able to produce "extensive deactivation of the limbic-paralimbic-neocortical system" (Fang et al., 2009).

Meanwhile, a series of reports using electroencephalogram (EEG) analysis to explore neurological effects of acupoint *tapping* (as contrasted with the traditional use of needles) showed normalized brainwave patterns upon activation of a traumatic memory that had disrupted such patterns prior to treatment (Diepold & Goldstein, 2009), normalization of theta waves after claustrophobia treatments (Lambrou, Pratt, & Chevalier, 2003), and decreased right frontal cortex arousal in treating trauma following motor vehicle accidents (Swingle, Pulos, & Swingle, 2004), all corroborated by improvements on pre-/post-treatment psychological measures. Together, these laboratory findings suggest that the stimulation of specific acupuncture points, with or without needles, can bring about precise, intended outcomes—such as the deactivation of an amygdala-based fear response to a specific stimulus.

Bingo! Or so it seemed. The primary mechanism in energy psychology appeared to be that after using a reminder phrase that brings about limbic-paralimbic-neocortical arousal, tapping on acupoints sends signals to the amygdala and other brain structures that immediately reduce that arousal. This would provide a plausible explanation for the rapid effects that have been widely reported by clinicians using the method, as well as an explanation for why the interventions can be targeted to bring about precise, desired outcomes. The reminder phrase selected determines the trigger–response pairing that will then be neutralized by the signals the acupoint stimulation sends to the limbic system.

However, while I found this explanation to have appeal, I quickly realized it was incomplete. It did not, in fact, account for the most critical piece of the puzzle. How do a few rounds of tapping while mentally activating a problematic response *permanently* change that response? Even if the tapping does send deactivating signals to the brain structures that maintain the unwanted response, resulting in temporary relief, wouldn't tapping be needed *every time* the trigger–response pairing was activated, in order to prevent the response? Yet follow-up investigations have shown the clinical benefits of energy psychology protocols persist with no further treatment (Church, 2013; Feinstein, 2012).

Therapeutic Reconsolidation: The Missing Piece of the Puzzle

Enter the findings about memory reconsolidation that began to emerge in the late 1990s from labs around the world. Hundreds of studies have shown that "a consolidated memory can return . . . to a labile, sensitive state—in which it can be modified, strengthened, changed or even erased!" (Nader, 2003, p. 65). Another, more powerful mechanism than *extinction* was being proposed to explain how the brain updates itself on the basis of new experience. The prevailing belief among neuroscientists had been that once a new learning is consolidated into long-term memory, it is permanently installed. It could be modified, or even eclipsed by subsequent experiences, as in extinction training, but it nonetheless remained and could be reactivated. Reconsolidation researchers were showing that if specific conditions were met after reactivation of an existing learning, that learning became labile, that is, capable of being altered or even completely erased and replaced with a new learning that integrated a current experience into the context of the original learning. The far-reaching implications of this discovery are delineated for clinicians in Ecker, Ticic, and Hulley's (2012) *Unlocking the Emotional Brain: Eliminating Symptoms at their Roots Using Memory Reconsolidation.*

The findings on memory reconsolidation show that despite the stubborn tenacity of deep emotional learnings, the brain has a mechanism for "updating existing learnings with new ones" (Ecker et al., 2012, p. 26). While core beliefs and mental models formed in the presence of intense emotion during childhood or later "are locked into the brain by extraordinarily durable synapses" that typically persist for the remainder of a person's life (p. 3), neuroscience research since 2004 has demonstrated that these core beliefs and mental models can be modified or totally eradicated. By facilitating a specific sequence of experiences, targeted emotional learnings can be activated and their synapses unlocked "for prompt dissolution of . . . retrieved learnings at their emotional and neural roots" (p. 8).

Through this process of "depotentiating" (deactivating at the synaptic level) the neural pathways maintaining implicit learnings that are at the basis of psychological problems, "major, longstanding symptoms can cease [because] their very basis no longer exists" (Ecker et al., 2012, p. 4). Whether in the lab, the consulting room, or the daily flow of life experiences, the deeply embedded learnings that "underlie and generate" (p. 14) a large proportion of the symptoms presenting in psychotherapy can be revised or altogether eradicated when a set of precise conditions has been met. Called the "transformation sequence" (p. 41), three interrelated experiences must occur:

1. The emotional memory or learning must be vividly accessed.

2. A "juxtaposition experience" that contradicts the implicit models or conclusions drawn from the original experience must concurrently be activated.

3. The juxtaposition pairing must be repeated several times.

Studies in labs and clinical settings, using both animal and human subjects, all point to this simple, commonsense sequence of steps as the way new experiences are incorporated into established models of how the world works and one's place in it. These steps seem to be nature's key for chemically unlocking the synapses that maintain deep learnings established in the past during highly charged emotional experiences, and for allowing them to be reconsolidated in a new way based on more recent experiences.

While not all psychotherapy facilitates this transformational sequence, Ecker et al. (2012) maintain that if the therapy produced basic markers of permanent change of an acquired response, these steps must have occurred "whether or not the therapist or client was cognizant of this sequence of experiences taking place" (p. 127). They maintain, in fact, that this model is a "meta-conceptualization" (p. 129) that transcends the theories and techniques of specific schools of psychotherapy, and that it can be applied to the implicit learnings that are at the foundation of a wide range of psychological symptoms, whether "formed in attachment, existential, social, traumatic, or other experiences" (p. 126).

How Energy Psychology Protocols Utilize Reconsolidation

In introducing the earliest acupoint tapping protocols, Callahan (1985) formulated a set of procedures that were, by intuition or by accident, remarkably attuned to the findings on memory reconsolidation that would emerge two decades later. Each of the steps in the transformation sequence identified by Ecker et al. (2012) occurs by following the core procedures of an energy psychology protocol. Even without the therapist or the client thinking in terms such as "juxtaposition experiences", "disconfirming knowledge", or "reconsolidation", the steps of the transformation sequence nonetheless occur.

Step 1: The emotional memory or learning must be vividly accessed. In a typical energy psychology treatment, the initial rounds of acupoint tapping most often involve activating the symptom or presenting problem using images, evocative phrases, or a felt sense of the problem. That scenario inevitably contains the implicit learnings underlying the symptoms. For instance, when the woman discussed above brought to mind being in a closed space by means of imagery and the reminder phrase "fear of elevators", the implicit belief that closed spaces are dangerous and to be avoided was activated. The formative experiences that established such a learning do not necessarily need to be accessed, but they frequently emerge. When the tapping has removed some of the emotional edge of the current problem, childhood memories involved with the presenting problem tend to spontaneously enter the client's awareness. When this happens, they generally become an area of focus, as occurred when the memory of being trapped in the appliance box came into the woman's mind. This allows the adaptive historical function of the symptom to be recognized and appreciated, a process that Ecker et al. (2012) use to normalize and humanize the client's symptoms and treatment. If, as is often the case, it proves necessary to address the original formative experiences to completely resolve the presenting problem, and the relevant memories do not arise spontaneously, techniques for bridging to earlier memories, such as following a current feeling or bodily sensation back to one of the first times it was experienced, are frequently used.

Step 2: A "juxtaposition experience" that contradicts the implicit models or conclusions drawn from the original experience must concurrently be activated. The second step in the sequence—generating an experience that disconfirms the earlier learning—is the most complex stage for most reconsolidation-oriented therapies, but it is where energy psychology protocols are shown to greatest advantage. Because stimulating selected acupoints rapidly reduces limbic arousal

(Fang et al., 2009; Hui et al., 2000, 2005), the emotional landscape changes *during* the exposure. A traumatic memory or trigger that produced a physiological threat response is vividly imagined, but the disturbing physiological response is no longer present. The brain is already experiencing a mismatch from learned expectations. The memory or trigger created a strong expectation that an unpleasant emotional reaction would be evoked, but the expected response did not occur, because acupoint stimulation had temporarily deactivated the limbic response. As the woman imagined being in an elevator without feeling the expected fear and racing heart, a mismatch occurred between her experience and her expectation. This juxtaposition of holding the troubling scene simultaneous with no physiological arousal is the mismatch that unlocks the neural pathway maintaining the old learning so it can be transformed by the new experiences in the next step. The mismatch or "disconfirming experience" in energy psychology treatments is generated simply by tapping on the skin—almost too easy to believe. The required mismatch is effected by bringing the trigger to mind while preventing the expected threat response from occurring via the deactivating signals the acupoint stimulation sends to the limbic system. Other therapies usually have to work much harder to create suitable mismatch experiences.

Step 3: The juxtaposition pairing must be repeated. Energy psychology protocols involve substantial repetition. Not only are as many rounds as necessary carried out to bring the SUD rating down to 0 or near 0 (in some cases having some subjective distress is considered adaptive), but every aspect of the problem that can be identified as evoking subjective distress is treated. In addition, therapists learning energy psychology are taught to challenge their positive outcomes. They might ask the client to try to reproduce the fear, pain, anger, or other disturbing emotion associated with the target memory or trigger by making the imagery more vivid or simply willing the earlier emotion to return. They might test the results by having the client imagine contexts that are even more severe than the original tapping scene and more likely to trigger distress. Back-home or other in vivo tests are also encouraged and discussed.

The Preliminary and Verification Phase

For clinicians to purposefully bring about what is termed "the therapeutic reconsolidation process" (p. 126), Ecker et al. (2012) describe a set of preliminary steps that are generally necessary to set up the transformation sequence outlined above and also a verification process that follows the transformation sequence. The three *preliminary* steps include a) identifying the target symptom, b) identifying the implicit learnings that maintain the symptom, and c) identifying knowledge within the client's experiences and beliefs that contradicts the learnings that maintain the symptom. Then, to *verify* that the transformation sequence has been successful, Ecker et al. turn to the same markers that neuroscientists use in laboratory studies to determine whether an emotional learning has been permanently eradicated via reconsolidation: the change was abrupt rather than incremental, the symptom-generating emotional reactions that had been triggered by specific cues and contexts are absent, and the change persists "without effort or counteractive measures" (p. 127). In what follows I will explore how these additional phases of treatment played into a case study.

Energy Psychology and Reconsolidation: A Case Study

In selecting a case to review in terms of the therapeutic reconsolidation model, I simply chose my most recent published case (Eden & Feinstein, 2014, pp. 221–224). As part of a book for the general public, it was not written to illustrate the reconsolidation process, and I thought it would be an interesting experiment to see how readily it fitted with the Ecker et al. (2012) model. I have structured the commentary so you can judge the results of this experiment for yourself. The descriptions of the case and the treatment are taken from the published version, edited and abridged only slightly to fit this context. The comments bridging it to the conditions necessary for therapeutic reconsolidation are new and are in italics.

Background. Jeremy was 36 when he married Melissa. He was eager to help raise her sons, aged 7 and 9. He had gotten to know them quite well during the year prior to the marriage, had taken them to baseball games, zoos, parks, and other local attractions, and had participated in their hobbies. The boys liked their stepdad and the attention he was giving them, and the new family was blossoming within an atmosphere of affection and promise. Melissa's ex-husband, Steve, the boys' biological father, had not been particularly eager to spend time with his sons during the marriage, but he also loved them. He had moved to another town several hours away after the divorce but had been reliable in taking the boys for the afternoon every other Sunday.

During his courtship with Melissa, Jeremy had never met Steve. But now that Jeremy had moved in with the family, the twice-monthly visits became a fixture in his life. He was civil enough toward his new wife's ex, but he avoided having much contact with him when the boys were being picked up or dropped off. During the first Christmas vacation after the marriage, Steve arranged to take the boys for a week, and the three of them flew to Orlando for a Disney marathon. The boys were so excited about it that they seemed to talk of little else for the week prior to and for the week following the trip. When Steve came for the next Sunday visitation, Jeremy could hardly look at him. He began to criticize Steve's parenting style to Melissa, point out his culpability in the divorce, and generally paint an ugly picture of the man who had fathered her children. At first Melissa acknowledged the truth in some of the observations, but over time Jeremy became increasingly vehement in his criticisms. This grew into a loaded theme in their interactions on the weekends that Steve would be arriving, and Jeremy began questioning the boys about their visits with their father, as if looking for more fodder for his rants. He was eventually unable to hide from the boys his disdain toward their father.

Jeremy's jealousy toward Steve continued to escalate, and the acrimony was seeping into other areas of the family. As Steve's visits approached, tension would descend onto the household. The boys were confused. Melissa began to judge Jeremy harshly. She had more than once called him a "spoiled brat". This was the state of things when they scheduled a couple counseling session with me.

Preliminary phase. Jeremy knew at some level that his reactions were not rational, but this knowledge was no match for the strength of his emotions. When Jeremy was triggered, Steve was an evil man sabotaging all of Jeremy's fine efforts with the boys and the family, and there was no other reality to consider.

After hearing both of their renditions of the problem, I spoke to the part of Jeremy that knew his reactions to Steve were extreme. I explained that when intense emotions are triggered, they are very real, whether rational or irrational. I suggested tapping to take the edge off the intensity of Jeremy's responses to Steve. Neither Jeremy nor Melissa had any experience with energy psychology, but the couple who referred them had worked with me and described the method, so they were game for anything that could help, however strange it might seem. While Jeremy was not open to considering that his assessment of Steve might be wrong, he was interested in feeling less consumed by his reactions. *We had accomplished only the first of the three preliminary steps—"identifying the target symptom"—before the first round of tapping. Jeremy knew his reactions to Steve were extreme and that was what he wished to change. As you will see, the next preliminary step, "identifying the implicit learnings that maintain the symptom", occurs during the tapping protocol.*

First round of tapping. The scene that Jeremy chose for the first SUD rating was from the previous Sunday, watching as Steve's car pulled into the driveway. He gave it a 10. *So we have activated the emotional reaction, but not yet completed the first step of the transformation process by identifying the emotional learning—the implicit meanings or models—that are driving the reaction.*

After four rounds of tapping, the SUD had gone down to a 7, but even after further tapping it seemed to be stuck there. I asked, "How do you know it is a 7?" Jeremy said that he felt pressure in his chest and a tightness in his throat. I asked him to explore the feelings in his throat. He said it was almost as if he were trying to hold back tears. I asked if he could remember one of the first times he had that feeling. He immediately recalled being 10 when his parents brought a foster boy into the family. It was to be a temporary arrangement until a permanent placement could be found, a favor for a relative of the boy, but it changed everything for Jeremy.

As an only child, Jeremy had enjoyed his parents' full attention and affection. Suddenly, that was history. The foster boy had many problems, both of Jeremy's parents held full-time jobs, and the limited time and resources they had available shifted from Jeremy to the new boy. Jeremy, at 10, did not have words or concepts that could help him come to grips with the loss. He felt emotionally abandoned by both of his parents, could not fathom why they had brought this troublesome person into their home, and he hated the foster boy. He began starting fights and creating acrimony wherever he could. This strategy seemed to eventually work. After about a year, the agency found a permanent placement for the boy and Jeremy never saw him again. All of this had faded from Jeremy's awareness. He hadn't thought about it for years, and no other circumstance in his adult life had triggered his unprocessed feelings around that phase of his childhood. He had never thought to mention it to Melissa, but the parallels between the foster boy and the situation with Steve became immediately obvious to all three of us.

This insight and its subsequent exploration accomplished the second preliminary step, "identifying the implicit learnings that maintain the symptom", as well as completing the first step of the transformation process, "vividly accessing the emotional learning". Jeremy now recognized that he was projecting onto Steve the model he had formed during his experience with the foster boy, admitting that he was afraid Steve was going to render him peripheral and alone, just as the foster boy had done. Notice that we are not going in the exact order of completing the preliminaries before starting the transformation process, nor do Ecker et al. (2012) imply that the steps are fixed. In fact, as you move into the transformation phase, additional information that corresponds with the preliminary topics for exploration organically emerges and may subsequently be utilized.

Neutralizing salient aspects of the problem. We tapped on every aspect of the memory we could identify, staying with each until subjective distress was down to a 0: Jeremy's loss of his parents' attention; his many times having held back tears when he felt lonely and abandoned; his confusion and puzzlement about what he had done wrong to deserve having all the attention withdrawn from him; the invasion into his family; his hatred for the new boy; the fights they had; his being punished for starting them and feeling like a bad boy after 10 years of being a good boy; and even his confusion when the new boy suddenly disappeared.

Fortunately, each round of tapping takes only a couple of minutes, so all of this was accomplished within that first session (I generally schedule two hours for initial sessions with couples). Jeremy was by then able to talk lucidly and calmly about the foster boy and the boy's invasion into his young life. *We now see Jeremy vividly having an initial set of juxtaposition experiences, the second step of the transformation process. His memories about the foster boy are no longer paired with feelings of anger, hate, jealousy, and abandonment. This was accomplished simply by evoking the memories and neutralizing the emotional responses using the acupoint tapping.*

Completing the transformation sequence. Now Jeremy could reflect on how Steve's visits with the boys were bringing up feelings that could be traced back to his experiences with the foster boy. *Finally, we get to the third preliminary, "identifying knowledge within the client's experiences and beliefs that contradicts the learnings that maintain the symptom". Jeremy was recognizing that his sense of Steve purposefully trying to destroy Jeremy's family seemed to have more to do with this earlier scenario than with the current one. He was now able to simultaneously hold two possibilities: the still somewhat emotionally charged framing from the old learning that "Steve is trying to destroy my family and upset my place in it", and the emotionally benign framing from the new learning that "Steve is just visiting with his boys like any father gets to do, and even though it sure reminds me of what I went through at 10, he really isn't a threat to my relationship with the boys".*

Focusing again on watching Steve's car pulling into the driveway, Jeremy gave it an SUD rating of three. A couple more rounds of tapping and it was down to a 0. *We have by now created juxtaposition experiences (the second step of the transformation process) enough times and in enough contexts (first with the foster boy and then with Steve) to accomplish the third step, which is the repetition of the juxtaposition experiences. The conditions have been met for Jeremy to permanently revise, through the therapeutic reconsolidation process, the deep emotional learnings from his childhood that were driving his reactions to Steve.*

Addressing fallout. We then briefly focused on Melissa's horror and sense of betrayal about Jeremy's shift over the recent months from an apparently ideal stepfather to an angry, jealous, irrational force in her home. Witnessing what we had gone through with Jeremy had already put all of this into a welcome new light, and by the end of the session, Melissa was able to review the strange course of their young marriage with no emotional charge.

Follow-up. On a follow-up session two weeks later, the issue had vanished. Jeremy was not triggered by Steve's next visit, the strong relationship Jeremy had established with the boys and with Melissa was back on track, and I had lost customers who could easily have spent a year or two in counseling. Such are the risks a therapist takes when diving right into the therapeutic reconsolidation process. *The verification phase of the treatment was accomplished in that the three markers of an emotional learning having been permanently eradicated were all present: the change was abrupt rather than incremental, the symptom-generating emotional reactions that had been triggered by specific cues and contexts were absent, and the change persisted without effort or counteractive measures.*

Discussion

The observations of Ecker et al. (2012) regarding therapeutic change, based on an understanding of the reconsolidation of emotional learnings, are consistent with the clinical reports emerging from energy psychology. One of the most controversial yet significant of these is that "transformational change through the erasure sequence does not rely on extensive repetition over time to effect change" (p. 32). The rapid outcomes seen in energy psychology treatments are consistent with Ecker et al.'s observations about "the swiftness with which deep, decisive, lasting change occurs through the therapeutic reconsolidation process" (p. 32). This, of course, "challenges traditional notions of the time required for major therapeutic effects to come about" (p. 32).

Another pertinent observation is that the "mismatch" component—the visceral experience that contradicts the client's existing emotional knowledge and becomes the basis for the new learning—"must feel decisively *real* to the person based on his or her own living experience . . . it must be experiential learning as distinct from conceptual, intellectual learning, though it may be accompanied by the latter" (p. 27). One of the most satisfying and frequently repeated experiences for energy psychology practitioners is watching the astonished expression on a person's face when bringing to mind a memory or trigger, or entering an in vivo situation, that 15 minutes earlier was met with the physiological components of terror but is now devoid of any emotional charge whatsoever.

Of particular interest with reconsolidation-informed therapies is the way that when an old emotional learning is erased, "erasure is limited to precisely the reactivated target learning, without impairing other closely linked emotional learnings that have not been directly reactivated" (Ecker et al., 2012, p. 25). Consistent with reports from energy psychology practitioners, after the learned fear response has been eliminated, "subjects still remembered the experiences in which they had acquired the conditioned fear response, as well as the fact of having had the fear, but the fear was not re-evoked by remembering those experiences" (p. 25). Ecker et al.'s (2012) observation is also clinically instructive. Energy psychology protocols treat every aspect of a problem that can be identified. It is not assumed that closely linked emotional learnings have been neutralized until they have each been addressed. For instance, a psychological aspect of the fear of elevators experienced by the woman from my earlier example was her childhood experience of being trapped in the appliance box. Both the current fear and the formative memory needed to be treated before it was likely that her phobia could be fully eliminated.

One final observation from Ecker et al. (2012)—that the treatment leads to an "increased sense of unified self and wholeness" (p. 33)—is also consistent with the outcomes reported by energy psychology practitioners. Not only are symptoms overcome, but when outdated emotional learnings are submitted to the therapeutic reconsolidation process, and old limiting beliefs and mental models transformed, new connections with neural networks that support optimal functioning are formed. Implicit memories and learnings enter the neocortex-mediated explicit memory system and integrate with neural pathways that support more adaptive coping strategies and an enhanced sense of integration. With little prompting, clients talk about themselves and their situation in more self-affirming ways. Their view of their world and their place in it becomes more complex yet more coherent and empowering.

Energy psychology protocols thus explicitly and organically fulfill the steps necessary for the therapeutic reconsolidation process. The tapping in itself does not erase or transform the embedded learning. But it does temporarily deactivate the limbic response to the memory, cue, or context that was evoking the target emotion and related learning. When the circumstances that triggered the emotion are experienced without the expected emotion occurring, the contradictory experience that is necessary for juxtaposition and therapeutic reconsolidation is unwittingly but fortuitously created. The outdated learning or model is then permanently eliminated or updated through the reconsolidation process. The client's felt sense is that a memory, cue, or context that had evoked a strong and unwanted emotional or behavioral reaction no longer triggers that reaction. The change is brought about rapidly, with precision, and it is lasting.

* * *

Comments on earlier drafts of this article by John Freedom and Robert Schwarz are gratefully acknowledged.

References

Benor, D. J. (2014). Energy psychology: Practices and theories of new combinations of psychotherapy. *Current Research in Psychology, 5*, 1–18. **doi:**10.3844/crpsp.2014.1.18

Callahan, R. J. (1985). *Five minute phobia cure: Dr. Callahan's treatment for fears, phobias and self-sabotage.* Wilmington, DE: Enterprise Publishing.

Callahan, R. J., & Callahan, J. (1996). *Thought Field Therapy (TFT) and trauma: Treatment and theory.* Indian Wells, CA: Thought Field Therapy Training Center.

Church, D. (2013). Clinical EFT as an evidence-based practice for the treatment of psychological and physiological conditions. *Psychology, 4,* 645–654. doi:10.4236/psych.2013.48092.

Church, D., Feinstein, D., Palmer-Hoffman, J., Stein, P. K., & Tranguch, A. (2014). Empirically supported psychological treatments: The challenge of evaluating clinical innovations. *The Journal of Nervous and Mental Disease, 202,* 699–709. doi:10.1097/NMD.0000000000000188

Craig, G. (2010). *The EFT manual.* Santa Rosa, CA: Energy Psychology Press.

Diepold, J. H., & Goldstein, D. (2009). Thought field therapy and QEEG changes in the treatment of trauma: A case study. *Traumatology, 15*, 85–93. doi:10.1177/1534765608325304

Ecker, B., Ticic, R., & Hulley, L. (2012). *Unlocking the emotional brain: Eliminating symptoms at their roots using memory reconsolidation.* New York, NY: Routledge.

Eden, D., & Feinstein, D. (2014). *The energies of love: Keys to a fulfilling partnership.* New York, NY: Tarcher/Penguin.

Fang, J., Jin, Z., Wang, Y., Li, K., Kong, J., Nixon, E. E., . . . Hui, K. K.-S. (2009). The salient characteristics of the central effects of acupuncture needling: Limbic-paralimbic-neocortical network modulation. *Human Brain Mapping, 30,* 1196–1206. doi:10.1002/hbm.20583

Feinstein, D. (2012). Acupoint stimulation in treating psychological disorders: Evidence of efficacy. *Review of General Psychology, 16,* 364–380. doi:10.1037/a0028602

Gallo, F. P. (1998). *Energy psychology: Explorations at the interface of energy, cognition, behavior, and health.* New York, NY: CRC Press.

Hui, K. K.-S., Liu, J., Makris, N., Gollub, R. W., Chen, A. J. W., Moore, C. I., . . . Kwong, K. K. (2000). Acupuncture modulates the limbic system and subcortical gray structures of the human brain: Evidence from fMRI studies in normal subjects. *Human Brain Mapping, 9,* 13–25. doi:10.1002/(SICI)1097-

0193(2000)9:1<13::AID-HBM2>3.0.CO;2-F

Hui, K. K. S., Liu, J., Marina, O., Napadow, V., Haselgrove, C., Kwong, K. K., . . . Makris, N. (2005). The integrated response of the human cerebro-cerebellar and limbic systems to acupuncture stimulation at ST 36 as evidenced by fMRI. *NeuroImage, 27*, 479–496. doi:10.1016/j.neuroimage.2005.04.037

Lambrou, P. T., Pratt, G. J., & Chevalier, G. (2003). Physiological and psychological effects of a mind/body therapy on claustrophobia. *Subtle Energies & Energy Medicine, 14*, 239–251.

Nader, K. (2003). Memory traces unbound. *Trends in Neurosciences, 26*, 65–72. doi:10.1016/S0166-2236(02)00042-5

Swingle, P. G., Pulos, L., & Swingle, M. K. (2004). Neurophysiological indicators of EFT treatment of post-traumatic stress. *Subtle Energies & Energy Medicine, 15*, 75–86.

Wolpe, J. (1958). *Psychotherapy by reciprocal inhibition.* Stanford, CA: Stanford University Press.

David Feinstein, PhD, a clinical psychologist, has been a pioneer in developing innovative therapeutic approaches, leading to nine national awards for his books on consciousness and healing.

He was recipient of the *U.S. Book News* Best Psychology/Mental Health Book Award of 2007. He has served on the faculties of The Johns Hopkins University School of Medicine and Antioch College.

His website is www.EnergyPsychEd.com.

USING NLP FOR MEMORY RECONSOLIDATION

A GLIMPSE OF INTEGRATING THE PANOPLY OF PSYCHOTHERAPIES

Bruce Ecker

Memory reconsolidation is the brain's innate process for unlocking stored learnings and conditionings at the synaptic level. Unlocking is of course a metaphorical term, but in this case the metaphor describes the very real cellular and molecular destabilization of encoding synapses. (For research reviews, see Agren, 2014 and Reichelt & Lee, 2013.)

That destabilization is the deconsolidation of the target learning, and it launches a process of reconsolidation or restabilization, which is completed in about five hours. During this period (known as the reconsolidation window), the target learning is susceptible to being unlearned and erased along with the unwanted responses that it generates (both external behaviors and internal states of mind), without any loss of personal autobiographical memory.

To the best of our scientific knowledge, reconsolidation is the core process in play whenever lasting, transformational change occurs in psychotherapy. There is no other known type of neuroplasticity that can eliminate a learned, well-established response pattern. The process of extinction temporarily suppresses but does not erase a target learning (Bouton, 2004), and is a fundamentally different neurological process than reconsolidation (as reviewed by Ecker, 2015).

The brain's requirements for triggering the reconsolidation and erasure of a specific target learning are well defined, as described below, but the brain does not care what particular techniques or procedures are used for fulfilling those requirements. That is why many different forms of psychotherapy (as well as experiences in other contexts) sometimes succeed in facilitating transformational change, even when the therapist is not informed about memory reconsolidation and is unaware of fulfilling its requirements.

Through acquiring such awareness, a clinician's ability to reliably and consistently facilitate transformational change can increase significantly. I experienced this myself and have seen it prove true for many clinical colleagues. For the psychotherapy field it is significant that empirical knowledge of how reconsolidation produces lasting change represents a major, unprecedented alternative to the multiplicity of theory-based models of change that have shaped the clinical landscape for over a century.

The therapeutic reconsolidation process

For flexible, consistent utilization of memory reconsolidation in psychotherapy, there is a general template that translates the laboratory findings into clinical application, consisting of a series of steps known as the *therapeutic reconsolidation process* (Ecker, Ticic, & Hulley (2012, 2013a). That process is fully natural and uses new learning to erase old learning. Chemical methods of erasure have also been studied (see Agren, 2014) but are in general less effective, less versatile, and less safe.

The case example below identifies how the steps of the therapeutic reconsolidation process, or TRP, are carried out by one of the core techniques of the neuro-linguistic programming (NLP) system of psychotherapy (Dilts, Grinder, Bandler, & DeLozier, 1980; Wake, 2008). The TRP begins with three preparatory steps of *accessing needed material*:

A. Identify symptom. Clarify with the client *what* to regard as the presenting symptom(s)—the specific behaviors, somatics, emotions, and/or thoughts that the client wants to eliminate—and *when* they happen, that is, the cues and contexts that evoke them. This information is critical to carrying out Step B.

B. Retrieve target learning. Bring into explicit awareness, as a visceral emotional experience, the details of the emotional learning or schema underlying and driving the presenting symptom. Knowledge of this material is critical to carrying out Step C.

C. Identify disconfirming knowledge. Find a vivid experience (past or present) that can serve as living knowledge that fundamentally contradicts the model of reality in the target emotional learning, such that both cannot possibly be true. The disconfirming material may be already part of the client's personal knowledge or may be created by a new experience.

As a result of Steps A, B, and C, client and therapist now have ready access to the materials needed for the three next steps, the *erasure sequence*, that yield a transformational change:

1. Reactivate target learning. Cues or contexts known to retrigger the target learning are used to reactivate it into foreground awareness. This is a bodily experience of emotional arousal combined with cognitive recognition of the content of the target learning.

2. Guide juxtaposition. With reactivation occurring, guide an experience that contradicts and disconfirms the target learning's model and expectations of how the world functions. This *juxtaposition* of the target learning with a vivid disconfirmation fulfills the requirement for *memory mismatch* or *prediction error* identified in many empirical studies of reconsolidation (e.g., Pedreira, Pérez-Cuesta, & Maldonado, 2004; Sevenster, Beckers, & Kindt, 2013; for an extensive list, see Ecker, 2015 or http://tiny.cc/7yutfx). The juxtaposition immediately destabilizes and unlocks synapses, rendering neural circuits susceptible to being updated by the disconfirming experience as new learning.

3. Nullify and erase via new learning. Guide a few repetitions of the juxtaposition in Step 2.

The next and final Step V seeks *verification of transformational change* by observing its three clear markers (the same markers that neuroscientists regard as confirming erasure of a target learning):

V. i. Symptom cessation. Unwanted behavior, emotion, somatics, or thoughts permanently cease to occur.

ii. Non-reactivation. The specific emotionally activated state and schema underlying symptoms can no longer be reactivated by cues and triggers that formerly did so.

iii. Effortless permanence. Non-recurrence of the emotional reaction and symptoms continues without counteractive or preventative measures of any kind.

The therapeutic reconsolidation process or TRP consists of those seven steps, A-B-C-1-2-3-V. The case example below adds NLP to the growing list of therapy systems that have been shown to carry out the TRP. As more and more therapy systems are added to that list, the validity of the TRP as a comprehensive framework of psychotherapy integration is demonstrated more extensively. For an updated list of psychotherapy systems that have been shown to guide the steps of the TRP, see http://bit.ly/15Z00HQ.

My further aim in the following case example is to show that, in addition to serving as a guide for consistently effective psychotherapy, the TRP is truly useful as a framework of psychotherapy integration. The TRP positions a therapist to see the multiplicity of therapy systems as a huge repertoire of ways of facilitating the same core process of transformational change. I hope to give readers a vicarious glimpse of the expanded capability and clinical dexterity that are gained by having the TRP as one's home base.

NLP Case Example

The client is a 45-year-old man whom I'll call Thomas. He described long-term PTSD in the form of a terrifying image and body sensation that were retriggered fairly often whenever he thought about clearing out "a whole room in our house piled *full* of books, papers, and unopened mail". He said he had created that accumulation and added, "This room has been a source of contention in my marriage for years."

Thomas was always stopped from putting this room in order because the thought of approaching that task triggered an overwhelming fear that he described by saying, "I feel I'm seeing a tidal wave coming right at me." He meant that literally, and the experience was quite destabilizing emotionally. Even describing this room situation to me was a delicate matter for Thomas, requiring pauses so that he could breathe and calm himself. It was clear to me that Thomas was describing PTSD symptoms, that is, the retriggering of traumatic memory. However, he had no idea at all about any original traumatic experience that had set up this horrible image and feeling of an oncoming tidal wave.

As I listened to Thomas describe this problem, I was considering his account in relation to the steps of the TRP, because the TRP is the framework I use for psychotherapy. I saw that Step A, symptom identification, was adequately accomplished, so I was wondering about Step B, eliciting explicit recognition of the emotional learning producing the symptom. I realized that Thomas had already revealed to me a key piece of that emotional learning: his emotional brain had evidently learned that approaching the piled-up room for clean-up work meant a tidal wave was coming right at him. That strong association between cleaning up the piled-up room and the horror of facing a tidal wave was the target learning in need of unlearning and dissolution by means of the therapeutic reconsolidation process. I was reminded of classical conditioning, in which the emotional brain learns to associate a normally harmless perception with a specific form of suffering.

Now that I had taken stock of the target learning responsible for Thomas's traumatic reactivation, Step B was carried out, and it was time for me to begin Step C, finding how Thomas could have an experience that decisively disconfirms the target learning. Usually I use the methods of Coherence Therapy to carry out the TRP, and for Step C in particular, Coherence Therapy provides an assortment of methods (Ecker et al., 2012). In this case, however, as I wondered how best to find an experience that would potently contradict the Pavlovian-like association of room and tidal wave, it was a method from NLP, not Coherence Therapy, that came to mind.

I proceeded immediately to guide the NLP technique, yet I did not feel I was switching out of one framework and into some other, different framework of psychotherapy. I was not thinking, "I need to switch over to NLP for this." I was staying in the core process of my home framework, the TRP. I knew what needed to be done next according to that process (Step C) and was scanning the various therapeutic methods in my personal repertoire for those that fit the client's material for that next step. In doing so, my internal process felt natural and seamless, and it was also very satisfying to have such a unifying framework guiding me to deliver an effective process of change. Otherwise, the extreme fragmentation of the psychotherapy field can feel anything but seamless as we strive to help our clients.

The NLP technique that I began guiding was very simple—so simple that there is far more involved in describing why it worked than how it was carried out. Bear in mind that my aim at this point was finding how to *create an experience* that would contradict and disconfirm Thomas's existing emotional learning that trying to clear out the piled-up room meant a tidal wave was coming at him. I was wondering how to create that experience when the NLP device of visualizing images on video screens came to mind. I began guiding Thomas to visualize two video screens at a moderate distance from him, so that they appeared smallish, with a sizable separation between them.

I said, "On one of the small screens is the image of the messy room. Do you have that? Good. On the other screen is the image of the scary tidal wave. Just see those images on those two screens. Is that workable?"

Yes, it was workable. For about ten seconds Thomas was silent as he internally attended to the imagery. I had no idea whether this approach would prove effective for him. Perhaps I would have to try some other way of fulfilling Step C. What Thomas said next, however, revealed that the visualization had the intended effect. He said, "Oh! I don't feel it anymore. It just now became really clear all of a sudden that the messy room is just a messy room, not a tidal wave. It doesn't feel overwhelming now."

The linkage of room and tidal wave had dissolved, and it never came back. The grueling reactivation disappeared and did not recur. In some cases, Step C, which completes the preparatory accessing sequence of the TRP, in turn precipitates Steps 1-2-3 of the erasure sequence, and that is what happened for Thomas, though I was not expecting this.

Two weeks later, he emailed to report that he had gone into the room many times and had not felt overwhelmed, and that having just completed a big project, he was now thinking about what to do with his available time, and "One of the first things that popped into my mind was to spend time cleaning out that messy room, which I felt very positively motivated to do and plan to tackle over the weekend." Three months after that email he sent me a handwritten thank-you card in which he wrote: "Steadily, I've been working on that room for hours at a time. It's not done yet. I'm about three quarters of the way through. It's not a matter of *if* I'm going to finish cleaning it up, it's a matter of *when!* My wife is dumbfounded by this change in behavior. …And needless to say, she's overjoyed!"

Looking Closely at the Process of Change

Thus, about one minute of guiding a simple visualization of two video screens produced a transformational change that freed this man from a potent trauma reactivation that had tormented him and ruled his behavior for many years. His follow-up reports fulfilled final TRP step V, the verification of markers of lasting change, but we also need to look closely at how and why the video screen visualization so effectively fulfilled TRP Steps C-1-2-3.

In other words, how did that visualization create the decisive disconfirmation experience that Thomas described when he said, "It just now became really clear all of a sudden that the messy room is just a messy room, not a tidal wave"? And how did that experience juxtapose with the target learning, as is necessary for profound unlearning to occur? Given that Thomas's familiar discomfort had so easily been retriggered merely by telling me about the room or the tidal wave, why wasn't it simply retriggered yet again by seeing the images of those two things on video screens in his mind's eye?

Here is my understanding of the effectiveness of the visualization (as well as many other specific techniques of NLP). The target learning had been powerfully maintaining Thomas's experience of a tidal wave coming whenever he approached the room to de-clutter it, but that learned version of reality was just one small bit of reality-defining material within his vast mind. Normally, his conscious awareness focused on that room-brings-tidal-wave schema only when the schema had been reactivated, and under those conditions of reactivation, his conscious awareness was merged into the schema, inhabiting and subjectively feeling the apparent reality that the schema compellingly created.

By encountering the components of the schema on video screens at a distance from himself and from each other, for the first time Thomas's conscious awareness was viewing from a position outside of the schema while attending to the contents of the schema. That "dissociation", as it is termed in NLP, is the critical effect of the video screen as a visualization device. A video or movie screen, as a visual format, cues the emotional brain into the context of, "I am outside of what I am seeing on the screen, and what is on that screen is not now actually happening to me."

Therefore as Thomas was seeing the images on the screens, his emotional state was not being governed by the target schema "room brings tidal wave", even though that schema was activated in the sense that its main features were overtly expressed. Viewing from that shifted vantage point outside of the schema, his consciousness was now free to recognize what the two separate screens were plainly showing him: that the room and the tidal wave were two separate, unrelated things. His mind was perfectly capable of recognizing and knowing that separateness, but not while his consciousness was inhabiting and merged with a schema in which room and tidal wave *were* tightly linked.

It is of course adaptive and survival-positive overall that learned, urgent emotional schemas normally dominate conscious experience and do not allow other contexts or versions of reality to register. Yet that dominance keeps many people stuck in endlessly re-experiencing the worst experiences of their lives, as Thomas was. The founders of NLP understood that non-problematic schemas or contexts can be cued into activation and inhabited as the locus of conscious awareness just as problematic schemas are. Many NLP techniques utilize ingenious ways of cueing a context that positions conscious awareness outside of the schema maintaining the problem. Working in the 1970s, the NLP founders did not know about memory reconsolidation, but they saw that skillful cueing of contexts was an effective way to create experiences that disconfirm and dissolve symptom-generating schemas. Knowledge of reconsolidation now deeply illuminates for us how and why such techniques can be so effective.

As mentioned, guiding Thomas through the visualization was much simpler than explaining why it worked. By beholding the room and the tidal wave from outside of the schema that linked them tightly together, Thomas in his wider mind effortlessly underwent the disconfirming experience that I was searching for. It was not merely a cognitive or factual insight that the room and tidal wave were unrelated things; it was an experiential knowing that had the quality of unmistakable, felt realness. That is the quality required in order for the erasure sequence, Steps 1-2-3, to be successful next.

Step 1, the reactivation of the target learning in the foreground of explicit awareness, was already in effect and had been from the start of Thomas's therapy session. Thomas was all too aware of the tight connection he felt between going toward that room to work on clearing it and seeing a tidal wave bearing down on him and terrifying him. That is why, as soon as the contradictory experience became apparent to him while visualizing the two video screens, he immediately experienced a juxtaposition of the target learning and the contradictory knowing, fulfilling Step 2. His learned emotional knowledge that approaching the room brought on the tidal wave collided with his now lucid knowledge that "the messy room is just a messy room, not a tidal wave".

Step 3 consists in a few repetitions of that juxtaposition. As a rule, this happens quickly in the client's internal process directly after the first juxtaposition in Step 2, as the client's attention flicks repeatedly back and forth between the two incompatible knowings in surprise and amazement. Even so, my standard practice with clients is to guide them explicitly through about three repetitions of the juxtaposition, to be certain that the two-sided experience is well formed and sustained, carrying out the unlearning process as fully as possible. Thomas, however, instantly gave such a decisive indication of unlearning and erasure of the target learning that I saw no need for overt repetitions.

Usually the first sign of successful erasure is the client's indication, following the juxtaposition experiences in Steps 2 and 3, that the target learning suddenly no longer has the feeling of emotional realness and is not reactivated even when thinking of or experiencing circumstances that have consistently retriggered it in the past. (For a description of the variety of clients' prompt responses that signal dissolution of target learning, see Ecker et al., 2012, p. 60.) Subsequently, the most conclusive marker of erasure is permanent non-reactivation in all actual situations that formerly were triggers, with no effort required to avoid reactivation.

Conclusion

The case examined here illustrates that for carrying out the therapeutic reconsolidation process, it can be sufficient to make explicit the emotional learning underlying the symptom without identifying the original experiences in which that emotional learning was formed. Knowledge of the latter is usually very helpful if accessible, but it is not necessary.

In most cases, the emotional learning maintaining the client's problem or symptom is significantly more complex than the relatively simple associative linkage described here. For a wide range of TRP case examples with more complex material, see Ecker et al. (2012, 2013a,b). Applying the TRP in such cases can be a non-linear, multi-faceted process requiring many sessions, but the core steps of process are still as described above.

As noted, attending to an emotional schema from an unmerged position outside the schema is termed "dissociation" in NLP. To avoid possible confusion, I should point out that this word is typically used with a different sense by therapists. In the therapeutic context, "dissociation" tends to denote a disconnection from emotionally problematic material such that it is suppressed out of awareness, whereas in NLP, "dissociation" describes a state of being aware of such material while yet experiencing differentiation from it and remaining unmerged with it. The two-screen technique I used with Thomas is a relatively simple form of NLP-type dissociation process, indeed much simpler than the "visual-kinesthetic dissociation" technique that is well known among NLP practitioners (Dietrich, 2000; Gray & Liotta, 2012; Hossack & Bentall, 1996; Koziey & McLeod, 1987).

The state of unmerged attending to significant problematic material allows contradictory knowledge to be accessed and brought into juxtaposition with that material. This juxtaposition experience is the crucial ingredient that triggers reconsolidation, destabilizing the synaptic encoding of the problematic learning and allowing profound unlearning and transformational change, as we have seen.

I believe that what I have been calling the unmerged attending type of dissociation is a key ingredient not only in NLP but also in several other forms of therapy, including EMDR, tapping, and progressive counting, and may be largely or wholly responsible for their effectiveness. The methodologies of EMDR, tapping, and progressive counting utilize a "dual focus" procedure in which conscious awareness is anchored to a sensory stimulus in the safe present environment while also attending internally to the traumatic emotional learning underlying the symptom (see, e.g., Lee, Taylor, & Drummond, 2006). In that way, conscious awareness is anchored outside of the target emotional learning while attending to it, as in NLP's dissociation techniques. The conjectures I have made here will of course need to be substantiated by suitably designed controlled studies.

I hope to have provided in this article a sense of how the therapeutic reconsolidation process can serve as a framework that integrates and guides our use of the kaleidoscopic pantheon of available forms of psychotherapy. There are so many inventive, artful and soulful methods to draw upon for guiding transformational change through the brain's innate process of memory reconsolidation.

References

Agren, T. (2014). Human reconsolidation: A reactivation and update. *Brain Research Bulletin, 105*, 70–82. doi:10.1016/j.brainresbull.2013.12.010

Bouton, M. E. (2004). Context and behavioral processes in extinction. *Learning & Memory, 11*, 485–494. doi:10.1101/lm.78804

Dietrich, A. (2000). A review of visual/kinesthetic disassociation in the treatment of posttraumatic disorders: Theory, efficacy and practice recommendations. *Traumatology, 6*, 85–107. doi:10.1177/153476560000600203

Dilts, R., Grinder, J., Bandler, R., & DeLozier, J. (1980). *Neuro-linguistic programming. Vol. 1: The structure of subjective experience.* Cupertino, CA: Meta Publications.

Ecker, B. (2015, in press). Memory reconsolidation understood and misunderstood. *International Journal of Neuropsychotherapy, 3.*

Ecker, B., Ticic, R., & Hulley, L. (2012). *Unlocking the emotional brain: Eliminating symptoms at their roots using memory reconsolidation.* New York, NY: Routledge.

Ecker, B., Ticic, R., & Hulley, L. (2013a). A primer on memory reconsolidation and its psychotherapeutic use as a core process of profound change. *The Neuropsychotherapist, 1,* 82–99. doi:10.12744/tnpt(1)082-099

Ecker, B., Ticic, R., & Hulley, L. (2013b). Unlocking the emotional brain: Is memory reconsolidation the key to transformation? *Psychotherapy Networker, 37*(4), 18–25, 46–47.

Gray, R. M., & Liotta, R. F. (2012). PTSD: Extinction, reconsolidation, and the visual-kinesthetic dissociation protocol. *Traumatology, 18,* 3–16. doi:10.1177/1534765611431835

Hossack, A., & Bentall, R. (1996). Elimination of posttraumatic symptomatology by relaxation and visual-kinesthetic dissociation. *Journal of Traumatic Stress, 9,* 99–110. doi:10.1007/BF02116836

Koziey, P., & McLeod, G. (1987). Visual-kinesthetic dissociation in treatment of victims of rape. *Professional Psychology: Research and Practice, 18,* 276–282. doi:10.1037/0735-7028.18.3.276

Lee, C. W., Taylor, G., & Drummond, P. D. (2006). The active ingredient in EMDR: Is it traditional exposure or dual focus of attention? *Clinical Psychology & Psychotherapy, 13,* 97–107. doi:10.1002/cpp.479

Pedreira, M. E., Pérez-Cuesta, L. M., & Maldonado, H. (2004). Mismatch between what is expected and what actually occurs triggers memory reconsolidation or extinction. *Learning & Memory, 11,* 579–585. doi:10.1101/lm.76904

Reichelt, A. C., & Lee, J. L. C. (2013). Memory reconsolidation in aversive and appetitive settings. *Frontiers of Behavioral Neuroscience, 7,* 1–18. doi:10.3389/fnbeh.2013.00118

Sevenster, D., Beckers, T., & Kindt, M. (2013). Prediction error governs pharmacologically induced amnesia for learned fear. *Science, 339,* 830–833. doi:10.1126/science.1231357

Wake, L. (2008). *Neurolinguistic psychotherapy: A postmodern perspective.* London, England: Routledge.

Bruce Ecker, MA, LMFT, is co-originator of Coherence Therapy, co-director of the Coherence Psychology Institute, and coauthor of *Unlocking the Emotional Brain: Eliminating Symptoms at Their Roots Using Memory Reconsolidation*; the *Coherence Therapy Practice Manual and Training Guide*; and *Depth Oriented Brief Therapy.* He is in private practice in Oakland, California, gives clinical trainings internationally, and has taught graduate courses for many years. Clarifying how lasting, transformational change takes place has been the theme of Bruce Ecker's clinical career. He has contributed extensive innovations in concepts and methods of experiential psychotherapy, and has driven the clinical field's recognition of memory reconsolidation research and how it translates into new capabilities of consistent therapeutic effectiveness and psychotherapy integration. For more information, visit www.CoherenceInstitute.org.

CREATIVE MEMORY RECONSOLIDATION

Courtney Armstrong

Watching a client transform from states of angst to enlightenment is exhilarating for a psychotherapist. Even more thrilling are those rare "Aha!" moments when a certain realization clicks into place, releases the client from the shackles of an imprisoning belief and liberates him or her toward change. We've all had those eureka experiences in our sessions, but why do they seem so elusive? Do people really make lasting change after they've had such epiphanies? More importantly, what can you do when the therapy process seems stuck and absolutely no flashes of insight are coming? Is there a certain set of conditions that seems to facilitate therapeutic breakthroughs in sessions? I believe that there is. It all starts with understanding the process of memory reconsolidation and engaging the emotional brain in a way that promotes positive shifts and ignites new neural networks.

Since the dawn of time, humankind has attempted to tame passion with reason, usually with limited success. Plato compared balancing emotion and reason to a small charioteer attempting to steer two horses running in opposite directions. Centuries later, albeit during the "Age of Reason", philosopher David Hume concluded, "Reason is, and ought only to be the slave of the passions, and can never pretend to any other office than to serve and obey them" (Hume, 1738–1739/2014, Book 2, Part 3, Section 3). Even modern neuroscientists acknowledge the futility of attempting to control emotions with rationality, as neuroscientist Joe LeDoux sings with his band, the Amygdaloids (2007): "An emotional brain is a hard thing to tame / It just won't stay in its place / Every time I think I got it / It gives me another face."

The Adaptive Emotional Brain

Sitting deep in the mid-brain between the cortex and brain stem, the emotional brain—or mammalian brain, as pioneering neuroscientist Paul MacLean called it—is where the majority of neural networks for our attachment schemas, implicit memories, and automatic patterns are stored. Most of the patterns stored in the emotional brain are learned experientially and activated unconsciously.

Contrary to what Freud theorized, the emotional brain is not merely driven by shadowy sexual urges or simplistic self-gratification, nor does it harbor "repressed" feelings. While it is true that the emotional brain drives our instincts for survival and pleasure, this "lower brain" isn't as self-serving as we've been led to believe. For example, neuroscientists Panksepp and Biven (2012) point out that the emotional systems of the midbrain also prompt us to be interested in connecting with others, giving and receiving CARE, pursuing PLAYful activities, and SEEKING experiences that inspire us and add to the quality of our lives. After all, life without emotion would be quite dull and seem rather meaningless.

While the emotional brain is generally adaptive and well intentioned, it isn't really fazed by quiet, rational discussion, intellectual insight, or analytical arguments—some of the staples of modern psychotherapy. Instead, the emotional brain learns from experience, association, stimulation of the senses, and repetition. Therefore, no matter how brilliantly our prefrontal cortex delivers intellectual insight and plans elegant coping strategies, the emotional brain is primed to override it all with neural patterns that persist until we intervene with something our emotional brain can understand—a compelling *felt experience*.

Orchestrating such felt experiences goes beyond simple emotional awareness or catharsis around the problem. Therapists must elicit an affectively engaging experience that changes the *emotional meaning* of an event. Hitting this neural sweet spot where cognition and emotion synthesize is what I believe creates that "Aha" moment.

A Cognitive–Experiential Approach to Change

Over 40 years ago, Seymour Epstein, a psychology professor at the University of Massachusetts, Amherst, proposed that humans have two separate systems for processing information: analytical–rational and experiential–intuitive. Our rational systems, or neocortex areas, operate via logical analysis, evaluation of factual evidence, and verbal processing. Meanwhile, the subcortical emotional areas learn through experiences and are conditioned through both external reward and punishment and internal affective states. For humans, emotional learning differs from simple behavioral learning in that our behavior and personalities are not just shaped by reward and punishment, but by the implicit beliefs our minds attach to an experience. Yet, as Epstein explains in his book, *Cognitive-Experiential Theory: An Integrative Theory of Personality* (2014):

> An experientially acquired belief may not be changed at all when it is made conscious because it continues to operate according to the same rules and attributes of the experiential system as it did before. . . . making an implicit experiential belief explicit is an important first step in correcting an experiential belief because once it is identified in the rational system, it can be treated experientially. (p. 235)

In other words, it's absolutely useful to assist clients in consciously identifying negative, implicit thoughts and beliefs, but to really change those beliefs, you have to appeal to the brain's emotional-experiential learning systems. Acknowledging the necessity of engaging both rational and experiential systems is especially relevant for intellectual clients who understand their problems all too well, but have not been able to change in spite of their insight, like my client Saundra.

Saundra's Sunrise

Saundra was an attractive, talented surgeon with a Mensa-level IQ who graduated at the top of her class from an Ivy League school. She had struggled most of her life with waves of severe depression and anxiety, but in recent years her mood swings had become more frequent and stormy, flooding her personal life and threatening to wreck her career. When she arrived at my office, Saundra clenched her jaw and gripped her wrist as she expressed feeling extremely disappointed with herself. "Intellectually," she lamented, "I understand what causes the depression and anxiety. Trust me, I've had years of therapy and tried dozens of medications. I realize my thoughts are irrational and know I developed these patterns because my family of origin was critical, abusive, and chaotic. But I'm 40 years old—when am I going to get over it?"

As Saundra described her history, I realized she had an excellent grasp of her issues and did not need more knowledge about her situation, nor did she need assistance in recognizing cognitive distortions. She saw them staring back at her in bold, living color and put lots of energy into reframing them. Yet her attempts to reason her way out of her feelings only added to her frustration and feelings of inadequacy. It occurred to me that what Saundra was really seeking was a new experience of herself, an experience that would cause her to believe there was more to her than negativity. As we talked, I began to search for experiences or subjects that elicited a smile on her face, passion in her voice, or animated movement in her body. What in Saundra's life made it worth coming to see me? What topics seemed to relax her or energize her?

Watching and listening for these cues, it became clear to me that the dearest things to Saundra's heart were her children. Describing her children was the only thing that seemed to brighten her eyes and broaden her affect into a slight smile. In addition, the rigidity in Saundra's posture softened whenever she talked about dabbling with painting or being outside in nature. Since she enjoyed painting, I assumed she was good at visualizing things, so I asked her to recall a place in nature where she had seen something that was beautiful and awe inspiring. She described watching the sunrise by a cool, calm lake in a wooded area near her home. As she described this scene to me, she released a deep sigh, closed her eyes, and leaned back into the curve of the couch. Her jaw relaxed and her clenched fingers unfolded as she rested her hands on her lap. She took another deep breath and whispered, "I could linger there for hours."

Because she was beginning to relax and indicated an interest in going further, I narrated the scene back to her, adjusting the pitch and tone of my voice so that it was melodic, soothing, and uplifting. I colorfully elaborated on the description of her sunrise, suggesting she could enjoy noticing how the crimson edges melted into pleasant pinks and golden oranges that glowed against the backdrop of an azure sky and the cool, calm lake. She dropped her tense shoulders as I continued using sensorily rich language to describe the balmy feel of the air and fresh pine scent of the trees, and made soft sound effects of the wind and birdsongs. It may mean donning an unfamiliar hat, but like an enchanting storyteller, narrating guided imagery with sound effects, animation in your voice, and sensory descriptive words is a great way to make an experience come alive for the emotional brain.

When I asked Saundra what she was noticing within herself, Saundra sighed as she murmured, "Feelings of serenity, peace and joy." I suggested to her that I did not think the sunrise dropped those feelings of peace inside of her. Instead, I told her I thought she was getting in touch with her true nature, who she really was underneath the clouds of depression. Tears streamed down her face as Saundra nodded and placed her hand over her heart, stating, "I do think that is who I am under all this darkness, but if I showed this side of myself to anyone, it got squelched. I am careful not to squelch my kids. I want them to express themselves and not feel so afraid, like I felt as a kid."

Her passion for being a loving, supportive parent informed our work in subsequent sessions as we used other types of imagery in which Saundra envisioned stepping into traumatic scenes from her youth and reparenting her younger self with the same nurturing, guiding, protective responses she would give to her children. Within two months, Saundra developed a new relationship with herself and her emotions. She reported fewer mood swings and was handling interpersonal situations more effectively. Rather than engaging in endless thought loops of self-talk when she felt discouraged, Saundra imagined her sunrise and sent herself feelings of love and reassurance to calm down. Saundra commented, "Other therapists told me I needed to learn to love myself, but nobody ever *showed* me how to do that." Saundra was right. She could never have *thought* her way into loving herself. She needed someone who could lead her and show her how to *evoke* the experience of self-compassion.

The Art of Evoking Emotion

Attempting to be there for my clients in this more creative, provocative way was not an easy transition for me to make. I was trained traditionally in cognitive–behavioral therapy and was very good at delivering it with the kind of empathy that would rival Carl Rogers. My practice was busy and my clients liked me, but to be honest, I rarely witnessed those crystallizing breakthrough moments. People would gain insight and try out the skills I suggested. They would feel better for a time, but the changes would not stick unless we met for months and the client put a lot of effort into consciously applying the skills between sessions.

That all changed several years ago when I stumbled upon a hypnosis workshop taught by an unconventional but brilliant therapist named Jon Connelly, who calls his method Rapid Resolution Therapy. I heard his method was especially effective for clearing the negative impact of trauma. On his website, I watched an impressive demonstration video of his work with a 9/11 World Trade Center bombing survivor that made me want to learn more. When I attended my first training session in Florida, I expected to learn about new scientific breakthroughs and pick up a few innovative techniques. What I was not expecting was an essentially theatrical performance led by this spellbinding 1960s peace activist-turned-therapist who presented as a fusion of artist, actor, stand-up comedian, and evangelical-like healer. It was Connelly who taught me the concepts I used in the imagery exercise with Saundra. His use of poetic words and dramatic performance art in his trainings *and* with his clients convinced me that therapy is less about the intervention and more about how we use ourselves in the session to create a therapeutic experience. He taught me not to get overly focused on why the client developed the problem, but instead to ask myself, "What is my intention for this client? What is the effect I want our conversation to have on them?"

Then it dawned on me. I learned a similar concept during my internship in graduate school 20 years ago when I worked with groups of at-risk students in New Orleans. The traditional cognitive–behavioral interventions I tried didn't faze those kids at all. I realized I'd better come up with a more entertaining song-and-dance routine fast, or those kids would fry up my self-esteem in no time and serve it back up to me in a gumbo steeped in red-hot humiliation. The magic started happening when I stopped hiding behind a detached therapist persona and began connecting with these students emotionally, crafting experiences that helped them face their fears and move closer to what they really wanted—feeling a sense of worth, purpose and connection to something larger than themselves.

After my stint in the New Orleans school system, I worked at hospitals and doctors' offices and eventually opened a private practice. While my time in the medical field was valuable, I realized I'd gotten so caught up in following the medical model and keeping up with managed care requirements that I'd lost the spontaneity that fueled the early years of my career. Connelly's work reminded me to listen to my clinical intuition, develop my own creative style, and be more emotionally engaging with clients. As I incorporated these qualities and a few of the methods I learned from him, I began having breakthrough sessions almost immediately. Hungry for a deeper understanding of why this approach was working so well, I began to devour books and research on trauma, positive psychology, experiential modalities, and affective neuroscience.

Fortunately, brain science seems to be validating what we have intuitively known as therapists: people heal through meaningful emotional experiences with others. But as I researched the phenomena of memory reconsolidation, I learned that the way we time and facilitate these emotional experiences in the session makes all the difference.

The Magic of Memory Reconsolidation

Although part of Saundra's treatment was to have her cultivating self-compassion, she couldn't fully embrace this until we had cleared up the emotional baggage from her past. Saundra had mixed feelings about reviewing past material, bemoaning that she'd replayed these events over and over with previous therapists and it only seemed to make her feel worse. I agreed that simply getting in touch with painful emotions and venting them through experiential reenactment techniques is counterproductive and can actually reinforce unwanted patterns and beliefs.

Thankfully, recent discoveries in neuroscience regarding the process of memory reconsolidation suggest that there is a less painful way to reconstruct memories and implicit beliefs; however, there appears to be a specific protocol that must be followed for the emotional brain to unlock and update these memories. I first learned about this research during conversations I had with neuroscientists Joe LeDoux and Daniella Schiller a few years ago as I was attempting to understand why Rapid Resolution Therapy (RRT) was working so well for my clients. LeDoux and Schiller suggested that the RRT process might be eliciting the process of memory reconsolidation and encouraged me to look at this research. Fascinated, I dived into the memory reconsolidation literature and was ecstatic when Ecker, Ticic, and Hulley published their excellent book *Unlocking the Emotional Brain* (2012). These were the first psychotherapists to translate the memory reconsolidation research into applications for psychotherapy. After comparing the memory reconsolidation findings against what they were discovering through their coherence therapy research, Ecker et al. boiled the memory reconsolidation sequence down to three essential steps. First, you must reactivate the emotional memory, which opens up the stored memory "file". Second, you have to simultaneously introduce a contrasting or "mismatch" experience that produces a prediction error—where the outcome is different from what the brain expects on the basis of the learned pattern acquired from the remembered experience. Third, you have to experientially repeat the new, desired pattern within five hours of the memory being recalled, or the memory reconsolidation window closes.

How is this different from traditional extinction therapy? First, researchers have demonstrated that reconsolidation and extinction are coded in the brain different-ly. Extinction seems to suppress a learned fear, but doesn't convince the emotional brain that the aversive stimulus won't show up again. Moreover, Gershman, Mon-fils, Norman, and Niv (2014) have theorized that our emotional brains operate like one big statistical prediction machine that doesn't just learn from association, but thinks in terms of probabilities based on past experience. These researchers suggest that when the prediction error only happens during one trial or is too dramatically divergent from what the animal expects, the animal simply believes there is a new *latent cause* for the new outcome. Thus, the new experience gets coded as a separate learning that competes with the original learning. Rather than removing aversive stimuli abruptly as is done with traditional extinction, Gershman, Jones, Norman, Monfils, and Niv (2013) theorize that the prediction error must be presented in gradual increments, or at least in a way that suggests the *original* latent cause of the event has been reversed.

Interestingly, Redondo et al. (2014) were able to diminish the association of fear with a memory in mice by simultaneously reactivating the fear memory while pre-senting the mice with a rewarding experience in the same environment where they learned the fear. Subsequent brain scans revealed that the mice had formed new connections between the amygdala (which tags the emotion to an event) and the hippocampus (which provides the context) that weakened the fear response and strengthened positive associations with the memory's environmental cues. Recall-ing a traumatic experience while simultaneously creating positive experiences in the session is what I learned to do with Rapid Resolution Therapy. Similarly, Eck-er et al. (2012) describe it as juxtaposing a mismatch experience with the earlier memory. They point out that because the memory reconsolidation protocol is a neurological construct, it is not limited to any single psychotherapy model. As long as therapists follow the transformation sequence—reactivating, mismatching, and revising with new learning—they are free to use their choice of experiential tech-niques to carry out the process.

In the following sections, I will illustrate creative ways you can "reactivate, mis-match, and revise with new learning" through a case example with Emily. Emily was a 28-year-old client who called me in desperation because she was having in-creasing trouble with social anxiety. The problem had worsened when a group of co-workers at her new job invited her to lunch and she had a severe panic attack. Emily understood that her fears were irrational, but no amount of positive self-talk and forcing herself to be social seemed to relieve her inner terror.

Reactivating the Emotional Memory

I explained to Emily that most of the time the reason why an emotional pattern has not changed is because it served an adaptive purpose at one time in someone's life. No matter how illogical it seems to the rational mind, the emotional brain is determined to protect us using strategies that worked earlier in our lives. To find the origin of Emily's social phobia, I asked her to follow the sensations associated with the anxiety to an earlier time when she could remember having similar feelings. Following the physical sensations usually leads to a more relevant memory because emotional memories are stored more as felt encounters than explicit verbal accounts. Once your client has located a relevant memory, you can explore the implicit beliefs and action tendencies that are associated with it. Emily described the feeling of having a pit in the bottom of her stomach, and dizziness, when she thought about going out in crowded, public places. She traced these sensations back to a memory when she was 11 years old and a group of kids bullied her in the school cafeteria at lunchtime. Emily coped by avoiding the cafeteria and catching up on her homework in the library. As a result, her parents and teachers praised her studiousness and good grades. Emily realized she was still repeating the same pattern of avoiding lunch with her peers, opting to sit at her desk catching up on work, and receiving praise from her boss for being so dedicated. Once Emily made this connection, she understood her mind had continued this pattern because it had been adaptive when she was younger. She had also internalized the implicit belief that her peers would not like her because she was "awkward and boring".

Now that Emily had reactivated this memory and the implicit beliefs associated with it, we needed to create a mismatch experience to open the memory reconsolidation and revise these unhelpful beliefs. One way to do this is to assist the client to create a new story around the original event that puts her in the role of a heroine or victor who survived a harrowing experience. Or, if your client is open to humor, you can even recast the story as a comedy of errors in which the client was an innocent bystander charged with a mistaken identity.

Mismatching with New Narratives

We are neurologically wired to organize our experiences into story. Dan Siegel (2010) posits that story can calm emotion as we engage our left hemisphere's drive to "order the details" of the affective and sensory input emanating from our emotional brain and right hemisphere. Siegel also asserts that the ability to provide a meaningful, coherent narrative of one's life promotes good mental health, which harkens back to Michael White and David Epston's (1990) narrative therapy, an effective therapeutic approach that assists clients in "restorying" their lives. The easiest way for the client to change the story is to give it a new ending. New endings provide a different context for the event, and yield new meanings and resolution. The new ending doesn't have to be dramatic, it just has to be a later moment in the client's life when he or she was out of danger, was in a better situation, or felt competent and empowered.

For example, the first time Emily told her story, she ended it by saying she hid in the library and avoided her peers. When I prompted her to consider ending the story with a positive experience that happened in her life later, she recalled that one of the boys who had teased her actually asked her to the prom in high school. This led her to remember that other members even invited her to a few parties too, even though Emily opted not to go out with them because they drank a lot and still seemed pretty closed-minded. Emily laughed as she retold the story, juxtaposing her middle school experiences with her high school experiences around this group of kids. She saw more clearly that they would do just about anything to "fit in" and was glad she didn't compromise her values to be accepted by them. As she retold the story from this updated perspective a few more times, she noticed that the memory didn't seem nearly as disturbing as it seemed the first time around. She commented, "Funny. As I'm retelling it now, the whole thing seems silly. They were just a bunch of goofy kids. Still are."

Revising with Play and Humor

Play has gained serious recognition as a therapeutic tool that fosters positive connections between people, decreases resistance, promotes a sense of mastery, and sparks creative problem solving. In fact, Panksepp (2009) has identified PLAY as one of our seven primary emotional systems and asserts, "Any therapist who can capture the therapeutic moment in mutually shared play episodes will have brought the client to the gateway of happy living" (p. 17). Therapists can stimulate the PLAY system by initiating amusing role-play games that assist clients in making new associations, rehearsing new behaviors, and building confidence. We know it's a good idea to rehearse new behaviors with clients in the session, but when you add a bit of fun and novelty to it, your clients will be even more likely to remember new responses and try them at home.

To continue reinforcing new learning while the memory reconsolidation time window was open, Emily and I acted out a humorous role-play to further reduce her anxiety and build her confidence. I suggested Emily play a woman with a snobby attitude, snubbing her at the lunch table while I played Emily.

Emily started the role-play by wrinkling her nose and saying, "Who invited you to have lunch with us, creep?"

I answered matter-of-factly, "Linda invited me."

Emily continued, "Well I hope you don't think I can be seen hanging out with you, especially while you're wearing those ugly black shoes. And you should really consider doing something different with your hair."

I smiled and replied, "Oh, what a shame. I fixed my hair this way just for you."

Emily laughed and we continued this jocular bantering for a few more minutes. Letting Emily play the character she feared reduced her anxiety because she realized how insecure a person would have to be to make such insensitive comments. Next we reversed roles. I began with silly, exaggerated insults, then gradually transitioned to more realistic scenarios Emily feared, such as stilted, awkward conversation. As we worked through her feared scenes, we practiced various ways of keeping a conversation going until she felt more confident. We also explored how Emily could use music to manage and reduce her anxiety before a social event.

Revising with Rhythm and Music

Neuroscience studies have shown that listening to music stimulates activity in the reward and pleasure centers of the brain, even if the music is sad. Music is often associated with episodic memories of previous events or times in one's life. Therefore, music from a particular time period can be used intentionally to bring up emotional memories or produce nostalgic feelings of happier times. You can also use music to entrain the brain to a preferred emotional state. For example, listening to music with a tempo of around 60–70 beats per minute (the rhythm of a relaxed human heartbeat) evokes calmer states of mind and elicits alpha–theta states of consciousness.

An activity my clients enjoy that is based on this concept of entrainment is creating a playlist of tunes that move them from a troubling emotional state to a positive emotional state. It parallels the memory reconsolidation process because the client reactivates the undesired state by starting the playlist with a couple of songs that match their current mood, followed by songs with rhythms that gradually evoke their desired frame of mind. Emily really liked this concept and compiled a playlist that began with songs that reflected feeling like a social reject like *Creep* by Radiohead and *How Soon is Now* by The Smiths. Next, she chose the song *Middle* by

Jimmy Eat World, which had encouraging lyrics and a faster beat. Emily ended her playlist with *Canned Heat* by Jamiroquai, the song that Jon Heder danced to in the film *Napoleon Dynamite*. In the film, Napoleon had been considered a social misfit, but when he danced to this song on the school's stage, his classmates cheered him on.

Holding this image of *Napoleon Dynamite* in her mind was both amusing and reassuring to Emily and further reduced her fears of social rejection. Emily made it her intention to listen to these songs in the morning before work to discharge her anxiety. At our next session, Emily said that revising her story with the new ending, recalling our humorous role-play, and listening to her playlist caused her to feel more comfortable around her co-workers. However, she still had not worked up the courage to actually join them for lunch, so we added movement and imagery as another means for revising her memories and reinforcing new patterns.

Mismatching with Movement

Incorporating body awareness and physical movement is another way to create mismatch experiences and change implicit patterns for your clients. Somatically focused interventions are especially relevant for clients who have trouble tuning into deeper feelings, hold their bodies in tense or powerless postures, struggle with recurring overactive responses, or have physiological complaints related to past trauma. In fact, trauma expert Peter Levine (1997) believes an explicit narrative of a traumatic event cannot even be formed until the implicit aspects of it are accessed and processed somatically. Inspired by Levine's Somatic Experiencing and Ogden's sensorimotor psychotherapy, I've created mismatch experiences by having the client complete the action their bodies wanted to take during an emotional event where they "froze". For some clients, acting out these new versions of their stories physically is more effective than simply retelling the story verbally.

Likewise, altering posture can change emotional and physiological states. For instance, Carney, Cuddy, and Yap (2010) demonstrated that participants who were instructed to hold an expansive, open posture that reflected power for just two minutes increased their levels of testosterone 20%, decreased cortisol levels by 25%, and were more open to taking risks. In contrast, participants who were instructed to hold a closed, contracted posture for two minutes demonstrated a 10% decrease in testosterone, a 15% increase in cortisol, and were more reluctant to take risks.

To coach Emily towards a posture that would increase her feelings of security and confidence, I encouraged her to broaden and relax her shoulders and lift her chin so she was looking up and out, rather than down at her feet. Then I asked her to retell the story of being bullied in middle school while holding this more secure posture, roll her eyes and shake her head and say, "Whatever!" as she imagined herself walking by this group and ignoring their teasing, seeing them as a bunch of goofy kids. Emily noticed that positioning herself in this more poised posture made even more difference to how she felt about herself and the memory. In fact, she said the memory no longer seemed troubling to her at all. Next, I suggested she hold this same posture as she imagined having lunch with her co-workers.

Revising Emotional Learning with Imagery

Research suggests the brain responds to an imagined experience almost as much as it does to a live encounter. In fact, Harvard researcher Stephen Kosslyn (2005) found that two thirds of the areas of the brain that are involved in visual perception of actual physical objects are also activated when we merely imagine the object. This is why we emotionally react to dreams, literature, movies, theater, and even video games. Similarly, you can create a mismatch experience and dramatically change the way a client feels about a situation, a relationship, and her identity by invoking an imagined experience in a session. Saundra was able to do this by invoking the image of the sunrise and associating more positive feelings with her identity. She also used imagery to revise traumatic memories from her childhood by imagining stepping into scenes from her past and compassionately guiding her younger self to realize her parent's hurtful behaviors were not her fault.

Because the SEEKING system (Panksepp & Biven, 2012) in the emotional brain is stimulated through the senses, creating a sensory representation of a desired state can fuel motivation and approach behavior. In light of this, I asked Emily to imagine feeling clear, secure, and at ease, having a friendly curiosity about people, and being interested in learning something about them whether she did this by quietly listening or initiating conversation herself. I suggested that if any person was rude or disrespectful to her, she had just learned something about that person, not herself. Then, I suggested that she identify something in nature or an animal in the wild that would represent her mind working this way. With her eyes still closed, Emily smiled and said, "A cat. They just hang out and don't take anything personally." To move Emily deeper into a calming, positive state of mind, I asked her to visualize the image of the cat as she took three slow, deep breaths. In Rapid Resolution Therapy, this process is called creating a *future model* and a *symbolic activator* (Connelly, 2014). Clients really enjoy using this imagery and find that recalling their symbolic image evokes the desired emotional state more quickly than verbal self-talk.

The next week, Emily practiced her confident postures and recalled her cat image as she took slow, deep breaths a few minutes before she out went to lunch with her co-workers. Although Emily said she didn't talk much the first time she went out to lunch with the others, she focused on listening and learning more about her co-workers as we had rehearsed in our sessions. Over the next several weeks, Emily's anxiety dissipated and she told me that one of her co-workers was turning out to be a pretty good friend. In fact, about a year later, he asked her to marry him.

Uniting the Psychotherapy Profession

We are in a most exciting time in the field of psychotherapy. Recent discoveries about the workings of the emotional brain and memory reconsolidation allow us to be intentional and effective with our clients in a way we have never been before. Additionally, I believe these neuroscience discoveries have the potential to unite the psychotherapy profession in an unprecedented way. Neuroscience studies now suggest that Freud wasn't far off the mark in his theories about subconscious learning, motives, and drives. Fortunately, though, we've learned the subconscious isn't completely hedonistic, and is actually an adaptive, well-intentioned, emotional brain. Skinner and the behaviorists were right in stating that our behavior is shaped by associative learning. But we know we aren't automatons, and can influence our behavior with our thoughts as the cognitive theorists proposed. However, the key is to integrate the best of what all the various theories have to offer and use our interventions more strategically.

As cognitive therapy proposes, we can still use our rational minds to identify maladaptive beliefs and behaviors. However, to eliminate problematic emotional responses at their roots we have to follow the brain's rules for memory reconsolidation and update implicit learnings through compelling, felt experiences as psychodynamic and humanistic theories have proposed. Once these implicit patterns are addressed and reconsolidated, new learning can be reinforced with subsequent cognitive-experiential interventions. As Ecker et al. (2012) observe, "With clear knowledge of the brain's own rules for deleting emotional learnings through memory reconsolidation therapists no longer have to rely largely on speculative theory, intuition or luck for facilitating powerful, liberating shifts" (p. 4). In other words, we don't have to guess at how to create "Aha" moments for our clients anymore; there are clear rules for how to achieve them. Eventually, I think our profession will agree on this basic premise, and the only way therapy models will differ is in the various techniques we use for creating these felt, transformational experiences.

References

Carney, D. R., Cuddy, A. J. C., & Yap, A. J. (2010). Power posing: Brief nonverbal displays affect neuroendocrine levels and risk tolerance. *Psychological Science,*

21, 1363–1368.

Connelly, J. (2014). *Rapid Resolution Therapy level I: Clinical hypnosis with rapid trauma resolution* [Manual issued to Foundation Training participants]. Tampa, FL: Author.

Ecker, B., Ticic, R., & Hulley, L. (2012). *Unlocking the emotional brain: Eliminating symptoms at their roots using memory reconsolidation.* New York, NY: Routledge.

Epstein, S. (2014). *Cognitive–experiential theory: An integrative theory of personality.* New York: Oxford University Press.

Gershman, S. J., Jones, C. E., Norman, K. A., Monfils, M. A., & Niv, Y. (2013). Gradual extinction prevents the return of fear: Implications for the discovery of state. *Frontiers in Behavioral Neuroscience, 7,* Article 164.

Gershman, S. J., Monfils, M.-H., Norman, K. A., & Niv, Y. (2014). *The computational nature of memory reconsolidation.* Manuscript in preparation.

Hume, D. (2014). *A treatise of human nature.* Retrieved from http://ebooks.adelaide.edu.au/h/hume/david/h92t/B2.3.3.html (Original work published 1738–1739)

Kosslyn, S. M. (2005). Mental images and the brain. *Cognitive Neuropsychology, 22,* 333–347.

LeDoux, J. E. (2007). An emotional brain [Recorded by The Amygdaloids]. On *Heavy mental* [mp3 file]. Retrieved from http://www.amygdaloids.com/heavy-mental

Levine, P. (1997). *Waking the tiger: Healing trauma.* Berkeley, CA: North Atlantic Books.

Panksepp, J. (2009). Brain emotional systems and qualities of mental life: From animal models of affect to implications for psychotherapeutics. In D. Fosha, D. J. Siegel, & M. F. Solomon (Eds.), *The healing power of emotion: Affective neuroscience, development and clinical practice* (pp. 1–26). New York, NY: W. W. Norton.

Panksepp, J., & Biven, L. (2012). *The archaeology of mind: Neuroevolutionary origins of human emotions.* New York, NY: W. W. Norton.

Redondo, R. L., Kim, J., Arons, A. L., Ramirez, S., Liu, X., & Tonegawa, S. (2014). Bidirectional switch of the valence associated with a hippocampal contextual memory engram. *Nature Online, 513,* 426–430. doi: 10.1038/nature 13725

Siegel, D. (2010). *The mindful therapist: A clinician's guide to mindsight and neural integration.* New York, NY: W. W. Norton.

White, M., & Epston, D. (1990). *Narrative means to therapeutic ends.* New York, NY: W. W. Norton.

Courtney Armstrong, MEd., is a licensed professional counselor and gives international trainings on a variety of topics for mental health professionals. She is the author of *The Therapeutic Aha!* to be published, by W. W. Norton in March 2015, as well as the book *Transforming Traumatic Grief.* Courtney contributes to the *Psychotherapy Networker* magazine, as well as other books and journals, and has made several radio and TV appearances. She offers several free resources for therapists on her website www.courtneyarmstronglpc.com.

MEMORY RECONSOLIDATION
UNDERSTOOD AND MISUNDERSTOOD

Bruce Ecker

Coherence Psychology Institute

Abstract

Memory reconsolidation is the brain's natural, neural process that can produce transformational change: the full, permanent elimination of an acquired behavior or emotional response. This article identifies and examines 10 common misconceptions regarding memory reconsolidation research findings and their translation into clinical practice. The research findings are poised to drive significant advancements in both the theory and practice of psychotherapy, but these benefits depend on an accurate understanding of how memory reconsolidation functions, and misconceptions have been proliferating. This article also proposes a unified model of reconsolidation and extinction phenomena based on the brain's well-established requirement of memory mismatch (prediction error) for reconsolidation to be triggered. A reinterpretation of numerous studies published without reference to the mismatch requirement shows how the *mismatch requirement and mismatch relativity* (MRMR) model can account for diverse empirical findings, reveal unrecognized dynamics of memory change, and generate predictions testable by further research.

Author information:

Bruce Ecker, MA, LMFT
Codirector, Coherence Psychology Institute
3640 Grand Avenue, Suite 209
Oakland, California 94610   USA
Tel: 510-452-2820
Fax: 510-465-9980
Email: bruce.ecker@coherenceinstitute.org

Acknowledgements

The author gratefully acknowledges neuroscientist Alejandro Delorenzi, psychotherapists Robin Ticic and David Feinstein, and two anonymous reviewers for reading earlier manuscripts and offering numerous suggestions that improved this article, and psychologist Sara K. Bridges for valuable advice.

First published as:

Ecker, B. (2015). Memory reconsolidation understood and misunderstood. *International Journal of Neuropsychotherapy, 3*(1), 2–46. doi: 10.12744/ijnpt.2015.0002-0046

Extensive research by neuroscientists since the late 1990s has found that the brain is innately equipped with a potent process, known as memory reconsolidation, that can fundamentally modify or erase a targeted, specific learning, even complex human emotional learnings formed subcortically, outside of awareness (Pine, Mendelsohn, & Dudai, 2014; for reviews see, e.g., Agren, 2014; Reichelt & Lee, 2013). Such learnings are found to underlie and drive most of the problems and symptoms addressed in psychotherapy and counseling (Toomey & Ecker, 2007; Ecker & Toomey, 2008), so the relevance and value of memory reconsolidation for the clinical field are profound.

To describe a particular learning as "erased" means that its behavioral, emotional, cognitive, and somatic manifestations disappear completely, and no further effort of any kind is required to maintain this nullification permanently. Such lasting, transformational change is the therapeutic ideal. There is growing evidence that in erasure, the neural encoding of the target learning is nullified (Clem & Huganir, 2010; Debiec, Díaz-Mataix, Bush, Doyère, & LeDoux, 2010; Díaz-Mataix, Debiec, LeDoux, & Doyère, 2011; Jarome et al., 2012). The discovery of an erasure process was something of an upheaval, reversing a firmly established conclusion, based on nearly a century of research, that subcortical emotional learnings were indelible for the lifetime of the individual (LeDoux, Romanski, & Xagoraris, 1989; Milner, Squire, & Kandel, 1998).

I began studying reconsolidation research findings in 2005, at about the 20-year point of my psychotherapy practice. Neuroscientists' densely technical accounts of their studies have been comprehensible to me, for the most part, thanks to my first career of 14 years as a research physicist, and it quickly became apparent to me that knowledge of reconsolidation could drive the evolution of the field of psychotherapy in major ways. The process that brings about erasure is so fundamental for potent, effective psychotherapy, and so sweeping in the advances that it delivers to the clinical field, that I refocused my clinical career on translating reconsolidation research into clinical practice. This has produced a versatile, integrative methodology of psychotherapy and a conceptual framework that maps out how knowledge of reconsolidation creates four major advances for the clinical field (Ecker, 2011; Ecker, Ticic, & Hulley, 2012, 2013a,b). These advances are: a new level of effectiveness for individual clinicians, the deep unification of seemingly diverse methods and systems of psychotherapy, clarification of the much-debated role of attachment in the therapeutic process, and a decisive breakthrough beyond nonspecific common factors theory and the almost 80-year-long "dodo bird verdict" that has appeared to limit all therapy systems to the same modest level of efficacy.

Understanding memory reconsolidation involves learning some new ways of thinking that differ from familiar concepts of psychotherapeutic change and may even seem counterintuitive initially. Therefore, various aspects of the reconsolidation framework are susceptible to misconceptions. I have been observing misconceptions as they have developed for nearly a decade as of this writing, and they are increasing as awareness of the importance of reconsolidation builds at an accelerating pace. In fact, sizable conceptual errors are being propagated widely in articles by science journalists in the popular media, in articles by psychologists in peer-reviewed journals, in posts by psychotherapists in online clinical discussion groups, and, surprisingly, even in articles and talks by some neuroscientists involved in reconsolidation research (Ecker, 2014).

Thus there is a growing need for a clear map of the new territory, showing where the path of understanding branches off into the various misunderstandings of memory reconsolidation. This article is an attempt to provide such a guide. For the clinical field to fully utilize the potential of memory reconsolidation for major advances, a clear and accurate understanding of it is necessary. Knowledge communities such as the clinical field can and historically do make collective errors in the development of new knowledge, locking onto limiting, polarized, or oversimplified notions that become unchallengeable for decades until, finally, a corrective movement forms. Reconsolidation is too important to fumble and delay in that way.

Understanding how memory reconsolidation can be utilized in psychotherapy (Ecker et al., 2012) is considerably simpler than understanding memory reconsolidation research findings, so many clinicians may choose to focus on the former and pass on the latter. The explanations of research findings in this article are for those with an appetite for more rigorous insights into how memory reconsolidation works. Though memory reconsolidation is a complex phenomenon, and there is still much for researchers to discover about the fine points of how it functions, its main features now appear to be fairly well established, particularly as regards its behavioral and experiential aspects, which are of primary interest to mental health clinicians.

This article covers the following common misconceptions regarding the major features of reconsolidation research findings and their translation into clinical practice:

Misconception 1. The reconsolidation process is triggered by the reactivation of a target learning or memory.

Misconception 2. The disruption of reconsolidation is what erases a target learning.

Misconception 3. Erasure is brought about during the reconsolidation window by a process of extinction. Reconsolidation is an enhancement of extinction.

Misconception 4. Anxiety, phobias and PTSD are the symptoms that memory reconsolidation could help to dispel in psychotherapy, but more research must be done before it is clear how reconsolidation can be utilized clinically.

Misconception 5. Emotional arousal is inherently necessary for inducing the reconsolidation process.

Misconception 6. What is erased in therapy is the negative emotion that became associated with certain event memories, and this negative emotion is erased by inducing positive emotional responses to replace it.

Misconception 7. The much older concept of corrective emotional experience already covers everything now being described as reconsolidation and erasure.

Misconception 8. To induce memory reconsolidation, therapists must follow a set protocol derived from laboratory studies.

Misconception 9. A long-standing emotional reaction or behavior sometimes ceases permanently in psychotherapy without guiding the steps that bring about erasure through reconsolidation, and this shows that reconsolidation isn't the only process of transformational change.

Misconception 10. Carrying out the steps required for reconsolidation and erasure sometimes fails to bring about a transformational change, which means that the reconsolidation process isn't effective for some emotional learnings.

The discussion of those topics will at some points (such as in the section on Misconception 3) go beyond a review of research findings to propose a new interpretation of the findings. Before delving into the misconception topics, however, a short overview is needed to provide the context that will make discussion of the misconceptions meaningful. In attempting to clarify both the reconsolidation research findings and their application to clinical work, this article spans a wide range of material, which in places may be more technical and laboratory focused than some clinical readers find useful. Clinical readers can skip ahead at such points.

Memory Reconsolidation in Context

Memory reconsolidation is the brain's innate process for fundamentally revising an existing learning and the acquired behavioral responses and/or state of mind maintained by that learning. In the reconsolidation process, a target learning is first rendered revisable at the level of its neural encoding, and then revision of its encoding is brought about either through new learning or chemical agents (for reviews see Agren, 2014; Reichelt & Lee, 2013). Through suitably designed new learning, the target learning's manifestation can be strengthened, weakened, altered in its details, or completely nullified and canceled (erased). Erasure through new learning during the reconsolidation process is the true unlearning of the target learning. When erasure through new learning is carried out in psychotherapy, the client experiences a profound release from the grip of a distressing acquired response (Ecker et al., 2012). The use of chemical agents to produce erasure is described later in this article.

In order to see the full significance of memory reconsolidation for psychotherapy, it is necessary to recognize the extensive role of learning and memory in shaping each person's unique patterns of behavior, emotion, thoughts, and somatic experience. Among the many types of learning and the many types of memory, the type responsible for the great majority of the problems and symptoms that bring people to psychotherapy is implicit emotional learning—especially the implicit learning of vulnerabilities and sufferings that are urgent to avoid, and how to avoid them. These learnings form usually with no awareness of learning anything, and they form in the presence of strong emotion, which greatly enhances their power and durability (McGaugh, 1989; McGaugh & Roozendaal, 2002; Roozendaal, McEwen, & Chattarji, 2009).

For example, if a small child consistently receives frightening anger from a parent in response to the child expressing needs, the child learns not to express or even feel needs or distress and not to expect understanding or comfort from others. This learning can occur with no representation in conscious thoughts or conceptualization, entirely in the implicit learning system. The child configures him- or herself according to this adaptive learning in order to minimize suffering in that family environment. Later in life, however, this same learned pattern has life-shaping, extremely costly personal consequences. The learnings in this example are very well-defined, yet they form and operate with no conscious awareness of the learned pattern or its self-protective, coherent emotional purpose and necessity. From outside of awareness these learnings shape the child's and later the adult's behavior, so the individual is completely unaware of living according to these specific learnings. The neural circuits encoding these learnings are mainly in subcortical regions of implicit memory that store implicit, tacit, emotionally urgent, procedural knowledge, not mainly in neocortical regions of explicit memory that store conscious, episodic, autobiographical, declarative knowledge (Schore, 2003).

As in the example above, the vast majority of the unwanted moods, emotions, behaviors, and thoughts that people seek to change in psychotherapy are found to arise from implicit emotional learnings, not in awareness (Toomey & Ecker, 2007). Common clinical phenomena that express implicit emotional learnings include insecure attachment patterns, family of origin rules and roles, unresolved emotional issues, compulsive behaviors or emotional reactions in response to an external or internal trigger, panic and anxiety attacks, depression, low self-esteem, fear of intimacy, sexual inhibition, traumatic memory and posttraumatic stress symptoms, procrastination, and many others.

Of course, some psychological and behavioral symptoms are not caused by emotional learnings—for example, hypothyroidism-induced depression, autism, and biochemical addiction—but it is implicit emotional learnings that therapists and their clients are working to overcome in most cases. There are also genetic or biochemical factors that may contribute to mood disturbances, but it is nevertheless the individual's implicit emotional learnings that are largely responsible for triggering specific bouts of emotional instability (Toomey & Ecker, 2009).

It is the tenacity of implicit emotional learnings, more than their ubiquity, that is the real clinical challenge. On a daily basis, psychotherapists encounter the extreme durability of original emotional learnings that fully maintain their chokehold decades after they first formed. Researchers too have observed that "A unique feature of preferences [the authors use that term to denote compelling, emotionally complex avoidances and attractions] is that they remain relatively stable over one's lifetime. This resilience has also been observed experimentally, where . . . acquired preferences appear to be resistant to extinction training protocols" (Pine et al., 2014, p. 1). The life-constraining grip of such patterns is the bane of psychotherapists and their clients, yet that very tenacity is a survival-positive result of natural selection. In the course of evolution, selection pressures crafted the brain so that any learning accompanied by strong emotion becomes encoded by enhanced, exceptionally durable synapses due to the emotion-related hormones that influence synapse formation (McGaugh, 1989; McGaugh & Roozendaal, 2002; Roozendaal et al., 2009).

So durable are implicit emotional learnings that they continue to function and drive responses even during states of amnesia and are only temporarily suppressed, not erased, by the process of extinction (nonreinforcement of a reactivated, learned expectation). Psychologists and neuroscientists have amassed extensive evidence that even after complete extinction of an emotionally learned response, the extinguished response is easily retriggered in various ways. This revealed that extinction training does not result in the unlearning, elimination, or erasure of the suppressed, original learning (making the term "extinction" something of a misnomer, suggesting as it does a permanent disappearance). Rather, the research found that extinction training forms a separate, second learning that competes against, but does not change, the original learning (see, e.g., Bouton, 2004; Foa & McNally, 1996; Milner et al., 1998; Myers & Davis, 2002). The learning formed by extinction training of a fear response is encoded in the brain's prefrontal cortex, a region that can suppress and temporarily override the nearby subcortical amygdala, which plays a central role in storing and reactivating fear-based learnings (Milad & Quirk, 2002; Phelps, Delgado, Nearing, & LeDoux, 2004; Santini, Ge, Ren, de Ortiz, & Quirk, 2004; Quirk, Likhtik, Pelletier, & Pare, 2003).

Many decades of studying extinction led researchers to the conclusion that implicit emotional learnings are permanent and indelible for the lifetime of the individual once they have been installed in long-term memory circuits through the process of *consolidation* (reviewed in McGaugh, 2000). There appeared to exist no form of neuroplasticity capable of unlocking the synapses of consolidated implicit memory circuits. The tenet of indelibility reached its peak influence with the publication of a research article on extinction studies by neuroscientists LeDoux, Romanski, and Xagoraris (1989) titled "Indelibility of Subcortical Emotional Memories." The indelibility model soon entered the literature of psychotherapy when van der Kolk (1994) published in the *Harvard Review of Psychiatry* his seminal article "The Body Keeps the Score: Memory and the Evolving Psychobiology of Posttraumatic Stress," in which there was a section titled "Emotional memories are forever." The conclusion that implicit emotional learnings persist for a lifetime meant that people could never become fundamentally free of flare-ups of childhood emotional conditioning. The worst experiences in an individual's past could at any time become reactivated and seize his or her state of mind or behavior in the present.

Then, several studies published from 1997 to 2000 suddenly overturned the model of irreversible memory consolidation and indelibility. Actually, a handful of earlier studies published from 1968 to 1982 had reported observations of the disappearance of well consolidated emotional learnings (Judge & Quartermain, 1982; Lewis, 1979; Lewis, Bregman, & Mahan, 1972; Lewis & Bregman, 1973; Mactutus, Riccio, & Ferek, 1979; Misanin, Miller, & Lewis, 1968; Richardson, Riccio, & Mowrey, 1982; Rubin, 1976; Rubin, Fried, & Franks, 1969). However, these unexplained challenges to the prevailing model of irreversible consolidation were seen as anomalies and received scant attention from memory researchers and clinicians at the time.

At the end of the 1990s, however, neuroscientists in several different laboratories resumed studying the effects of reactivating an established emotional learning (Nader, Schafe, & LeDoux, 2000; Przybyslawski, Roullet, & Sara, 1999; Przybyslawski & Sara, 1997; Roullet & Sara, 1998; Sara, 2000; Sekiguchi, Yamada, & Suzuki, 1997). Using sophisticated new techniques as well as the field's advanced knowledge of exactly where in the brain certain emotional learnings form and are stored in memory, researchers again demonstrated the full elimination of any expression of a target learning. In addition, they demonstrated that such erasure of the learning became possible because consolidated, locked memory synapses had returned to a decon-solidated, unlocked, unstable or "labile" state, allowing erasure of the learning by chemical agents that disrupt only synapses that are in an unstable, nonconsolidated condition. The longstanding tenet of irreversible consolidation was disconfirmed.

The destabilized state of deconsolidation was found to exist only soon after the target learning had been reactivated by a suitable cue or reminder. Yet, long after such a reactivation, an implicit learning is found to be once again in a stable, con-solidated state. Thus the detection of a deconsolidated, destabilized state of memory soon after its reactivation implied the existence of a natural process of *reconsolida-tion*, the relocking of the synapses of a destabilized memory, returning the memory to stability. Subsequent studies found that the labile state of deconsolidation lasts for about five hours—a period widely known now as the reconsolidation window—during which the unstable target learning can be modified or erased (Duvarci & Nader, 2004; Pedreira, Pérez-Cuesta, & Maldonado, 2002; Pedreira & Maldonado, 2003; Walker, Brakefield, Hobson, & Stickgold, 2003).

If, following the reactivation and destabilization of a target learning, there is no new learning and no chemical treatment, then after its reconsolidation (that is, more than about five hours later) the target learning is found to have increased strength of expression (e.g., Forcato, Fernandeza, & Pedreira, 2014; Inda, Mura-vieva, & Alberini, 2011; Rossato, Bevilaqua, Medina, Izquierdo, & Cammarota, 2006; Stollhoff, Menzel, & Eisenhardt, 2005). For that reason, researchers regard reconsolidation as having two biological functions: (a) It preferentially strengthens recent learnings that are most frequently reactivated and destabilized, and (b) it allows new learning experiences to update (strengthen, weaken, modify, or nullify) an existing learning. The latter function is the one utilized for bringing about nulli-fication and transformational change in psychotherapy. When a learned, unwanted emotional reaction is erased, there is no loss of memory of events in one's life (as shown by Kindt, Soeter, & Vervliet, 2009, and as illustrated by a clinical example later in this article). There is evidence that the destabilization/restabilization pro-cess and the updating/erasure process occur through different molecular and cel-lular processes (Jarome et al., 2012; Lee et al., 2008).

With that background, we can now examine the misconceptions of the recon-solidation process listed above.

Ten Common Misconceptions

Misconception 1: The Reconsolidation Process Is Triggered by the Reactivation of a Target Learning or Memory

As noted earlier, in the reconsolidation discovery studies of 1997 to 2000, a state of deconsolidation was found to exist only soon after the target learning had been reactivated by a suitable cue or reminder. This observation was interpreted by the researchers to mean that each reactivation of a target learning deconsolidates its neural circuits, launching the reconsolidation process.

That conclusion may have been sensible based on the initial few studies, but it turned out to be incorrect. Pedreira, Pérez-Cuesta, and Maldonado (2004) were first to show that reactivation alone does not bring about deconsolidation and reconsolidation. They concluded, "at odds with the usual view, retrieval per se is unable to induce labilization of the old memory" (p. 581), and they demonstrated that what the brain requires to trigger the reconsolidation process is reactivation plus another critical experience, described below. Subsequently, this same two-step requirement has been demonstrated in at least 22 other studies that I have tallied as of this writing. They are listed in Table 1. In the discovery studies of 1997 to 2000, researchers had fulfilled this two-step requirement without awareness of doing so, as shown later in this section.

The early interpretation that reactivation by itself produces deconsolidation spread widely among both neuroscientists and science journalists and became a reconsolidation meme. Despite the post-2004 piling up of decisive evidence revealing that this original conclusion was incorrect, it has continued to be asserted in new writings by not only science journalists but also by some prominent researchers who were involved in the original studies, as well as by many later reconsolidation researchers. As of this writing, more than 10 years since the mismatch requirement was first detected and published, new research articles continue to be published that lack any consideration of the mismatch requirement's role in the reported results (e.g., Wood et al., 2015).

It is perhaps understandable that science journalists would latch on to and continue to spread the misconception that reactivation in itself destabilizes the reactivated learning, if they were unaware of what the ongoing research was revealing. It is less clear why the error would continue to be voiced by researchers. From my point of view as a clinician observer witnessing this situation unfold for almost a decade, I cannot escape the impression that many reconsolidation researchers appear unaware of sizable amounts of research published in their own area of specialization. Some of the more significant reconsolidation research articles, such as that of Schiller et al. (2010), assert that reactivation induces reconsolidation and reference none of the studies in Table 1 that have shown that view to be incorrect. Commenting here on this situation is hopefully warranted by the importance of assuring that research findings critically important for clinical application are not obscured.

What, then, is the second step that must accompany reactivation? Pedreira et al. (2004), followed by all of the studies listed in Table 1, have shown that in order to induce reconsolidation, reactivation must be accompanied or followed soon by what researchers term a *mismatch* experience or *prediction error* experience. This is an experience of something distinctly discrepant with what the reactivated target memory "knows" or expects—a surprising new learning consisting of anything from a superfluous but salient novelty element to a direct contradiction of what is known according to the target learning. It makes sense from an evolutionary perspective that deconsolidation and reconsolidation, being the brain's process for updating learnings and memories, would be triggered only by new information that is at odds with the contents of an existing learning (Lee, 2009). Lee wrote, "reconsolidation is triggered by a violation of expectation based upon prior learning, whether such a violation is qualitative (the outcome not occurring at all) or quantitative (the magnitude of the outcome not being fully predicted)" (p. 417). It would be biologically costly, with no benefit, if the brain launched the complex neurochemical process of reconsolidation when there is no new knowledge requiring a memory update. The studies listed in Table 1 have shown that the brain evolved so as to launch de/reconsolidation *only when an experience of something discrepant with a reactivated, learned expectation or model of reality signals the need for an update of that existing knowledge.* This empirical finding of a critical role of mismatch or prediction error can be regarded as a neurobiological validation of a central feature of the learning models of both Piaget (1955) and Rescorla and Wagner (1972).

Thus, what shifts a particular learning into a deconsolidated, destabilized state, allowing its expression to be modified or erased by new learning during an approximately five-hour window, is not simply reactivation of that learning, but the experience of that reactivated learning encountering a mismatch or prediction error. As stated by Agren (2014) in reviewing research on reconsolidation of emotional learnings in humans, "it would appear that prediction error is vital for a reactivation of memory to trigger a reconsolidation process" (p. 73). Likewise, Delorenzi et al. (2014) commented, "strong evidence supports the view that reconsolidation depends on detecting mismatches between actual and expected experiences" (p. 309). Exton-McGuinness, Lee, and Reichelt (2015) review the role of prediction errors in memory reconsolidation studies and sum up their position by stating, "We propose that a prediction error signal . . . is necessary for destabilisation and subsequent reconsolidation of a memory" (p. 375). That is the research finding that translates into major advances for the psychotherapy field (Ecker, 2011; Ecker et al., 2012, 2013a,b).

For those advances to materialize, it is necessary for clinicians to understand well what the brain regards as an experience of mismatch or prediction error. Misconceptions abound on this point as well. The following example shows the meaning of mismatch at the basic level of classical conditioning in the laboratory, as

Table 1

Studies demonstrating that both memory reactivation and memory mismatch (prediction error) are necessary for inducing memory destabilization (deconsolidation) and reconsolidation, and that memory reactivation alone is insufficient.

Year	Authors	Species	Memory type	Design and findings
2004	Pedreira et al.	Crab	Contextual fear memory	Reactivated learned expectation of visual threat must be sharply disconfirmed for memory to be disrupted by cycloheximide.
2005	Frenkel et al.	Crab	Contextual fear memory	New experience modifies memory expression only if preceded by a memory mismatch experience.
2005	Galluccio	Human	Operant conditioning	Memory is erased only by being reactivated along with a novel contingency.
2005	Rodriguez-Ortiz et al.	Rat	Taste recognition memory	Novel taste following reactivation allows memory disruption by anisomycin.
2006	Morris et al.	Rat	Spatial memory of escape from danger	Reactivation allows disruption of original memory by anisomycin only if learned safe position has been changed, creating mismatch of expectation.
2006	Rossato et al.	Rat	Spatial memory of escape from danger	Reactivation allows disruption of original memory by anisomycin only if learned safe position has been changed, creating mismatch of expectation.
2007	Forcato et al.	Human	Declarative memory	Memory of syllable pairings learned visually is destabilized and impaired by new learning only if, after reactivation by presentation of context, presentation of a syllable to be paired does not occur as expected, creating mismatch.
2007	Rossato et al.	Rat	Object recognition memory	Memory is disrupted by anisomycin only if reactivated in presence of novel object.
2008	Rodriguez-Ortiz et al.	Rat	Spatial memory of escape from danger	Reactivation allows disruption of original memory by anisomycin only if learned safe position has been changed, creating mismatch of expectation.

Table 1 cont.

2009	Forcato et al.	Human	Declarative memory	Memory of syllable pairings learned visually is labilized and lost only if reactivation is followed by learning revised novel pairings.
2009	Pérez-Cuesta & Maldonado	Crab	Contextual fear memory	Reactivated learned expectation of visual threat must be sharply disconfirmed for memory to be disrupted by cycloheximide.
2009	Winters et al.	Rat	Object recognition memory	Memory is disrupted by MK-801 only if reactivated in presence of novel contextual features.
2010	Forcato et al.	Human	Declarative memory	Memory of syllable pairings learned visually destabilizes and incorporates new information only if, after reactivation, the expected opportunity to match syllables does not occur, creating mismatch.
2011	Coccoz et al.	Human	Declarative memory	Memory of syllable pairings learned visually destabilizes, allowing a mild stressor to strengthen memory, only if, after reactivation, the expected opportunity to match syllables does not occur, creating mismatch.
2012	Caffaro et al.	Crab	Contextual fear memory	New experience modifies memory expression only if preceded by a memory mismatch experience.
2012	Sevenster et al.	Human	Associative fear memory (classical conditioning)	Reactivated fear memory is erased by propranolol only if prediction error is also experienced.
2013	Balderas et al.	Rat	Object recognition memory	Only if memory updating is required does reactivation trigger memory destabilization and reconsolidation, allowing memory disruption by anisomycin.
2013	Barreiro et al.	Crab	Contextual fear memory	Only if memory reactivation is followed by unexpected, mismatching experience is the memory eliminated by glutamate antagonist.

Table 1 cont.

2013	Díaz-Mataix et al.	Rat	Associative fear memory (classical conditioning)	Reactivated fear memory is erased by anisomycin only if prediction error is also experienced.
2013	Reichelt et al.	Rat	Goal-tracking memory	Target memory reactivated with prediction error was destabilized and then disrupted by MK-801, but not if brain's prediction error signal was blocked.
2013	Sevenster et al.	Human	Associative fear memory (classical conditioning)	Reactivated fear memory is destabilized, allowing disruption by propranolol, only if prediction-error-driven relearning is also experienced.
2014	Exton-McGuinness et al.	Rat	Instrumental memory (operant conditioning)	Memory for lever pressing for sucrose pellet was disrupted by MK-801 only if the reinforcement schedule during reactivation was changed from fixed to variable ratio, creating prediction error.
2014	Sevenster et al.	Human	Associative fear memory (classical conditioning)	Reactivated fear memory is destabilized, allowing disruption by propranolol, only if prediction-error-driven relearning is also experienced, and termination of prediction error terminates destabilization.

demonstrated by Pedreira et al. (2004) and other studies listed in Table 1. Clinically relevant learnings are often far more complex, and the guiding of mismatch experiences in psychotherapy looks very different, as a rule, from the laboratory instances described in this article, but the principles of mismatch are usefully clarified at this basic level.

Consider a target learning that was created by several repetitions of turning on a blue light and delivering a mild electric shock several seconds later, during the last half-second of the light being on. Subsequently, if the blue light is turned on again, the learned expectation of the shock is reactivated immediately, along with fear and the physiological expressions of fear, such as a mouse's freezing or a human's change of skin conductance. However, this reactivation does not deconsolidate and destabilize the memory circuits of this learned association of light and shock, because no mismatch experience has occurred as yet. While the blue light stays on without any shock being delivered, a mismatch or prediction error has not occurred because the shock might still occur. The target learning is in a state of expectancy of the shock. Mismatch occurs when the blue light is turned off with no shock having been experienced. Only then are perceptions discrepant with what the target learning "knows." Now the synapses encoding the target learning unlock into a modifiable state, because now it is definite that no shock occurred as expected while the blue light was on.

Understanding the mismatch requirement allows us to interpret correctly the results of various studies that were misinterpreted by the researchers because they analyzed their studies without reference to the mismatch requirement. The simple logic of the situation, as stated by Agren (2014), is that "the studies that have shown effects of reconsolidation . . . must somehow have induced a prediction error" (p. 80). Ecker et al. (2012) articulated the same principle: "Whenever the markers of erasure of a learning are observed, both reactivation and a mismatch of that learning must have taken place, unlocking its synapses, or erasure could not have resulted. This logic can serve as a useful guide for identifying the critical steps of process in both the experiments of researchers and the sessions of psychotherapists" (p. 23).

Therefore, identifying the presence or absence of mismatch in each of the many published studies of reconsolidation that lacks consideration of the mismatch requirement is an exercise necessary for bringing the field of reconsolidation research to maturity from its present fragmented condition. The remainder of this section begins that unifying exercise by describing several key studies, analyzing the presence or absence of mismatch in them, and reinterpreting their results accordingly. This analysis of mismatch in published studies yields instructive insights into how mismatch may function.

The study by Nader, Schafe, and LeDoux (2000), which repeated the basic design of some other early studies (Przybyslawski et al., 1997, 1999; Roullet et al., 1998), is often regarded as the one that brought the initial research to a tipping point of establishing the reconsolidation phenomenon conclusively. Nader et al. used the same classical conditioning procedure as described in the example just above, but with an audible tone rather than a blue light. They taught rats to expect a shock during the last half-second of a 30-s tone. Later, their procedure accomplished memory reactivation with the *onset* of the 30-s tone, and it accomplished memory mismatch with the *offset* of the tone with no shock occurring, triggering destabilization of the target learning and launching the reconsolidation process.

However, the researchers were unaware of the mismatch requirement (which was discovered four years later by Pedreira et al., 2004) or of the crucial role of this mismatch in triggering deconsolidation of the target learning. It was by chance that their procedure happened to include the needed mismatch. Memory erasure resulted from anisomycin administered soon after that mismatch experience (but not when administered 6 hr later, when the reconsolidation window was no longer open), confirming that memory destabilization (deconsolidation) had occurred, because anisomycin destroys only nonconsolidated synapses.

Understandably but erroneously, Nader et al. concluded that memory reactivation was sufficient for triggering destabilization. If their design had included reactivation by the tone together with the expected shock, eliminating the mismatch of expectations, no deconsolidation or erasure would have occurred. Such failure to achieve destabilization of a reactivated target learning has been reported in many studies (e.g., Bos, Becker, & Kindt, 2014; Cammarota, Bevilaqua, Medina, & Izquierdo, 2004; Hernandez & Kelley, 2004; Mileusnic, Lancashire, & Rose, 2005; Wood et al., 2015), and we can now recognize that this failure was due to an absence of mismatch or prediction error in the procedure used. (For example, as reported by Hernandez and Kelley in 2004, a rat's memory that pressing a certain lever brings a sugar reward was indeed reactivated when the rat was once again placed in the chamber with the lever, pressed it, and received a sugar pellet, but this reactivation provided the expected reinforcement and entailed no experience of prediction error, so memory destabilization did not occur.) In these studies, too, the researchers made no mention of a mismatch or prediction error requirement in their interpretation of results. Instead, they concluded incorrectly that the particular type of memory under study was not subject to reconsolidation. Subsequently, other studies successfully demonstrated reconsolidation for those types of memory (see, e.g., Wang, Ostlund, Nader, & Balleine, 2005).

All 23 studies listed in Table 1 have shown that reactivation alone does not launch the reconsolidation process, but reactivation plus mismatch does. This point was particularly emphasized by Forcato, Argibay, Pedreira, and Maldonado (2009) in titling their article, "Human Reconsolidation Does Not Always Occur When a Memory Is Retrieved," and by Sevenster, Beckers, and Kindt (2012), who titled theirs "Retrieval Per Se Is Not Sufficient to Trigger Reconsolidation of Human Fear Memory." The latter authors characterized their next published study by stating, "we show in humans that prediction error is (i) a necessary condition for reconsolidation of associative fear memory and (ii) determined by the interaction between original learning and retrieval" (Sevenster, Beckers, & Kindt, 2013, p. 830).

Reconsolidation can also be triggered by a mismatch of *when* events are expected to occur, with no change in *what* occurs, as demonstrated by Díaz-Mataix, Ruiz Martinez, Schafe, LeDoux, and Doyère (2013). On Day 1 in their study, rats heard a 60-s tone and received a momentary electrical shock at the 30-s point, midway through the tone. For each rat this was repeated 10 times to create a reliable conditioned response of fear to the tone. On Day 2, each rat heard the tone and received the shock again just once, reactivating the learned association of tone and shock. The shock occurred at the same 30-s point for some rats, but for others it occurred at the 10-s point. Immediately after this reactivation experience, researchers administered a chemical agent (anisomycin) that disrupts nonconsolidated memory circuits. On Day 3, the tone was played again for each of the rats five times with no accompanying shock, and the strength of fear responses was measured. Rats that had unchanged shock timing on Day 2 reacted with fear on Day 3 fully as strongly as they had done on Day 2, indicating that anisomycin had no effect and, therefore, that the reactivation without mismatch on Day 2 had not destabilized the target learning. In contrast, rats whose shock timing had been changed on Day 2 reacted on Day 3 with only half as many fear responses as on Day 2, indicating that anisomycin had significantly impaired the target learning and, therefore, that the reactivation with timing mismatch on Day 2 had indeed destabilized the target learning.

This important finding that temporal mismatches trigger reconsolidation will figure significantly in other discussions later in this article. Díaz-Mataix et al. did identify the prediction error that played a critical role in their procedure, and they concluded from their observations that new information must accompany reactivation in order to destabilize the target learning. That conclusion corroborates what was demonstrated in at least sixteen prior studies listed in Table 1, so it unclear why Díaz-Mataix et al. describe their finding as though it is a new discovery and cite only one of prior studies (Sevenster et al., 2012).

A target learning that has been destabilized by mismatch can be erased not only by chemical agents, but also by a counterlearning experience with no use of chemical agents. It is this endogenous approach that is most desirable for psychotherapeutic use and which has been applied extensively in that context (Ecker et al., 2012). In laboratory studies, endogenous erasure or modification of a target learning has been demonstrated with both animal and human subjects (e.g., Galluccio, 2005; Liu et al., 2014; Monfils, Cowansage, Klann, & LeDoux, 2009; Schiller et al. 2010; Steinfurth et al., 2014; Walker et al., 2003; Xue et al., 2012).

Monfils et al. (2009) used three pairings of a 20-s audio tone (the conditioned stimulus, CS) and half-second footshock (unconditioned stimulus, US), with 3 min between pairings, to train rats to respond to the tone with fear. One day later, the target learning was reactivated by the CS/tone, but there was no accompanying US/shock, which is a mismatch of the expectation of the US. So far, the procedure is basically the same as that of Nader et al. (2000), described above, but rather than disrupt the target learning chemically at this point, Monfils et al. continued to present the CS without US repeatedly. CS2, the second tone, was presented 10 min or

1 hr after the first one, but then additional CS tones came at 3-min intervals, for a total of 19 CSs. That procedure successfully and robustly erased the rats' learned fear of the tone.

Note that if the initial 10-min or 1-hr interval had been a 3-min period like all of the ensuing intervals, the repetitive CS counterlearning procedure would have been a standard multitrial extinction training, which is well known not to bring about erasure. Thus the longer interval between CS1 and CS2 was critically important for achieving erasure through reconsolidation rather than suppression through extinction. The fact that erasure occurred implies that the target learning was destabilized and erasable during the series of CSs, which in turn implies that the longer interval from CS1 to CS2 resulted in a mismatch of expected and actual timing. (The discussion of results provided by Monfils et al. does not refer to the concept of mismatch or prediction error, however.)

The key role of a temporal mismatch in inducing destabilization in both Monfils et al. (2009) and Díaz-Mataix et al. (2013) makes it clear that the brain learns the temporal features of new emotional experiences no less than it learns other characteristics, and that mismatches of timing can be highly effective for inducing reconsolidation in cases where the target learning has distinct temporal structure. In other recent research, networks of dedicated "time cells" in the hippocampus have been found to measure and remember time intervals (Jacobs, Allen, Nguyen, & Fortin, 2013; MacDonald, Lepage, Eden, & Eichenbaum, 2011; Naya & Suzuki, 2011; Paz et al., 2010).

The important observations made by Monfils et al. (2009) will be revisited and utilized later in this article to address fundamental questions of what governs whether reconsolidation or extinction occurs and why extinction fails to produce erasure. It is noteworthy too that the erasure procedure used by Monfils et al. was subsequently adapted for use with human subjects by Schiller et al. (2010), who demonstrated the first endogenous erasure of a fear learning in humans in a controlled study. The Appendix to this article provides a detailed examination of the mismatches involved in their procedure.

Fulfillment of the mismatch requirement is evident in the successful inducing of reconsolidation in a wide range of experimental procedures. For example, an associative fear learning can be triggered into reconsolidation by a reexperiencing of only the unconditioned stimulus (US) without the conditioned stimulus (CS) (Díaz-Mataix et al., 2011; Liu et al., 2014). The target learning, consisting of experiencing first the CS followed by the US, is mismatched if the US occurs without the CS. That mismatch consists of both the absence of the expected CS and also, importantly, a change in the expected temporal sequence of events, because the target learning expects the US to occur after the CS, not without the prior occurrence of the CS. Another example is the case of having two different co-occurring CSs, both of which have been paired with the same US. Debiec, Díaz-Mataix, Bush, Doyère, and LeDoux (2013) showed that reexposure to either one of the CSs can trigger the reconsolidation of the memory of the other. Here the expected co-occurrence of both CSs is mismatched when only one CS is presented. None of the authors referenced in this paragraph explained their results in terms of the mismatch requirement, however. They discussed their results as though the triggering of reconsolidation can be attributed to reactivation alone.

Even researchers who are well aware of the mismatch/prediction error requirement can overlook the occurrence of mismatch in their own procedures. For example, Pine et al. (2014) provided an ingenious and intricate demonstration that reconsolidation occurs for complex, unconscious emotional learnings in humans— and in doing so they have supplied the strongest empirical support to date for the anecdotal clinical observations reported by Ecker et al. (2012, 2013a,b)—but they commented, "Our results seem to counter a recent theory that new learning (or the generation of a prediction error) is required during reactivation in order to trigger reconsolidation. . . . Here, no new learning took place during the reminder" (p. 11). However, the "reminder" (reactivation) that they used for triggering reconsolidation on Day 2 of their procedure contained three distinct temporal mismatches relative to the original learning on Day 1: a reversal of overall sequence, an overall duration of the series of trials that was one-fourth as long, and the introduction of a 10-min delay within the overall sequence. Thus, due to these temporal mismatches of the original learning, its reactivation was actually accompanied by an abundance of new learning, triggering destabilization and reconsolidation. As noted above, we know from Díaz-Mataix et al. (2013) that even a single temporal mismatch can be an effective destabilizer.

As this section's final example of how the mismatch requirement can account for diverse reconsolidation phenomena, there have been several studies of how the age or strength of a target learning effects the triggering of memory destabilization (Boccia, Blake, Acosta, & Baratti, 2006; Clem & Huganir, 2010; Debiec, LeDoux, & Nader, 2002; Eisenberg & Dudai, 2004; Frankland et al., 2006; Inda et al., 2011; Milekic & Alberini, 2002; Steinfurth et al., 2014; Suzuki et al., 2004; Winters, Tucci, & DaCosta-Furtado, 2009). Reviewing all results of these studies is beyond the scope of the present article, other than to summarize that, as a rule, stronger reactivation is required in order to destabilize stronger or older target learnings. Some of the studies in this area successfully destabilized both young and older target learnings (up to 8 weeks after acquisition), but others failed to destabilize older memories. Lee (2009) commented, "it is also possible that all memories undergo reconsolidation regardless of their age, but that previous studies have failed to use sufficiently intense memory reactivation conditions for older memories" (p. 416).

The results found by Suzuki et al. (2004) can serve to illustrate the further research possibilities that become apparent as a result of asking the question: If the mismatch requirement is responsible for experimental observations, what are those observations showing about how mismatch functions under various circumstances? Suzuki et al. taught rats to fear a test chamber (context/CS) by placing each rat in the chamber for 2.5 min and then administering a 2-s footshock (US). Rats in one group received just one shock; those in another group received three shocks separated by 30 s. All rats were removed from the context/CS 30 s after their final footshock. Then, either 1 day, 1 week, 3 weeks, or 8 weeks later, immediately after administration of anisomycin, rats were placed in the context/CS for various amounts of time and then removed with no shock, in order to reactivate the fear learning and disrupt it if it had been destabilized by the reactivation. One day later their fear level was measured during a 3-min reexposure back in the context/CS. This procedure resulted in the following findings:

For fear memory created by a single context-shock pairing, a 1-min shock-free reexposure to the context did not destabilize the fear learning, but a 3-min reexposure did destabilize it if memory age was 1 day, 1 week, or 3 weeks. The implication is that a 1-min shock-free reexposure did not create a mismatch experience, but a 3-min reexposure did create a mismatch. This is suggestive of a temporal structure in the target learning. The 2.5-min period of initial exposure to the context/CS fits that possibility well, because relative to that learned 2.5-min period, the 1-min reexposure could have been too short to be experienced as a nonreinforcement, so it would not create a mismatch experience, but the 3-min reexposure would.

If memory age was 8 weeks, a 3-min reexposure no longer caused destabilization, but a 10-min reexposure did destabilize. This possibly implies that memory of the 2.5-min period lost definiteness over time and therefore required a longer reexposure for decisive nonreinforcement and mismatch to be experienced.

For fear memory created by three context-shock pairings instead of one, a 3-min reexposure no longer caused destabilization, but a 10-min reexposure did destabilize. Here the challenge is to understand how a stronger fear training would alter the timing memory. Three 2-s shocks coming every 30 s is a grueling minute that might feel to a rat much longer than a minute spent sniffing around curiously in a harmless place, just as a human also experiences time periods very differently depending upon the presence or absence of pain. The prior 2.5-min duration may have been distorted or blurred retroactively by this long, traumatic minute, such that the longer 10-min reexposure was necessary for decisive nonreinforcement and mismatch to be experienced.

The interpretations sketched above are not the only possible ways in which the mismatch requirement could have resulted in the observations made by Suzuki et al. (2004). They are offered here heuristically, by way of showing how the mismatch requirement can be logically applied to illuminate how experimental procedures interact with the inherent properties of the brain's memory systems.

The experimental procedures discussed in this section in relation to the mismatch requirement illustrate a principle that is critical for understanding reconsolidation phenomena: *What does, or does not, constitute a mismatch experience depends entirely on the specific makeup of the target learning at the time of mismatch.* That is a principle that I will refer to henceforth as *mismatch relativity*. It is essential for understanding the effects of reconsolidation procedures used in both laboratory studies and therapy sessions. In the small minority of reconsolidation research articles that do address the mismatch requirement, I have never seen mismatch relativity articulated explicitly; rather it is either tacitly assumed or asserted in an abstract manner (as in Bos et al., 2014, and Sevenster et al., 2013, 2014; for example, Bos et al. state, "The experience of a prediction error upon reactivation critically depends on the interaction between the original learning of the fear association and the memory retrieval" [p. 6]). Mindfulness of mismatch relativity is critical for consistent outcomes in utilizing reconsolidation in psychotherapy to bring about transformational change. Only by attending closely to the specific elements of a symptom-generating emotional learning can a psychotherapist reliably guide mismatch experiences that disconfirm those specific elements, as is necessary for their nullification and dissolution.

A question often asked by clinicians learning about reconsolidation is: When my panicky therapy client drives on the highway and the feared terrible fiery crash doesn't happen, that seems to be a mismatch experience, as needed to launch reconsolidation, yet it doesn't unlock or erase the learned fear. Doesn't this show that the model is incorrect? To clarify this, we need to apply the mismatch relativity principle and examine whether or not a mismatch experience actually took place. That begins with examining the detailed makeup of the target learning in question. In this case, the target learning is not that a car crash happens on every drive; rather it is that a crash *might* happen unpredictably on *any* drive. That learning is not mismatched or disconfirmed by an accident not happening on any one drive or on any number of drives. A safe, uneventful drive creates no prediction error and therefore does not induce deconsolidation, so the target learning is not revised and the model has not failed to apply.

This example naturally raises the question: For that target learning, what *would* be a mismatch experience? The knowledge that a crash might happen unpredictably on any drive is true as a recognition of existential reality, so no mismatch or disconfirmation of that knowledge is possible. However, that knowledge is not the entire learning maintaining the panicky dread of a fiery car crash. Some other learning is responsible for that emotional intensity, and it is for elements of that learning that mismatches *can* be created. The most common form of this other learning, though not the only possibility (see Ecker, 2003, or Ecker & Hulley, 2000, for an account of diverse learnings underlying anxiety and panic symptoms), is suppressed traumatic memory of the same or a similar kind, such as a car crash, a fiery explosion, the death of high school classmates in a head-on collision, a terrible scare from skidding on ice on a mountain road or from being pulled along very fast at 3 years old in a little wagon tied to the bicycle of an older sibling, and so forth. The suppressed state of the traumatic memory preserves its emotionally raw, unprocessed quality, including desperate fear and helplessness. De-suppression of the memory (in small enough steps to be tolerable) reveals a set of specific elements, each of which is a particular learning. It is these component learnings that can now be subjected to a mismatch experience. For example, the helplessness felt and learned in the original situation can in many cases encounter a mismatch experience through the technique of empowered reenactment, which is widely used in trauma therapy to create a vivid experience of potent self-protection in the original scene. For a detailed clinical example of that kind, see Ecker et al. (2012, pp. 86–91).

In summary of this section, the research findings on memory reconsolidation represent a nontheoretical set of instructions for bringing about transformational change in a target learning. These instructions specify that in order for a target learning to become destabilized and susceptible to being unlearned and nullified, it must be both reactivated and subjected to a mismatch or prediction error experience. The mismatch relativity principle has been introduced here, within the exercise of analyzing the occurrence of mismatch in published studies, to emphasize that what is, and what is not, a mismatch experience is always defined in relation to the specific elements of the target learning and what the target learning "knows" or expects. This exercise of examining the role of mismatch in published studies will continue in each of the next two sections. (For numerous examples of creating mismatch experiences in psychotherapy, see Ecker et al., 2012, Chapters 3–6.)

Misconception 2: The Disruption of Reconsolidation Is What Erases a Target Learning

As soon as a reactivated target learning encounters a single brief but vivid mismatch experience, the target learning is deconsolidated and for about five hours is open to being changed or erased at the level of its synaptic encoding. Erasure is the focus of this article, because it is erasure that is experienced clinically as liberating, transformational change, that is, complete and permanent disappearance of an unwanted behavior or state of mind.

As noted above, erasure of a deconsolidated target learning has been accomplished by researchers either by guiding new learning that nullifies the target learning or by applying chemical agents. Those two processes of erasure are fundamentally different.

Chemical agents used for this purpose are those that block some step in the complex cellular and molecular process by which a memory circuit restabilizes into a consolidated state (for a review, see Reichelt & Lee, 2013). Administered just before or after a target learning is destabilized, these chemical agents selectively act upon only deconsolidated, destabilized memory circuits without affecting consolidated ones. This blockage of the reconsolidation of the target memory circuits impairs and destroys these circuits, erasing the target learning by disrupting the very process of reconsolidation. This disruption takes effect not immediately upon administration, but when restabilization would normally happen, about five hours after initial destabilization.

In contrast, erasure by new learning is understood by researchers as de-encoding and/or reencoding the target learning's synapses, unlearning and nullifying the prior content of that learning, but leaving the neurons and synapses operating normally and allowing the natural restabilization/reconsolidation of the circuits to occur. This results in memory circuits that no longer contain the target learning. Erasure by new learning occurs through the *utilization* of the reconsolidation process rather than through its disruption. One might characterize this type of erasure as disrupting the *content* of the target learning, but the reconsolidation process itself is not disrupted. Thus, referring to this type of erasure as a "disruption of reconsolidation" is a misconception and a misrepresentation of the actual process.

Most of the chemical agents successfully used in animal studies to disrupt reconsolidation are unsuitable for use with humans due to toxicity, side effects, or slowness of action (Schiller & Phelps, 2011). However, with human subjects the beta-adrenergic blocker propranolol is safe and has been tested in numerous studies ranging from Pavlovian (associative) fear conditioning to genuine PTSD conditions in clinical trials, as reviewed by Agren (2014). Results have varied widely for both associative fear conditioning and genuine PTSD. For associative conditioning, full erasure by propranolol was demonstrated by Kindt et al. (2009) and Soeter and Kindt (2011), but Bos et al. (2014) measured no reduction of fear at all. Bos et al. acknowledged, "The current findings clearly indicate that we did not trigger reconsolidation during memory reactivation" (p. 6). They offered the speculation that the cause of the negative result appeared to be a failure of their reactivation procedure to generate the required memory mismatch/prediction error experience, and they drew the lesson that "Future studies may benefit from protocols that are explicitly designed to assess and manipulate prediction error during memory retrieval" (p. 7). For PTSD, Brunet et al. (2011) measured a significant reduction of symptoms due to propranolol, but Wood et al. (2015) reported no reduction of symptoms using either propranolol or mifepristone, a glucocorticoid blocker that interferes with the neural (and other) effects of the stress hormone cortisol. Wood et al., in discussing various possible causes of their negative results, gave no consideration or mention of the requirement for memory mismatch. It seems probable that in chemical disruption/PTSD studies that did achieve symptom reduction, the procedure included mismatch unwittingly. For example, Brunet et al., unlike Woods et al., had subjects speak out their account of a traumatic experience to an interviewer, thus creating what trauma therapists term *dual focus*, an experiential state in which attention is simultaneously directed to a safe external environment and an internal traumatic memory. Dual focus maintains a dissociation and subjective distance between conscious attention and the attended contents of traumatic memory, and appears to be a critical ingredient in some trauma treatment procedures that achieve rapid, lasting depotentiation of traumatic memory and cessation of PTSD symptoms (see, e.g., Lee, Taylor, & Drummond, 2006). Dual focus creates memory mismatch in the form of a strong perception of safety concurrent with traumatic memory reactivation, as well as through facilitating internal accessing of existing personal knowledge that contradicts the contents of the traumatic memory schema (Ecker, 2015).

For clinical purposes, a natural process of erasure through unlearning rather than through chemical agents is of course greatly preferable, as a rule. The clinical feasibility and effectiveness of erasure through new learning have been demonstrated for symptoms and target learnings of many kinds, including but not limited to anxiety and posttraumatic symptoms (Ecker et al., 2012; Gray & Liotta, 2012; Xue et al., 2012). Thus, in the endogenous clinical context in particular it is a misconception to describe erasure as occurring through the disruption of reconsolidation, though the chemical approach is exactly that.

At the opposite end of the terminology spectrum, researchers sometimes use the phrase, "the enhancement of reconsolidation." This phrase denotes not a strengthening of the reconsolidation process itself, but a strengthening of the behavioral expression of a target learning that results, after its reconsolidation, from various procedures applied during the period of destabilization (for reviews, see Delorenzi et al., 2014; Forcato et al., 2014). The phrase therefore is essentially synonymous with "reconsolidation-induced enhancement of memory expression." Here we have yet another way in which the word reconsolidation is used by researchers, and again we see that for accurate understanding, readers of reconsolidation literature must consider carefully what an author's phrasing actually is intended to mean.

Misconception 3: Erasure Is Brought About During the Reconsolidation Window by a Process of Extinction: Reconsolidation Is an Enhancement of Extinction

Reconsolidation and extinction are different phenomena, with distinctly different effects, but misconceptions have developed for reasons described in this section.

In the process that has been known for a century as extinction, the target learning is not revised or erased, but only suppressed temporarily by new counterlearning, and the new learning is encoded in its own memory circuitry that is anatomically separate from, and in competition with, the circuits of the target learning. Later, however, the target learning wins that competition and reemerges into full expression (Bouton, 2004; Foa & McNally, 1996; Milner et al., 1998). In contrast, during the reconsolidation process, a target learning is destabilized and rendered susceptible to being revised fundamentally by new learning, which can either weaken it, strengthen it, alter its details, or fully nullify and erase it, and these changes are lasting, as described earlier.

Researchers have determined that reconsolidation and extinction are distinct and even possibly mutually exclusive processes at the behavioral, neural, and molecular levels (Duvarci & Nader, 2004; Duvarci, Mamou, & Nader, 2006; Merlo, Milton, Goozée, Theobald, & Everitt, 2014). "Reconsolidation cannot be reduced down to facilitated extinction" was the conclusion of Duvarci and Nader (p. 9269).

Despite those signature differences in process and effects produced, confusion about the relationship between reconsolidation and extinction nevertheless arises because to a degree they share certain operational and procedural patterns:

First, while the nullification learning that contradicts and erases a destabilized target learning can have any convenient procedural design, in many studies it has had the same design as a conventional extinction training—a series of numerous identical counterlearning/unreinforced trials—so it can be confused with and mislabeled as an extinction training, even though extinction is not actually involved.

Second, extinction, like reconsolidation, begins with the two-step sequence of reactivation and nonreinforcement (that is, a recueing of the target learning followed by nonoccurrence of what the target learning expects to happen, such as playing an audio tone without also delivering the mild electric shock that had previously been paired with the tone). It can be confusing and difficult to see how reconsolidation and extinction are two separate phenomena if they share the same initiating sequence of reactivation and nonreinforcement.

The main aim of this section is to dispel those two confusions, as well as to review various research findings that clarify the nature and relationship of reconsolidation and extinction and their differential triggering. In addition, the discussion will explore these questions: Are the empirical findings on reconsolidation and extinction understandable entirely, or only partially, in terms of the mismatch requirement and mismatch relativity (MRMR)? Does it prove instructive to consider how the findings would have to be understood in order for them to be entirely consistent with MRMR? The heuristic exploration of those questions in this section extends significantly the degree to which the mismatch/prediction error requirement has been applied, to date, to the interpretation of experimental findings.

Extinction-like procedure used for nullification learning. As noted earlier, for inducing erasure, some reconsolidation researchers have used a format of nullification learning during the reconsolidation window that has the same procedural structure as classical extinction training: a series of numerous identical counterlearning (nonreinforcement) experiences. The result of this procedure is not extinction (temporary suppression of the target learning), but rather the permanent erasure of the target learning, such that even strong recueing (reinstatement) cannot reevoke the target learning into expression. Nevertheless, these researchers have unfortunately labeled this procedure as "extinction" by naming it with such phrases as the "memory retrieval-extinction procedure," "extinction-induced erasure," "extinction during reconsolidation," or other phrases containing "extinction" (e.g., Baker, McNally, & Richardson, 2013; Clem & Huganir, 2010; Liu et al., 2014; Monfils et al., 2009; Quirk et al., 2010; Schiller et al., 2010; Steinfurth et al., 2014; Xue et al., 2012). Such labeling is a source of much misunderstanding of reconsolidation and extinction.

We are faced with these empirical facts: When a repetitive counterlearning procedure is applied to a target learning that is in a stable state when the procedure begins, the result is extinction—the target learning is suppressed but is intact and later reemerges into expression. However, when the same repetitive counterlearning procedure is applied to a target learning that is already in a destabilized/deconsolidated state, the result is erasure—the target learning's encoding is rewritten according to this new counterlearning, permanently nullifying the content of the target learning (Monfils et al., 2009; Schiller et al., 2010). Thus a particular learning procedure (repetitive counterlearning) can have extremely different neurological and behavioral effects depending on whether or not it is carried out during the reconsolidation window. So, any label for the erasure procedure that includes the term "extinction" is a misnomer that invites the misconception that reconsolidation utilizes and enhances the process of extinction.

The use of repetitive counterlearning during the reconsolidation window could more appropriately be labeled "nullification learning," "update learning," or "erasure learning," rather than "extinction training," to avoid conceptual errors and confusion. However, the "extinction" labeling has already become standard among researchers who use this particular procedure and is probably here to stay.

The great significance and usefulness of the reconsolidation window lies in the fact that, during that window, to unlearn is to erase, regardless of the specific form of the unlearning or nullification experience. The repetitive counterlearning procedure is a convenient protocol under the highly simplified conditions of laboratory studies but is not suitable in general for nullification of the far more complex emotional learnings encountered in real-life psychotherapy. There is a potentially unlimited number of formats in which nullification learning can occur in psychotherapy (for many examples of which, see Ecker et al., 2012).

The triggering of reconsolidation versus extinction. As already described, both reconsolidation and extinction begin with the two-step sequence of reactivation and nonreinforcement, that is, a recueing of the target learning followed by nonoccurrence of what the target learning expects to happen. What, then, determines whether reconsolidation or extinction is the result?

We know that the experience of mismatch (prediction error) is what triggers destabilization and reconsolidation, as discussed earlier. This seems to imply that when memory reactivation plus nonreinforcement create a mismatch experience, reconsolidation is triggered, whereas when reactivation plus nonreinforcement occur without creating a mismatch experience, the extinction process begins. Therefore, in order to understand what causes the triggering of reconsolidation versus extinction, it may be necessary to understand why reactivation with nonreinforcement creates mismatch in some circumstances but not in others. With that question in mind, it is instructive to examine a range of instances where reconsolidation or extinction was induced.

Many observations of the triggering of reconsolidation versus extinction have been made in animal studies through reactivating a CS-US target learning by presenting the unreinforced CS only, and then promptly applying a chemical agent that disrupts nonconsolidated or deconsolidated learnings but has no effect on stable, consolidated memory circuits. The findings of many such studies can be summarized in terms of how the effect of reactivating a target learning with CS-only presentations depends on their time structure. In the studies summarized here, the target learning was formed by two or more CS-US pairings with 100% reinforcement.

Reconsolidation is triggered. After a single brief CS presentation, there is no extinction learning and the target learning is still at full strength (Nader et al., 2000; Eisenberg, Kobilo, Berman, & Dudai, 2003; Jarome et al., 2012; Merlo et al., 2014; Pedreira et al., 2004). In this case, prompt application of a chemical agent that blocks consolidation (and reconsolidation) disrupts the target learning, which is found to be significantly weakened or completely erased 24 hr later, indicating that the target learning was destabilized (deconsolidated) by the CS presentation, triggering the reconsolidation process. This implies that unreinforced reactivation by a single CS presentation does create a mismatch experience.

Extinction is triggered. After a single prolonged CS or a series of many short CS presentations, an influential extinction learning exists and largely suppresses the target learning, so the behavioral expression of the target learning is significantly diminished. In this case, prompt application of a consolidation-blocking chemical agent disrupts the newly formed, not yet consolidated extinction learning, and this restores the target learning to full strength (see, e.g., Eisenberg et al., 2003). The return of the target learning to full strength implies that the target learning was unaffected by the chemical agent and therefore was not in a destabilized state when the chemical agent was administered after the single prolonged CS or the series of many short CSs. This in turn implies that although the first of the many short CS presentations must have created a mismatch experience (as in the single brief CS situation), mismatch must have been terminated promptly by the ensuing CSs, restabilizing the target learning, despite the fact that each CS in itself would seem to be a nonreinforced reactivation that should maintain mismatch. These logical inferences have been corroborated by several studies, described below.

Neither reconsolidation nor extinction is triggered. For an intermediate number of unreinforced CS presentations, the target learning remains at full strength and a variety of chemical interventions that either disrupt or enhance reconsolidation or extinction have no effect on subsequent target learning expression/ This is understood to mean that neither reconsolidation nor extinction is underway (Flavell & Lee, 2013; Merlo et al., 2014; Sevenster, Beckers, & Kindt, 2014). Merlo et al. (2014) commented, "In the continuum of possible retrieval conditions, reconsolidation and extinction processes are mutually exclusive, separated by an insensitive phase where the amount of CS exposure terminates the labilization of the original memory, but is insufficient to trigger the formation of the extinction memory" (p. 2429).

Of the many studies that have reported the kinds of findings summarized above, very few also addressed the question of *why* one, or a few, or many nonreinforced CS reactivations have the observed effects of triggering or not triggering the destabilization and reconsolidation of a target learning. Here the focus of discussion now turns to an examination of why reactivation with nonreinforcement creates mismatch and triggers destabilization in some circumstances and not in others.

MRMR model of triggering reconsolidation or extinction. The critical role of mismatch in triggering reconsolidation was first reported by Pedreira et al. (2004), as noted earlier. A mismatch exists when there is a significant discrepancy between what is expected and what is actually experienced. Thus reconsolidation and all of its complex cellular and molecular machinery is an experience-driven phenomenon.

A growing number of experimental observations require a view of mismatch as being a fluid, dynamical quality of experience that can vary on a moment-to-moment basis with the passage of time and with new experiences (see, e.g., Jarome et al., 2012; Merlo et al., 2014; Sevenster et al., 2014). The following paragraphs apply that dynamical view of mismatch and offer the proposal that the reconsolidation/extinction dichotomy may be largely or completely governed by the mismatch requirement and mismatch relativity (MRMR), as defined earlier.

To explore this proposal and show that MRMR potentially could be responsible for a wide range of reconsolidation and extinction phenomenology, what follows is a discussion of how several significant research findings can be understood as being entirely MRMR effects. The discussion shows specifically how reactivation with nonreinforcement creates mismatch, triggering destabilization, in some circumstances and not in others.

Single CS-only presentation. First consider the simplified case in which the sequence of reactivation and mismatch (nonreinforcement) occurs only once and is not repeated. For example, if a conditioned stimulus (CS, such as a blue light, an audio tone, or a particular physical environment) has previously been paired repeatedly with a mild electrical shock (unconditioned stimulus, US) just before the CS turns off, what happens subsequently if the CS turns on and then turns off unreinforced (no shock), just once?

The CS turning on immediately reactivates the target learning, generating the expectation of receiving a shock. Several studies have shown that the time period from CS onset to CS offset (with no US) controls whether reconsolidation or extinction occurs, and that whichever process occurs is triggered by CS offset and does not begin before CS offset (Kirtley & Thomas, 2010; Lee, Milton, & Everitt, 2006; Mamiya et al., 2009; Pedreira & Maldonado, 2003; Pedreira et al., 2004; Pérez-Cuesta & Maldonado, 2009; Suzuki et al., 2004). In these studies, the CS onset-to-offset time that originally created the target learning (with CS-US pairing) was short, typically in the 1- to 5-min range. Subsequently, CS onset and offset with no shock induced reconsolidation if the CS onset-to-offset time was less than about one hour (destabilizing the target learning, making it revisable by new learning during the next five hours), but it induced extinction if the CS onset-to-offset time was more than about an hour (that is, the target learning remained stable and a separate counterlearning formed in competition with the target learning).

To my knowledge, researchers have not proposed or identified a mechanism that explains the observations that short versus long periods of CS onset-to-offset induce reconsolidation or extinction, respectively. If MRMR (mismatch requirement and mismatch relativity) are the cause, they would operate as follows.

Consider first the case where, after the target learning was formed by a series of CS-US pairings (100% reinforcement), there is a single unreinforced CS reexposure with short duration of onset-to-offset (about equal to the CS onset-to-offset time in the original CS-US training), triggering reconsolidation. As noted earlier in describing the study by Nader et al. (2000), the absence of the expected US creates a decisive US mismatch that destabilizes the target learning.

Next, consider the case where a single short CS-only presentation occurs after the target learning has been formed by a partial reinforcement schedule. Partial reinforcement results in the subject expecting not that the US will *always* occur following the CS, but only that it *might* occur. In this case MRMR predicts that a single short CS-only presentation would not constitute a decisive mismatch and would therefore not induce destabilization. The target learning would remain stable, as was found to be the case by Sevenster et al., (2014), who used a 50% reinforcement schedule to create a fear learning and showed that a single, short CS-only presentation did not induce destabilization. (Learnings created by partial reinforcement require significantly more extinction trials to suppress, as compared with learnings created by continuous reinforcement, because the initial trials are not experienced as a decisive mismatch or prediction error. This is the "partial reinforcement extinction effect", e.g., Pittenger & Pavlik, 1988.)

A special case of learnings formed by partial reinforcement is single-trial learning, which again results in the expectation that the US *might* occur following the CS, not that it will always occur. Here too, a subsequent single CS-only reexposure does not create a decisive US mismatch. This was the case in a study of conditioned taste aversion in rats reported by Eisenberg, Kobilo, Berman, and Dudai (2003). A single training trial produced lasting avoidance behavior, but a single CS-only reexposure did not destabilize the target learning (as evidenced by no disruption of the target learning from anisomycin administered immediately after the CS reexposure). When Eisenberg et al. used a series of two CS-US pairings to create the target learning instead of one pairing, creating strong US-expectancy due to the 100% reinforcement, the same single CS-only presentation now did trigger destabilization, allowing disruption by anisomycin, implying that now a mismatch was created.

The foregoing examples and those below illustrate that the principle of mismatch relativity emphasizes a detailed consideration of all features of the target learning, in order to predict accurately whether or not a given reactivation procedure creates a decisive mismatch/prediction error experience in relation to the target learning in question. Mismatch relativity also alerts us to understand that any given successful experimental destabilization procedure reveals not the inherent, fundamental properties of the brain's reconsolidation process, but only a way of creating mismatch relative to the particular features of the target learning created by the researchers.

Next we have to consider why, according to MRMR, a single long-duration, unreinforced CS causes extinction rather than reconsolidation. For example, Pedreira et al. (2004) found that a 2-hr CS presentation failed to destabilize the target learning into reconsolidation and instead produced an extinction learning. The original target learning began with a 5-min exposure to the CS (the training chamber), and then the US, a simulated predator, was presented every 3 min, 15 times. The fact that a 2-hr unreinforced CS reexposure did not trigger reconsolidation means, according to MRMR, that the 2-hr CS did not function as a mismatch of the target learning's 5-min exposure before the US began to appear. Why it did not function as a mismatch can be inferred from mismatch relativity: Relative to the original learning experience with its 5-min CS exposure, a 2-hr CS reexposure presumably was an experience that qualitatively differed subjectively from the original learning to such a degree that the 2-hr reexposure experience registered as a contextually unrelated experience, not as a mismatch or even as a reminder of the 5-min experience encoded in the target learning. Thus the experience of mismatch, which would have occurred with CS offset for some time after the 5-min point, no longer occurred with CS offset at the 2-hr point. Due to the relativity of mismatch, an experience that is too greatly dissimilar to the original learning experience does not function as a reminder or mismatch of it, so the target learning does not destabilize, which causes the new learning driven by the unreinforced CS to form separately as an extinction learning.

This example suggests the possibility that the presence or absence of mismatch can change over time during CS presentation, which will figure importantly in the analysis of multitrial extinction below. The *general principle of mismatch relativity* is that experience B is a mismatch of expected experience A if B resembles A enough to register as a reminder and repetition of A, while also containing saliently discrepant or novel features relative to those of A.

Testable predictions arise from the MRMR interpretation above. For example, the original learning could be created by a 2-hr CS with the US occurring in the final minutes, with a repetition of that CS-US beginning 30 min later, and so on three or four times. Mismatch relativity predicts that now a 2-hr CS-only reexposure *would* serve as a reminder and mismatch and would achieve destabilization; and perhaps now a 5-min CS reexposure without US would fail to do so because the dissimilarity might be too great for the short reexposure to serve as a reminder of the extremely long duration in the target learning.

If the mismatch requirement and mismatch relativity govern whether reconsolidation or extinction occurs, then there is no absolute time duration of unreinforced CS reexposure that defines the boundary between the two phenomena. Rather, the time boundary (the largest and smallest unreinforced CS reexposure durations that function as a mismatch and trigger reconsolidation) would depend on the original learning's CS duration. That predicted dependency of the reconsolidation/extinction time boundary on the time structure of the original training serves as another test of the MRMR model and could be directly measured by extending existing studies to vary the reinforced CS duration in the original learning while measuring the maximum and minimum unreinforced CS reexposure durations that trigger reconsolidation.

Multiple CS-only trials. The foregoing paragraphs addressed reconsolidation and extinction having a shared initiating sequence in the case of single-trial, non-reinforced CS reexposure. Next, consider the case of a series of numerous identical counterlearning experiences of reactivation and nonreinforcement, that is, the classical extinction procedure. It is well known that the multitrial extinction procedure does not destabilize or erase the target learning, yet, as discussed above, a single short CS-only trial does do so (for a target learning created by multiple CS-US presentations). This raises the question: Given that the first CS-only presentation mismatches and destabilizes, how does the state of the target memory evolve with each successive CS-only presentation, such that there is no destabilization and no erasure resulting from the series?

It will be assumed in what follows that the target learning was formed originally by a series of CS-US pairings having the same time structure as in the subsequent extinction procedure. This assumption allows for an unambiguous delineation of the logic of MRMR in this instance, but it does not limit the relevance of MRMR to only these assumed conditions as a special case.

The question requiring an answer is this: Why does the standard extinction procedure fail to destabilize and then erase the target learning, given that the first CS-without-US in the series mismatches and destabilizes the target learning and the ensuing series of CS-without-US experiences could be expected to then function as a nullification learning that erases the target learning? MRMR implies that because the result of multiple-trial counterlearning *is* extinction rather than erasure, it must be the case that multiple-trial counterlearning does not sustain a mismatch experience long enough for erasure to occur. The question therefore becomes: Why does multiple-trial counterlearning not sustain a mismatch that keeps the target learning destabilized and allows erasure to occur, even though every unreinforced trial in the series seems to be a mismatch of the expected CS-US pairing? The answer to that question has emerged from several recent studies (Jarome et al., 2012; Merlo et al., 2014; Sevenster et al., 2014).

Jarome et al. (2012) paired sound and footshock to create a learned fear of the sound in rats, and then, 1 day later, applied anisomycin immediately following either a single unreinforced CS or two unreinforced CSs that were separated by 1 hr. (Longer periods were also tested.) On the next day, tests of fear in response to the CS showed that after single-CS reexposure, the fear learning had been largely disrupted and erased by anisomycin, indicating destabilization had occurred, but after the two-CS exposure there was no reduction in fear due to anisomycin. This implies that the second CS rapidly changed the neurological condition of the target learning, either returning the target learning to stability (according to the standard interpretation of anisomycin's effect) or, alternatively and more conjecturally, launching the updating/erasure process and thereby altering the prevailing molecular mechanisms such that even though destabilization persisted, anisomycin no longer caused disruption (T. J. Jarome, personal communication, 24 November, 2014).

Sevenster et al. (2014) also demonstrated rapid changes in target memory condition caused by successive nonoccurrences of the US when it was expected according to the original training. A fear learning was created in human subjects by pairing an image with a wrist shock, and the effects of 0, 1, and 2 nonreinforcements by CS-only presentations were studied. Whether the target learning was destabilized was determined by administering propranolol, which disrupts destabilized CS-US fear learnings in humans (Kindt et al., 2009; Soeter & Kindt, 2011). This revealed that a single nonreinforcement functioned as a mismatch and destabilized the target learning, launching reconsolidation, but 0 and 2 nonreinforcements did not. This indicates again, as in Jarome et al. (2012), that a target learning destabilized by an initial unreinforced CS presentation is restabilized by the second unreinforced CS presentation. Here, however, the time interval from first to second CS was 40 s rather than 1 hr.

Importantly, in addition to measuring the level of fear in response to each unreinforced CS presentation, during each unreinforced CS presentation Sevenster et al. (2014) also measured subjects' subjective rating of their US-expectancy, that is, the felt level of anticipation that the shock would occur at the end of the current 7-s CS image presentation. US-expectancy was rated by subjects on a scale from −5 (certainty of not happening) to 0 (uncertain) to +5 (certainty of happening). This revealed that as the first nonreinforcement was about to happen, average US-expectancy was strong at +3.8, which created a mismatch experience when the US did not occur, but as the second nonreinforcement was about to happen, average US-expectancy had decreased sharply to 0.9, close to the "uncertain" level and presumably too low to create a mismatch experience when the US did not occur. The first US nonoccurrence had created new learning that reduced the US-expectancy created by the original training, and it was this reduced US-expectancy that then encountered the second US nonoccurrence. The direct implication is that immediately after the first nonoccurrence of the US when the US would be expected on the basis of the original learning, subjects were in the experience of mismatch, so the target learning was found to be destabilized, but immediately after the second nonoccurrence of the US when it would be expected according to the original learning, subjects were not in an experience of mismatch, so the target learning was found to be stable.

Thus the presence or absence of a mismatch experience evidently switches destabilization on or off, respectively, in real time. By comparing their measurements of fear and US-expectancy, Sevenster et al. also showed that the sharp drop in self-reported US-expectancy was not accompanied by a decrease in physiologically measured fear. This means that with accumulating unreinforced CS presentations, US-expectancy began to decrease, evidently returning the target learning to stability, before there had been enough counterlearning to initiate the formation of an extinction learning. This is consistent with other studies indicating that reconsolidation and extinction are mutually exclusive phenomena (e.g., Duvarci & Nader, 2004; Duvarci et al., 2006; Merlo et al., 2014). Thus after two US nonoccurrences, the target learning was stable and neither reconsolidation nor extinction was occurring.

Observations by Merlo et al. (2014) provide further corroboration that accumulating unreinforced CSs switch off reconsolidation before extinction is in effect. After 1, 4, 7, and 10 presentations of an unreinforced CS, Merlo et al. tested a conditioned fear learning in rats for susceptibility to alteration by various chemical agents applied locally in the basolateral amygdala (BLA). After the fourth CS presentation, the target learning was no longer chemically alterable, meaning that it was no longer in a destabilized state in the BLA. Furthermore, there were no behavioral or molecular markers of extinction, so neither reconsolidation nor extinction was occurring. Merlo et al. infer from these findings that the target learning's state (stable or unstable) may be reset on a moment-to-moment basis as CS-only presentations accumulate.

In light of the studies just reviewed, there is now growing evidence indicating why the multiple-trial counterlearning of conventional extinction training does not sustain mismatch or destabilization and does not erase the target learning: A target learning's state of destabilization and erasability evidently is maintained by the ongoing presence of the experience of mismatch or prediction error and can quickly terminate if the experience of mismatch or prediction error terminates. Thus the mismatch requirement first identified by Pedreira et al. (2004) functions as a dynamic on/off switch. The destabilized state can be toggled on/off or off/on as mismatch is subjectively present/absent or absent/present, respectively. (Destabilization lasts for a time window of about five hours, as described earlier, if, once destabilized, the target learning is not further recued by additional experiences.)

In this picture of dynamic mismatch bipolarity, the principle of mismatch relativity governs how each successive unreinforced CS affects the target learning. In other words, the target learning consists of expectations that can be revised by an individual CS in the series if that CS deviates from the expectations extant just prior to that CS. The evolving expectational content of the target learning must be considered in detail in order to understand the effect of each successive CS.

In short, the studies by Jarome et al. (2012), Merlo et al. (2014) and Sevenster et al. (2014) indicate that MRMR principles determine the effects of the multiple-trial extinction procedure, as follows. With a target learning created by CS-US pairings with continuous (100%) reinforcement, the subject has the expectation that the US always accompanies the CS. The first CS-without-US presentation is therefore a decisive mismatch (that is, the nonoccurrence of the US creates strong surprise and a felt inability to anticipate accurately) because the learned expectation that the US always accompanies the CS has now encountered the mismatching current perception that the US does *not* always accompany the CS. This has two effects. First, this strong mismatch abruptly destabilizes the target learning. Second, the nonoccurrence of the expected US creates new learning that the US does not always accompany the CS. This new learning persists and results in a sharply reduced US-expectancy during the second unreinforced CS presentation. The second US nonoccurrence is therefore not experienced as a mismatch, because now there is no surprise or prediction error felt. Rather, there is now an experience that this US nonoccurrence is in accord with the expectation that the US might or might not happen. This termination of mismatch terminates destabilization, because destabilization is dynamically maintained in real time by the persisting experience or context of mismatch. The target learning shifts into a stable state. (Whether the new learning created by the first US nonoccurrence immediately updates the target learning's model of the CS-US association is not yet known, though molecular findings by Monfils et al., 2009, and Jarome et al., 2012, seem to imply that the destabilization event does not also launch updating. Possibly, updating is launched only if mismatch saliently persists after destabilization occurs.)

In that way, the multitrial extinction procedure destabilizes and then quickly restabilizes the target learning before erasure can occur. With the third unreinforced CS, presumably there would no longer be any surprise or mismatch whatsoever. With the target memory in a stable state as CS repetitions continue, the target learning remains intact and the new learning created by the ongoing series of harmless CS presentations forms separately. That is the MRMR account of standard multitrial extinction.

Standard multitrial extinction training was converted into an effective erasure procedure in studies by Monfils et al. (2009) and Schiller et al. (2010), as described in a previous section, simply by increasing the time interval between the first and second CS-only presentations. Why that seemingly minor alteration of extra time in the first interval could make such a qualitative and drastic difference in outcome becomes apparent by applying the MRMR model and examining the timing difference in terms of its mismatch effects. That exercise is carried out here next for the Monfils et al. study, as this section's final and most intricate example of applying the MRMR model. The Schiller et al. study, which had human subjects, is described in the Appendix of this article.

In the procedure that Monfils et al. (2009) used with rats, the original fear acquisition consisted of three CS-US (tone-shock) pairings every 3 min, with CS duration of 20 s, ending with a half-second shock. On the next day, the interval between the 19 CS-only presentations was also 3 min, except for a longer initial interval between CS1 and CS2 of 10 min or 1 hr, both of which resulted in long-term erasure of the learned fear, which could not be reevoked later by either the CS or the US. The control group did not have the longer initial interval, making the procedure a conventional extinction training, and for these rats the learned fear was later reevoked.

The functioning of the erasure procedure is understood as follows according to the MRMR model. It can be reliably assumed, based on many other studies as described earlier, that CS1 created a US mismatch that quickly destabilized the target learning. Therefore, after CS1 the target learning was open to being updated by any variations in the procedure relative to the original training. An immediate and salient variation was the appearance of CS2 defining a 10-min or 1-hr interval since CS1, far longer than the 3-min interval expected based on the original acquisition training. The already destabilized target learning was updated according to that longer interval, so the timing expectation going forward was now that after each colored square there would be *either* 3 min or the longer time (10 min or 1 hr). The longer interval defined by CS2 also was a mismatch of timing expectations, and that second mismatch experience, coming while the target learning was already destabilized, would only have made the destabilized state more robust.

However, as discussed earlier, CS2 would not create a US mismatch as CS1 had done. Thus CS2 ended the US mismatch while creating a timing mismatch. Did the target learning restabilize due to the termination of US mismatch, or did it remain destabilized due to the timing mismatch?

One indication comes from Jarome et al. (2012), who largely replicated this situation with two CSs 1 hr apart, as described earlier. Anisomycin applied immediately after the second CS did not reduce fear in response to another CS 1 day later. That is usually understood as meaning that the target learning was stable, because anisomycin disrupts a destabilized memory. However, while anisomycin disrupts a memory that is newly destabilized but not undergoing updating, its effect on a memory during the updating process is not known. On the cellular and molecular level, the process that destabilizes the target learning and the process that updates/erases it appear to be two distinct though coupled processes (Jarome et al., 2012;

Lee et al., 2008). Updating occurs through a molecular mechanism that potentially alters the molecular processes involved in the memory's dynamical progression. Anisomycin is a protein synthesis blocker. If the updating/erasure mode eliminates the protein synthesis that a nonupdating memory requires for restabilization, then anisomycin would not have a disruptive effect on a destabilized memory that is undergoing updating, as Timothy J. Jarome (personal communication, 24 November, 2014) has pointed out.

Only further research can settle the question of whether the target learning in Monfils et al. (2009) was stable or unstable after CS2, so here the MRMR account must branch to follow both possibilities.

If CS2 caused restabilization due to elimination of US mismatch, the fact that erasure then resulted from CS3 to CS19 implies that CS3 must have destabilized the target learning yet again. That in turn implies that a new mismatch experience was created by CS3, which in turn directs us to identify the procedural elements that created that mismatch. CS3 occurred 3 min after CS2, which created another timing mismatch because an interval of 10 min or 1 hr was expected after the updating driven by the longer interval from CS1 to CS2. This timing mismatch created by CS3 onset would have redestabilized the target learning. (This is a prediction of MRMR that could be tested by extending the Jarome et al. study to include a CS3 that occurs 3 min after CS2, and conducting molecular tests for destabilization promptly after CS3.) Having been destabilized by CS3, the target learning would then be updated by the 3-min interval from CS3 to CS4, as well as by CS4 itself as an experience that the CS is harmless. The condition required for erasure to be occurring is having the target learning in a destabilized state concurrent with a fresh or freshly remembered experience that contradicts and disconfirms the target learning's expectations or model of how the world functions. Erasure of the CS-US association may have been underway following CS3, and more so when the destabilized target learning encountered CS4. The next 3-min interval from CS4 to CS5 would have been as expected, ending the experience of mismatch, which may have terminated the destabilized state and, with it, the erasure process also. That would imply that erasure was fully accomplished by CS1 through CS4, and that CS5 through CS19 were not needed, which could be tested by repeating the Monfils et al. (2009) experiment without CS5 through CS19 and seeing whether or not the results are unchanged.

If, on the other hand, CS2 maintained prior destabilization by creating a timing mismatch, it is probable that CS2 began the erasure process. Then, after CS2, the effects of the procedure's time intervals and CSs would be the same as described in the previous paragraph (with the exception that CS3 would now maintain rather than reinitiate destabilization). Thus the question of whether or not CS2 restabilizes the target learning does not influence the outcome, according to the MRMR model.

There is an additional possibility for how the updating process could affect the unfolding dynamics of the target learning. Engagement of the updating/erasure process possibly could maintain the destabilized state even without an ongoing experience of mismatch. In order for the adaptive process of updating to proceed, destabilization must be in effect during the new learning that is driving the updating (otherwise what occurs is not updating but a separate encoding of new learning, as in extinction). Therefore, because the adaptive success of updating depends on destabilization, it is likely that whenever new learning during destabilization is driving updating, the destabilized state is maintained directly by molecular signals from the updating/erasure process and is no longer dependent on an ongoing experience of mismatch, so that updating will not be prematurely terminated by an absence of mismatch causing a return to stability. This could be termed *maintenance of destabilization by updating*, or MDU. Presumably, at the point where no further encoding, reencoding, or de-encoding is occurring for updating, the molecular signals driving MDU cease, and the updated target learning then returns to stability promptly. It is well established that a target learning returns to stability after about five hours if there has been destabilization but no updating (such as by a single short CS-only presentation; Duvarci & Nader, 2004; Pedreira et al., 2002; Pedreira & Maldonado, 2003; Walker et al., 2003), but if updating has also occurred, it is possible that restabilization occurs through a different molecular process with a different temporal characteristic.

If MDU is included in the MRMR framework, the picture becomes one of memory mismatch initiating and maintaining destabilization until memory updating is occurring, from which point destabilization is maintained directly by the updating process and continues until updating terminates either due to saturation of encoding or cessation of new learning input. The MRMR account of the erasure procedure used by Schiller et al. (2010; see Appendix) more strongly requires and implies MDU. Obviously, further studies are needed to test these possibilities and clarify how the stability status of the target learning evolves with each successive CS presentation in various procedural configurations.

The above analysis of results of Monfils et al. (2009) illustrates how assuming the results of experimental procedures to be governed by MRMR principles can illuminate previously unrecognized dynamics and resolve dilemmas of interpretation and apparent inconsistencies between studies. The foregoing MRMR accounts are offered heuristically, to indicate the kinds of phenomenology that are brought into consideration by the MRMR framework.

The MRMR model has the systemic implication that the neural and molecular processes of reconsolidation or extinction are under the direct control of brain regions and circuits that assess, detect, and signal mismatch (prediction error) occurring between learned expectations and currently experienced temporal, spatial, and/or somatosensory perceptions (as well as, in the human clinical context, attributed meanings). A direct indication of that supervening role of mismatch detection can be seen in the findings of Reichelt, Exton-McGuinness, and Lee (2013) and Sevenster et al. (2014). The latter showed, as described above, that the switching off of reconsolidation during a series of unreinforced CSs (reminders) can be directly attributed to a sharp decline in US-expectancy and corresponding termination of the experience of mismatch. Reichelt et al. demonstrated that a successful mismatch procedure for destabilizing goal-tracking memory in rats, allowing chemical disruption, became ineffective as a result of impairment in the ventral tegmental area, a brain region that is believed to be critical for generating prediction error signals but is not a site of memories undergoing reconsolidation. Understanding how mismatch signals are generated and how they supervene upon the machinery of reconsolidation and extinction may prove to be particularly fruitful for arriving at dexterous control of these phenomena. For a discussion of prediction error signal generation and ideas for future research, see Exton-McGuinness et al. (2015).

In summary, from the MRMR perspective, the triggering of reconsolidation versus extinction by any particular reactivation procedure is to be understood in terms of the presence or absence of a mismatch (prediction error) experience at each point of the procedure. In addition to identifying what may control the reconsolidation/extinction dichotomy, the MRMR model provides a new, fundamental understanding of classical extinction by identifying why repetitive counterlearning creates a separate learning in competition with the target learning, rather than erasing the target learning. The MRMR account potentially unifies a broad range of reconsolidation and extinction phenomena.

Misconception 4: Anxiety, Phobias, and PTSD Are the Symptoms That Memory Reconsolidation Could Help to Dispel in Psychotherapy, but More Research Must Be Done Before It Is Clear How Reconsolidation Can Be Utilized Clinically

This section really comprises a blend of two misconceptions. First is the view that for clinical use, reconsolidation could be suitable for helping to dispel learned *fears* of various kinds, with symptomology such as PTSD, phobias, panic attacks and anxiety. This impression probably stems from the consistent tendency of researchers to comment in their research articles that reconsolidation has significant potential for treatment of PTSD and anxiety disorders. Researchers have to be ultraconservative in what they write so that everything they propose is firmly based on what is known according to the current state of research. Reconsolidation is relevant as a candidate treatment only for conditions that are maintained by memory, and for a brain researcher there is no risk that PTSD could be unrelated to memory and therefore no risk of a departure from the required empiricism. Furthermore, fear is the most reliably detectable and measurable type of negative emotional response, so that researchers preferentially envision applications of the reconsolidation process to fear symptomology. Clinicians, however, regularly observe phenomenology showing that an extremely wide range of other conditions also are rooted in and driven by implicit memory (Ecker et al., 2012; Ecker & Toomey, 2008; Toomey & Ecker, 2007; Schore, 2003; Siegel, 2006). Nevertheless, it is not conventional practice for neuroscience researchers to reference that body of knowledge.

In fact, reconsolidation research has already demonstrated that the process applies to many types of learning other than fear learnings—for example, appetitive (pleasure) learnings (Stollhoff et al., 2005), operant (instrumental) learnings (Exton-McGuinness, Patton, Sacco, & Lee, 2014; Gallucio, 2005), spatial learnings (Rossato et al., 2006), object recognition learnings (Rossato et al., 2007), motor task learnings (Walker et al., 2003), taste recognition learnings (Rodriguez-Ortiz, De la Cruz, Gutierrez, & Bermidez-Rattoni, 2005), human declarative learnings (Forcato et al., 2007), human episodic learnings (Hupbach, Gomez, Hardt, & Nadel, 2007), and emotionally compelling human preferences (Pine, et al., 2014), among others. In fact, to my knowledge, as of this writing, all tested types of learning and memory have been found to submit to the process of reconsolidation.

That is extremely good news for psychotherapy, as the learnings that underlie and drive individuals' problems and symptoms are of many different kinds and not necessarily fear-based. Examples from my own practice of non-fear-based implicit emotional learnings brought into direct awareness include: the expectation to be allowed no autonomy, with reliance on secrecy and lying to maintain personal power; the heartbreak-laden memory of father abandoning the family when the client was 4 years old and the ensuing conviction that the cause was her own deficiency; and the expectation of severe devaluing and derision from others for any mistake or misstep, generating paralyzing states of shame and inhibition.

The second misconception in this category is this: In reconsolidation research articles, the authors typically comment that much more research must be done before it is clear how reconsolidation can be utilized in psychotherapy. This is hardly the case. In reality, for over a decade before neuroscientists' discovery in 2004 of the sequence of experiences that triggers reconsolidation (Pedreira et al., 2004), psychotherapists had been knowingly guiding clients through that sequence, having recognized from clinical observations that it was responsible for transformational therapeutic change (as described below). Furthermore, since 2006, psychotherapists have been translating reconsolidation research findings into successful therapeutic methodology. In 2006 I gave a keynote address to a conference of psychologists and psychotherapists (Ecker, 2006), describing the critical sequence of experiences that is required, according to reconsolidation research, for erasing a target emotional learning. In that talk, a clinical case example from my practice illustrated the guiding of that sequence and the resulting permanent disappearance of a longstanding, intense emotional reaction. In subsequent years, many articles and conference talks have presented the critical sequence in many clinical case examples of using it to decisively dispel a wide range of symptoms and problems (e.g., Ecker, 2008, 2010, 2013; Ecker, Ticic, & Hulley, 2012, 2013a,b; Ecker & Toomey, 2008; Sibson & Ticic, 2014).

Note that according to current neuroscience, memory reconsolidation is the only known process and type of neuroplasticity that can produce what we have been observing clinically: the abrupt, permanent disappearance of a strong, longstanding, involuntary emotional and/or behavioral response, with no further counteractive measures required. So, in psychotherapy we have been guiding the same well-defined sequence of experiences and observing the same distinctive signs of erasure as reconsolidation researchers have. We have applied the process successfully to the real-life, highly complex emotional learnings that underlie and maintain symptoms of many different types (see citations in the previous paragraph). Also, successful clinical use of protocols designed to induce reconsolidation and erasure have been reported by Högberg et al. (2011) and Xue et al. (2012). The latter demonstrated, in a controlled study, a strong degree of elimination of heroin addicts' cue-induced craving for heroin.

Thus the new era of the psychotherapy of memory reconsolidation is well underway. It had a curious birth: From 1986 to 1993, my clinical colleague Laurel Hulley and I closely scrutinized the occasional therapy sessions in our practices in which abrupt, liberating change had somehow occurred—the lasting cessation of a problematic pattern of emotion, behavior, cognition and/or somatics. Finally we identified a sequence of experiences that was always present, across a wide range of clients and symptoms, whenever such transformational change occurred. We developed a system of therapy focused on facilitating that key sequence of experiences right from the first session of therapy, and found that working in this way made our sessions far more consistent in producing transformational therapeutic breakthroughs. We began teaching this methodology in 1993 at a workshop in Tucson, Arizona, followed by our first published account of it in the volume *Depth Oriented Brief Therapy* (Ecker & Hulley, 1996). Subsequently the same sequence of experiences emerged in reconsolidation research, providing corroboration of our clinical observations by empirical, rigorous studies. It seemed remarkable that the same process for erasing emotional learnings had been discovered independently in the therapeutic domain of subjective, experiential phenomenology and in the laboratory domain of research on animal memory circuits. In hindsight that convergence now seems most natural, because any process of lasting change that is truly innate to the brain would inevitably be apparent in both domains.

Our psychotherapy system, now known as *coherence therapy*, guides the series of experiences required by the brain for reconsolidation and erasure to occur, creating transformational change (Ecker & Hulley, 2011). It is the only system of psychotherapy that explicitly calls for and maps directly onto the process identified in reconsolidation research, but there are many other systems of therapy in which the same process also takes place, albeit embedded within methodologies conceptualized quite differently. It is clear that no single school of psychotherapy "owns" the process that induces memory reconsolidation, because it is a universal process, inherent in the brain. In any therapy sessions, the occurrence of transformational change can now be presumed to mean that reconsolidation and erasure of the target response have occurred, whether or not the therapist was knowingly guiding that process. Toward confirming that universality, we began an ongoing project of explicitly identifying the embedded steps of the reconsolidation and erasure process in published case examples of various forms of psychotherapy (Ecker et al., 2012; see Chapter 6).

Thus, knowledge of memory reconsolidation can enhance the effectiveness of individual psychotherapists, but more importantly, it also translates into a unifying framework of psychotherapy integration in which the many different systems of therapy form a huge repertoire of ways to guide the brain's core process of transformational change. This framework gives practitioners of different therapies a shared understanding of their action and a shared vocabulary for their action. Of course, not all systems of psychotherapy are equally consistent and reliable in fulfilling the sequence required by the brain for erasure of a target learning, and this too becomes apparent through this unified framework.

Misconception 5: Emotional Arousal Is Inherently Necessary for Inducing the Reconsolidation Process

Quite a few psychotherapies of focused, transformational change have emerged since the 1980s, and one of the tenets they have in common is that the client's engagement in therapy needs to be emotional for deep, lasting change to take place. Perhaps this important clinical tenet contributes to the view maintained by some clinical psychologists that for inducing memory reconsolidation, emotional arousal is necessary (see, e.g., Lane, Ryan, Nadel, & Greenberg, in press). However, the research shows that the reconsolidation process does not inherently involve emotional arousal. As noted earlier, successful deconsolidation and erasure have been demonstrated for learnings of many types, some of which have no emotional content per se, such as neutral declarative learnings (set of syllable pairings: Forcato et al., 2009), object recognition learnings (Rossato et al., 2007) and motor task learnings (Walker et al., 2003). In such cases no emotional arousal is involved either in the reactivation and mismatch of the target learning, triggering the reconsolidation process, or in the new learning that then revises the target learning. The brain clearly does not require emotional arousal per se for destabilizing and erasing the existing learning. That is a fundamental point.

If the target learning happens to have emotional components, then its reactivation (the first of the two steps required for deconsolidation) of course entails an experience of that emotion. Naturally, target learnings or schemas in psychotherapy usually are emotional, so observable emotion accompanies reactivation and is a key marker of adequate reactivation. However, this emotional arousal is not inherent in the reconsolidation process, and is present only because the target learning happens to involve emotional material. Clinical psychologists and psychotherapists sometimes conflate the emotional nature of target learnings in therapy with the inherent phenomenology of the reconsolidation process, as Lane et al. (in press) appear to do. For an accurate understanding of memory reconsolidation this distinction is important, though from a pragmatic clinical perspective it may seem to be hair-splitting.

Emotional arousal is not inherently required in any of the steps that erase a target learning. When researchers create a new learning to nullify and erase a target learning, this new learning necessarily consists of experiences that sharply contradict the target learning's expectations and model of the world. Prior to erasure, the target learning is deconsolidated by a mismatch experience that typically consists of either an initial, brief instance of that same contradictory experience or some salient novelty not predicted by the target learning. For example, the target learning in the human study by Schiller et al. (2010) was a learned fear, specifically the classically conditioned expectation that the appearance of a yellow square on a computer screen would be accompanied in a few seconds by an electric shock to the wrist. For nullification of that learned fear after it had been mismatched and destabilized by a novelty (see Appendix for details), subjects were repeatedly given the contradictory experience of seeing a yellow square appear and disappear with no shock occurring. The simple experience of seeing each yellow square disappear was not an emotionally arousing experience, yet precisely for that reason it erased the fearful expectation of the shock.

Likewise, in psychotherapy we observe that erasure results from a contradictory experience that sharply disconfirms the target learning, and we observe that in some cases the contradictory experience is not in itself emotionally arousing, even though the target learning is strongly emotional. This is possible because the target of unlearning and nullification is the target learning's schema or model of reality (the semantic knowledge in the target learning), not the emotions generated by that model. This important point is illustrated by the following case vignette from my psychotherapy practice, which shows successful nullification and erasure of an emotional target learning resulting from a contradictory knowledge that is not emotional.

The client, a married woman, aged 50 and the mother of one child, sought therapy to dispel her aversion to sexuality with her husband, her depression, and her panic attacks, all of which had been afflicting her for at least a decade. I was using coherence therapy, in which the nonconscious, implicit emotional learnings that underlie and drive a given symptom are first brought into direct, explicit awareness, and then subjected to the process of memory reconsolidation and erasure, creating transformational change.

Session by session, into explicit awareness was emerging a complex array of underlying, implicit emotional learnings, some of which involved traumatic memories from various developmental stages of her life. In her first session I found that she would dissociate and become glazed and wooden in response to even a small step of interior exploration. She had a total of 45 sessions and was symptom-free at the end. This vignette focuses only on the particular emotional learning that emerged in her ninth session. This learning had formed when she was 18 years of age and had become pregnant by her boyfriend while living with her parents in a conservative town. She was living in shame and "desperate loneliness," did not want the baby or the boyfriend, and was struggling to decide about having an abortion when she had a miscarriage.

Wanting to find the emotional learnings she had formed in this ordeal, I gently guided her into experientially revisiting and reinhabiting that situation imaginally, and voicing her thoughts and feelings in present tense. This technique is often useful for bringing the implicit meanings of the original experience into explicit awareness. She seemed absorbed in the subjective reality of this material, and her voice was soft but somber as she said, "In this town, a girl who's been pregnant outside of marriage is just ruined, completely ruined."

In order to elicit fully and explicitly the learning she had formed, I asked softly, "What does 'ruined' really mean? What's going to happen to you now?"

After a silence, in an even quieter voice she said, "The rest of my life as a woman is ruined. I'll never marry, and I'll never have children." There it was, the specific learning she had formed. According to this learning, which had been implicit and outside of awareness for decades, having sex had results that had ruined the rest of her life. Immediately I understood that this dire model of her future was a potent source of both her depression and her sexual aversion.

With this clarity about the makeup of this target learning, I saw a possible way to create a contradictory experience: use of the brain's automatic detection of mismatches, a background process that is always scanning current conscious experience. So in reply to her words, I said, "Please say that again."

Somberly, and clearly feeling the emotional reality of the words, she said again, "The rest of my life as a woman is ruined. I'll never marry, and I'll never have children." As soon as she spoke the words this time, her wider conscious knowledge networks registered this information, which was new to her conscious networks though it was old in her implicit memory system. Her head made an abrupt movement, and in a sharper, louder voice she said with obvious surprise, "Wait—that's not true! I *did* marry! I *did* have a child!"

This first encounter between the target learning and vivid contradictory knowledge was the mismatch experience or prediction error needed for deconsolidating the target learning. This both-at-once experience of the target learning and vivid contradictory knowledge is termed a *juxtaposition experience* in coherence therapy to emphasize the simultaneous activation of the two as copresent conscious experiences.

Note that in this instance, the mismatching knowledge—"I *did* marry! I *did* have a child!"—was familiar, ordinary knowledge that was very real to her experientially, as real and certain as her own existence, but it was not inherently emotional in quality. It would not normally induce emotional arousal by itself. For successful mismatch, the knowledge or experience utilized must feel decisively real to the person on the basis of his or her own living experience, but that does not require this mismatching knowledge to be emotionally arousing in itself, even though the target learning is strongly emotional. (As noted above, the emotional quality of the target learning is extraneous and incidental to the reconsolidation process, not inherent in it.)

Presumably the neural encoding maintaining "My life as a woman is ruined, I'll never marry, I'll never have children" was now rapidly destabilizing, opening that set of learned meanings to being rewritten and erased by the knowledge, "I *did* marry! I *did* have a child! My life *isn't* ruined!"

She said in almost a whisper, "That just feels *huge*." Then her head tipped back against the top of her chair, and she gazed at the ceiling with blinking eyes. Then her eyes closed, and after about ten seconds she said, "I feel tingling and buzzing all over my body. It's weird—I can feel the skin between my toes. It's huge, it's huge." Internally she was repeatedly beholding and marveling at the new realization, which served as the several repetitions of it needed for rewriting the now deconsolidated target learning. For good measure, I soon created an explicit, out-loud repetition by jokingly saying, "I'm seeing an image of you running down the street waving your arms and shouting, 'I *did* get married! I *did* have a child! My life *wasn't* ruined!'" She laughed heartily at that, but even before I said it, her mood had shifted into a happy lilt that I had never seen in her before. Her contradictory knowledge was not emotional in itself, but the liberating effect of its use in the reconsolidation process certainly was.

I then reminded her that in our previous session she had raised a major question: "Why did I start feeling unbearable sadness and depression when I became pregnant with my son 13 years ago?" I asked her, "Does today's session help you see why?" Her eyes widened with this further powerful realization that the later pregnancy had reevoked her emotional memory of the much earlier one, reimmersing her in the complex emotional miseries that accompanied that pregnancy and the miscarriage. She said, "Ohhh—that's an amazing insight."

After that session, her longstanding depressed mood was gone and did not return. This confirmed that the targeted learning had been producing that mood, and that erasure or dissolution of that learning had been accomplished—meaning that "I'll never marry, I'll never have children" no longer felt real or true in any memory network. Her depressed mood had been the conscious surface of the unconscious despair and grief generated by the target learning.

That session was also the beginning of the end of her sexual aversion, which was dispelled after several more sessions that revealed a number of other episodes in her life where great suffering had resulted from or accompanied sex. Finally she no longer felt any urge to avoid her husband's overtures, though she did feel vulnerable and cautious about entering into a new level of sexuality with him. Those of course were natural, appropriate feelings, and I coached her on expressing to him her need for him to sensitively honor her pace and her cues.

Her panics attacks proved to be based in yet other emotional learnings. They ceased after the discovery and dissolution of those other learnings through juxtaposition experiences tailored to them.

The main purpose of the case vignette above is to show that the disconfirming knowledge or experience used for creating a mismatch experience and then nullifying the target learning does not necessarily have to be emotional in itself. The vignette also illustrates the lifelong durability of original emotional implicit learnings or schemas, as well as their dissociated, encapsulated state, which keeps them insulated from and immune to new experiences and new knowledge formed later in life. By being retrieved into conscious, explicit awareness, emotional implicit learnings become fully available for contact with other, disconfirming knowledge that can induce transformational change through juxtaposition (mismatch) experiences.

Thus, for consistently guiding decisive change through the reconsolidation process in therapy, the required reactivation of a target learning has to be its reactivation *as a conscious, explicit experience of the retrieved, specific elements of the target model* (such as "I'll never marry or have children, so my life as a woman is ruined"), not merely the retriggering of a still nonconscious, unretrieved implicit schema.

Such implicit learnings are often retriggered in day-to-day life *without* conscious awareness, and often life also provides strong disconfirmations, but because the schema remains outside of awareness, there is no juxtaposition experience—no conscious coexperiencing of both the old and new knowledge of what's real—and therefore no change takes place.

In psychotherapy, when an implicit schema maintaining symptom production becomes a conscious, explicit experience, the schema continues to feel subjectively completely real and compelling, and it persists in driving symptom production. This continues until the schema encounters a mismatch and disconfirmation experience, creating the conscious juxtaposition described above. Then abruptly the schema can lose its feeling of emotional realness and its power to control behavior or state of mind, and symptoms cease. Now the schema is not retriggered by situations and cues that formerly triggered it. I and other practitioners of coherence therapy have observed this clinical phenomenology many, many times (Ecker & Hulley, 1996; Ecker & Toomey, 2008; Ecker et al., 2012). Thus, conscious, subjective awareness and attention appear to function as the arena where separate, differing schemas (learnings, knowings, representations of reality) can come into mutual contact and undergo a combined semantic evaluation that allows for a revision of one schema by the other through the reconsolidation process.

Our clinical observations suggest that the brain and mind appear to operate according to a metarule that allows dissociated schemas to differ but requires consistency between schemas that are experienced concurrently in the same field of awareness (Ecker & Hulley, 2011). Guiding a juxtaposition experience cooperates with this metarule in order to transform a symptom-generating schema. When two mutually contradictory schemas are juxtaposed consciously, the schema that more comprehensively or credibly models reality, and therefore more usefully predicts how the world will behave, reveals the other schema to be false, and the falsified one is immediately transformed accordingly. Maximizing predictive power is well known to be a primary function and organizing principle of the brain (Clark, 2013; de-Wit, Machilsen, & Putzeys, 2010; Friston, 2010).

The previous paragraph emphasizes that a conscious, vividly experienced juxtaposition is found to be critically important in the psychotherapeutic utilization of memory reconsolidation. That emphasis could appear to be at odds with recent research and recent reviews of research: Delorenzi et al. (2014), Pine et al. (2014), and Santoyo-Zedillo, Rodriguez-Ortiz, Chavez-Marchetta, Bermudez-Rattoni, & Balderas (2014) have demonstrated that a target learning can be reactivated *without* coming into conscious awareness or behavioral expression, and that even under such conditions a mismatch/prediction error can then take place and destabilize the target learning, allowing it to be updated by new learning or disrupted chemically. How can these findings be reconciled with the clinical picture, in which the unconscious learnings maintaining symptoms are not dissolved until they come into conscious juxtaposition with contradictory knowledge?

There are several dynamics that might provide answers to that question (Ecker & Toomey, 2008). First and foremost, researchers have shown that the stronger and/or older the target learning is, the stronger must be the reactivation in order for destabilization to occur (Frankland et al., 2006; Suzuki et al., 2004). The target learnings in psychotherapy typically are both very old and also very strong, as they involve (and were formed in the presence of) intense emotion and urgent contingencies. Reactivation that produces conscious, bodily felt emotion, expectations, and meanings (as facilitated in therapy) is much stronger than reactivation that remains outside of awareness, which may be why conscious juxtaposition is observed to be necessary for achieving transformational change in therapy.

Another relevant dynamic is the active suppression and dissociation of emotional learnings that have strongly distressing content, which is the case for many of the target learnings that figure significantly in psychotherapy. Such active, self-protective suppression and dissociation could insulate these nonconscious, implicit learnings from direct juxtaposition with contradictory experiences in everyday life, preventing them from being updated. That insulation is removed in therapy by gently and gradually bringing these learnings into conscious awareness, allowing juxtapositions and transformational change to occur.

There is yet another reason why the versatile clinical utilization of memory reconsolidation requires first bringing a target learning into conscious experience. Researchers know the detailed makeup of the target learning, having created it themselves. This knowledge allows them accurately to reactivate and mismatch the target learning, destabilizing it, and also to then conduct new learning designed precisely to nullify and erase it. In sharp contrast, clinicians are in the dark at the start of therapy, with no knowledge of the makeup of the target learning driving symptom production. Therefore it is only by bringing the target learning into explicit awareness and verbalization that its makeup can be known, and only then and not before can the therapist design and guide experiences of mismatch and nullification learning.

In summary, this section began by explaining that the reconsolidation and erasure process does not inherently involve or require emotion in either the target learning or the new learning that is juxtaposed with and nullifies it. In psychotherapy, however, the target learnings usually are richly emotional, so emotional arousal accompanies the therapeutic reconsolidation process as a rule, but this presence of emotion should not be conflated with the intrinsic nature of the reconsolidation process. The examination of juxtaposition phenomenology then continued into a clarification of why therapeutically effective juxtapositions have to be conscious experiences, even though reconsolidation research has shown that under special laboratory conditions, the process can take place outside of awareness.

Misconception 6: What Is Erased in Therapy Is the Negative Emotion That Became Associated With Certain Event Memories, and This Negative Emotion Is Erased by Inducing Positive or Neutral Emotional Responses to Replace It

As the clinical example in the previous section shows, what is erased through the reconsolidation process is a specific, learned schema or model or template of reality, verbalized in the example as "I'll never marry or have children, so my life as a woman is ruined." That schema was the target for erasure, and the mismatch that deconsolidated and then nullified it consisted of experiencing a sharp disconfirmation of that specific schema. With dissolution of the schema, the negative emotions that it was generating (despair, grief, and depression) disappeared, though those emotions were not themselves the target for mismatch or erasure, and the mismatch did not consist of creating a positive or neutral emotion instead of despair and depression.

Notice also that the client's negative emotion was arising directly from her existing model of the rest of her life, not from episodic memory (event memory) of the traumatic pregnancy and miscarriage. In other words, the traumatic experience resulted in her model (which is semantic memory), and that model in turn generated and maintained her emotional symptoms. Erasure of that model caused no loss of autobiographical memory.

Therapy clients' unwanted symptoms and problems are of course not limited to negative emotions, but can also be behaviors, thoughts, dissociated states, somatic sensations or conditions, or any combination of these. In any case, the target for erasure is not the manifested symptom or problem. The target is the learned implicit schema or semantic structure that underlies and drives production of the symptom. Erasure occurs when the target schema is activated as a conscious, explicit experience and is directly disconfirmed by a concurrent, vivid experience of contradictory knowledge. In other words, erasure does not occur simply through evoking a nonsymptomatic state when normally the symptom would be occurring (with one important exception, discussed at the end of this section). The occurrence of a symptom does not in itself bring the underlying, symptom-generating schema into conscious, foreground awareness, as is necessary for guiding the erasure process in therapy, so methods for evoking a nonsymptomatic state are not likely to disconfirm the underlying schema. The woman in our example might arrive at a session in a depressed mood, and there are techniques of somatic therapy, positive psychology, or mindfulness practice that could be used to shift her into a depression-free sense of well-being. However, that would not disconfirm and dissolve the

141

underlying implicit schema maintaining her depression, "I'll never marry or have children, so my life as a woman is ruined." Her depression would therefore recur.

An example of the misconception that negative emotion is erased by inducing positive or neutral emotion is the view of Lane et al. (in press) that "changing emotion with emotion" characterizes how the system of psychotherapy known as emotion-focused therapy carries out reconsolidation and erasure. Rather, "changing old model with new model" is the core phenomenology of erasure through reconsolidation in any system of therapy. Emotions then change *as a derivative effect* of change in semantic structures (models, rules, and attributed meanings), just as in our example the client's depression disappeared as a direct result of dissolution of her target schema. In therapy, mismatch consists of, and erasure results from, a direct, unmistakable perception that reality is fundamentally different from what one currently knows and expects reality to be.

There is one important exception to the rule that lasting change does not result from evoking a nonsymptomatic state when normally the symptom would be occurring. The exception is target learnings that consist of a learned expectation of having a strongly problematic response in a particular kind of situation. Perhaps the most common instance of this is the "fear of fear" that typically accompanies or even largely maintains phobias. In such cases there is a primary learned fear, such as a terror of bees stemming from a traumatic experience of being attacked by a swarm of bees in childhood, as well as a secondary learned, fearful expectation of suffering intense fear if a bee appears. The primary learning is the fearful expectation of being painfully stung by bees; the secondary learning is the fearful expectation of feeling terrorized by any bee. That secondary fear of fear is often the major force maintaining a phobia.

The expectation of feeling intense fear if a bee appears can be mismatched, disconfirmed, nullified and erased by using techniques that allow the person to encounter a bee in photos or imagination without feeling any fear. The absence of the expected terror is the mismatch experience. Clinically such techniques are found to dispel longstanding phobias abruptly and permanently (see, e.g., Gray & Liotta, 2012). However, guiding a therapy client into a neutral or positive emotion instead of the usual problematic emotion brings about lasting change only when the problematic emotion arises from a learned expectation of experiencing the problematic emotion, as in fear of fear. This is a special case that does not apply in the great majority of clinical cases.

Misconception 7: The Much Older Concept of Corrective Emotional Experience Already Covers Everything Now Being Described as Reconsolidation and Erasure

The familiar concept of the corrective emotional experience, introduced by Alexander & French (1946), denotes a therapy client's experiencing of something that was needed in earlier stages of development for well-being or healthy development but was missing: some new experience that could significantly undo and repair the effects produced by harmful experiences in the past. Most often this concept is applied in attachment-focused therapies, where it is typically understood as implying that the therapist's empathy and nonjudgmental acceptance can create corrective emotional experiences of interpersonal relationship that repair early interpersonal traumas and the patterns of insecure attachment learned in those ordeals.

What, then, is the relationship between the concept of the corrective emotional experience as it is widely understood, and the process of profound unlearning through memory reconsolidation? Are they the same, or are there significant differences? Is the reconsolidation framework just old wine in a new bottle?

To answer that question, we have to translate it into more specific terms: Does the guiding of a corrective emotional experience automatically and inherently include the creation of the juxtaposition (mismatch) experience that is required for erasure through memory reconsolidation?

The answer to that question is no: corrective emotional experiences do not necessarily include juxtaposition experiences. In a juxtaposition experience, the client lucidly experiences *both* the problematic original learning or schema *and* a contradictory, disconfirming new learning in the same field of awareness—not just the desired new experience by itself. In widespread clinical practice, corrective emotional experiences often consist of the desired new experience by itself.

Both therapists and clients are prone to what I have described as a counteractive tendency or reflex (Ecker, 2006, 2008; Ecker et al., 2012), an urge to avoid and suppress unwanted states of mind by building up preferred states of mind. Corrective emotional experiences are all too easily shaped by the counteractive tendency: the client's attention is fully engaged in the desirable new experience and disengaged or dissociated from the unwanted reaction or ego-state and its core schema. This disconnection from the problematic target schema during a corrective emotional experience is the very opposite of the explicit, foreground, experiential awareness of that schema that is needed for reliably guiding juxtaposition and transformational change. Corrective emotional experiences structured in that counteractive, one-sided manner can feel deeply meaningful and satisfying in the moment, but they cannot result in lasting change if the core schema underlying the problem remains intact, as it does if it is not being subjected to a juxtaposition that dissolves it. In short, as widely carried out by clinicians, a corrective emotional experience might supply the material for one side of a potential juxtaposition experience but does not inherently access and reactivate the other side—the emotional learning underlying the problem—to actually create the juxtaposition.

On the other hand, if we regard juxtaposition experiences to be the true corrective emotional experiences, then we have a definition that does inherently call for all of the ingredients needed for inducing memory reconsolidation and a lasting transformation of the emotional learning maintaining unwanted emotions, behaviors, thoughts, and somatics. A therapist who understands that reconsolidation and transformational change require juxtaposition guides a one-sided corrective emotional experience into becoming a two-sided juxtaposition experience by eliciting concurrent, direct awareness of the problematic learning that is thereby disconfirmed by the desired new experience.

For example, a client accidentally knocks over a small clock in the therapist's office and apologizes anxiously and profusely. The therapist says with a relaxed, warm smile, "It's really OK. To me that's a very small thing and not a problem at all. Little accidents like that happen for all of us, including me. Can you see that I'm not at all upset?" The client takes this in and feels much relieved to recognize that with the therapist he is safe from negative judgments, anger, humiliation, or rejection over such things. Probably most therapists would regard that as a corrective emotional experience for this person. However, if the insecure attachment learnings underlying the client's fearful apology have not yet been made conscious and explicit, this new experience is not being juxtaposed with those learnings, so transformational change is not occurring. In order for that positive new experience to help bring about transformational change, the therapist has to guide the client into experiential, embodied awareness and verbalization of the underlying target learning, such as, "Mom's rage and disgust at me for any accident or mistake mean I'm worthless if do anything wrong, and I expect anyone else to react to me that way too." Then the therapist guides a juxtaposition experience, for example by saying empathically, "All along you're expecting that anyone would go into rage and disgust at you for any little thing you do wrong, just as Mom did so many times, and yet here you're having an experience of me feeling it's really no big deal at all that you accidentally knocked over this little clock. Can you hold both of those at once, and see what that feels like?" That explicit, experiential juxtaposition gives the new experience its maximum influence toward actual unlearning and dissolution of the target learning.

New experiences that can disconfirm and dissolve existing problematic schemas arise not only in the form of the therapist's responses, but also in the course of the client's daily life, and these are fully as useful for juxtaposition as the client's experience of the therapist. (For a detailed case example, see Ecker et al., 2012, pp. 43–61.)

As a final comment on this topic of how the reconsolidation framework illuminates the concept of corrective emotional experiences, the drawbacks of the term "corrective" are worth noting. The term implies that the client's existing learnings and responses, formed in earlier life experiences, are "incorrect." However, when we bring these existing learnings into awareness and verbalization in therapy, making their content explicit, it always becomes apparent that the client's implicit emotional learning system did its job faithfully and properly in (a) forming those learnings adaptively in response to what was subjectively experienced, and (b) maintaining and utilizing those learnings ever since they were formed until the present day, however many decades that may be. Emotional implicit learnings are specially formed so as not to fade out for the life of the individual, as noted earlier. To describe a therapy client's core beliefs or schemas as incorrect, maladaptive or pathogenic is actually to accuse the process of natural selection of having those attributes, because a person's persistent beliefs and schemas exist due to the proper functioning—not the malfunctioning—of the emotional brain.

Misconception 8: To Induce Memory Reconsolidation and Erasure, Therapists Must Follow a Set Protocol Derived From Laboratory Studies

Memory reconsolidation research tells us that a well-defined sequence of experiences is required by the brain in order to destabilize a target learning and then unlearn and eliminate it: the target learning must first be reactivated into conscious awareness, then destabilized by a mismatching experience, then updated and re-encoded by new learning that nullifies it. That is a sequence of three experiences, but each is defined without reference to any particular procedure for bringing it about. Researchers and clinicians are free to devise any suitable means for creating those experiences, and the creative possibilities are unlimited. The brain does not care what concrete conditions or procedures induce those experiences. Hundreds of studies of reconsolidation have been published by neuroscientists as of this writing, and across them there is a great diversity of concrete procedures used.

Likewise, many clinical methods for guiding the critical sequence of experiences have been described by Ecker et al. (2012), who propose that the 3-step sequence is the core process shared by many different-seeming therapy systems that produce transformational change. Thus, as noted earlier, memory reconsolidation serves as a new framework of psychotherapy integration, and within that framework, the many therapies of transformational change are seen as a broad range of methods for guiding the one core process, giving clinicians great versatility in how they do so. Current neuroscience is consistent with that picture, in the sense that reconsolidation is the brain's only known process for eliminating (not merely suppressing) an established learned emotional response. Thus the view that a set protocol is dictated by the memory reconsolidation process could not be further from the reality.

Misconception 9: A Long-Standing Emotional Reaction or Behavior Sometimes Ceases Permanently in Psychotherapy Without Guiding the Steps That Bring About Erasure Through Reconsolidation, and This Shows That Reconsolidation Is Not the Only Process of Transformational Change

As implied in the previous section, various therapy systems involve concepts and methodology that make no reference to memory reconsolidation or the sequence of experiences required by the brain to induce it, yet their methodologies do result in that sequence of experiences occurring with some degree of consistency, resulting in transformational change. A close examination of the moment-to-moment process in published case studies makes the occurrence of the required steps apparent (Ecker et al., 2012, see pp. 126–155). Practitioners of such therapy systems might maintain that they have not guided those experiences when in fact they have done so. It is a well-known meme in the clinical field that how therapists conceptualize what they do, and what they actually do, are not necessarily the same.

In my own psychotherapy practice I have occasionally seen transformational change result from sessions where I did not think the key sequence had occurred. In such cases I have made a point of then engaging my client in closely examining, in hindsight, the internal events that led to the shift or breakthrough. All such hindsight enquiries have revealed that a juxtaposition experience in fact occurred serendipitously, without being recognized or verbally labeled at the time. Thus my own clinical experience suggests and upholds the hypothesis that transformational change of an acquired response is always the result of a juxtaposition experience—that is, of the reconsolidation process—even when there has been no explicit guiding of the steps required for erasure.

A memorable example of such hindsight verification of juxtaposition emerged from a colleague's case consultation. Her therapy client was a woman, aged 32 and married for five years, who was struggling with her obsessive attachment to and compulsive pursuit of the man who had been her major love through her early twenties. This problem developed after she and this man happened to cross paths again two years earlier. There had been no physical intimacy in these two years, owing solely to the man's lack of responsiveness, but the woman's emotional infidelity was significant and was causing her much guilt.

The therapist had used a number of different types of therapy for many sessions, with little or no effect on the client's heavy preoccupation with her former boyfriend. Most recently there had been several sessions in which the therapist had an uncomfortable sense of flailing and being ineffectual. Then the client came into the next session and reported that a major shift had occurred. Her preoccupation and her pursuit of this man had stopped. This breakthrough was mysterious for both client and therapist. The client could offer nothing more than to speculate, "I think what you said sunk in somehow, that when an investment goes badly, sometimes it's best to cut your losses." This referred to an offhand, momentary comment made by the therapist in the previous session, a comment that seemed more like advice than therapy. It was counteractive in nature (an attempt to build up a cognitive understanding to override the emotionally driven symptom), was not dwelt upon, and the focus of the session had moved on. Yet the client indicated that the comment had somehow led to her liberating shift.

Soon after that, the therapist consulted with me and mentioned all of this. I suggested a way for her to guide her client to look more closely into the process that had occurred internally: She could ask, "If it was new for you to hear that ending it with him could be OK even though you had an emotional investment in it from long ago, what were you previously believing or expecting about how it would *not* be OK to end it?" This would be using the disconfirming knowledge to find the constructs or schema that had been disconfirmed, which is a reverse engineering of coherence therapy's usual process of first finding the client's symptom-generating schema and then, on the basis of the details of that schema, finding vivid contradictory knowledge to create a juxtaposition experience. But when a transformational shift occurs serendipitously, it is typically the disconfirming knowledge that becomes apparent first, while the disconfirmed schema is still unknown. Subsequently the disconfirming knowledge can be used to bring the now defunct schema into explicit awareness, as I guided the therapist to do in this case.

My colleague then briefed me on what emerged when she pursued, with some persistence, the enquiry I had suggested. The offhand comment happened to reach precisely into an unconscious schema that the client now put into words by saying, "I was struggling to keep my emotional investment in that relationship from being lost because I'd really put my heart and soul into that relationship, and on some level I felt that if it ended, I'd be losing so much of myself that I would die or just be an empty shell or ghost forever. But when you said it's OK to get out of an investment even if you take a loss, all of a sudden that changed, because I saw, 'Oh—people do that all the time. It's *not* a disaster, it's just practical.' I saw that I *could* let go and lose that investment in him, and I wouldn't turn to dust."

That account points clearly to a juxtaposition experience that had formed in response to the therapist's offhand comment. The woman reported also that it was not a struggle to persist in not contacting the man, though she did feel "a quiet sadness" each time she would have contacted him but did not do so. The nonreactivation of the symptom-generating schema or ego-state and the effortlessness of remaining symptom-free are key markers of erasure and transformational change.

Thus, when the steps required for reconsolidation and erasure have not been overtly or deliberately guided in therapy and yet transformational change is observed to occur, this does not imply that a process other than reconsolidation is responsible for the change. Extensive clinical experience indicates rather that an unnoticed, nonverbalized juxtaposition experience is implicated and can probably be revealed by the type of inquiry illustrated in the example above.

Informational and psychoeducational comments made to a client in therapy tend to result in mere intellectual knowledge and therefore do not, as a rule, represent an effective method for setting up the disconfirming *experiential* knowledge required to create a juxtaposition experience. The example above shows that juxtaposition experiences can sometimes form, unbeknownst to the therapist, even in clinical situations where we would not imagine that they could do so, such as in response to an offhand, commonsense comment.

Misconception 10: Carrying Out the Steps Required for Reconsolidation and Erasure Sometimes Fails to Bring About a Transformational Change, Which Means That the Reconsolidation Process Is Not Effective for Some Emotional Learnings

In psychotherapy there are four distinct situations in which the reconsolidation process can appear to fail to produce decisive change when actually the process is not failing, but rather is not in fact taking place for some specific, identifiable reason:

1. Resistance to dissolution. In some cases, the therapist has indeed guided the sequence of experiences necessary for reconsolidation and erasure, but the target learning does not dissolve and remains in force (continues to retrigger, feel real, and produce symptoms). We will see below that in such cases, the shift is prevented by a blockage or resistance that can be cleared away, allowing dissolution to occur when the sequence is guided once again. The blockage is a separate, distinct phenomenon that does not imply a fundamental failure of the reconsolidation process.

2. Multiple symptom-generating schemas. In other cases, in response to the necessary sequence of experiences, the target learning does dissolve and no longer activates or feels real, but the symptom produced by that target learning continues to occur. This means that there is at least one other emotional learning or schema, distinct from the one that has been dissolved, that also produces the same symptom. It is common for therapy clients to present a symptom or problem that is driven by more than one emotional schema. A symptom ceases to occur only when all of its underlying emotional learnings have been nullified.

3. Nonimplementation. In other cases, the therapist believes he or she has guided the required sequence of experiences, but has not actually done so. As explained below, the necessary experiences have aspects that can be misperceived, particularly by clinicians who are relatively new to guiding this process.

4. Not based in learning. One other situation in which the reconsolidation process can erroneously appear to be failing is where the client's problem or symptom is not rooted in acquired, underlying emotional learning. This category includes autism spectrum and other conditions that have genetic causes, or purely physiological conditions such as depression caused by hypothyroidism. For dispelling or moderating such conditions, the memory reconsolidation process does not apply and should not be used, so it cannot correctly be said to fail in such cases. A very wide range of symptoms has been dispelled decisively in therapy by the reconsolidation process (Ecker et al., 2012, p. 42), which shows how pervasively emotional learnings are the underlying cause of presenting problems.

In the case of resistance to dissolution, the erasure sequence is well fulfilled by juxtaposition experiences, as required by the brain for dissolution of the target learning, and yet dissolution does not occur because it is blocked by another, distinct dynamic. The erasure of an emotional learning is the profound unlearning and dissolution of what has seemed to be a reality. For example, after dissolution of an implicit emotional learning verbalized as "Dad never talking to me or playing with me means I'm unlovable and don't matter," the individual now either has *no* way of making sense of being neglected by Dad, or realizes emotionally that "I *was* lovable and *did* matter, and yet Dad never talked to me or played with me." Such alterations of personal reality entail difficult emotional adjustments, particularly when the target learning is a core element of a deeply vulnerable area, such as primary attachment relationships, identity, or sense of justice, for example. Even if the series of experiences required for dissolution has occurred as required, dissolution is blocked by the emotional brain if the emotional consequences of dissolution do not feel tolerable, whether or not those consequences are recognized consciously.

Thus the unlearning and dissolution process is not governed by mechanistic neurological processes. Higher-order, abstract meanings that are distressing can block it. For example, many times I have seen a therapy client hold back from a liberating shift because of an accompanying realization that if the shift were to occur, it would mean that decades of life were wasted by living according to unconscious, life-choking beliefs that have turned out to be completely false. That abstract meaning of "life wasted" tends to produce initially intolerable emotional pain of grief and injustice. If any consequences of dissolution feel unworkably distressing, the dissolution is blocked.

This unconscious blockage can be understood as a self-protective response to the expected consequences of the change. The therapist considers that such resistance may be occurring when he or she is reasonably confident that genuine juxtaposition experiences have occurred (with both the target learning and contradictory knowledge experienced concurrently and vividly), yet the target learning remains in effect (continues to feel real and to generate the client's symptoms). Then the therapist's task is to guide the client gently to bring awareness to the specific distress that is expected to result from dissolution (such as disorientation, loss, grief, pain, or fear), making dissolution too daunting to allow. The expected distress itself consists of meanings, models and ego states that now become the focus of transformational change. When, as a result of this work, there is no longer any intolerable emotional consequence to dissolution, the juxtaposition experience is repeated and dissolution readily occurs.

In other words, the dissolution of any one emotional schema necessarily takes places within the whole ecology or network of interconnected meanings and models that constitute the person's experiential world, and that world may first have to be prepared so as to make the emotional consequences of dissolution tolerable and acceptable. At that point, the required sequence of experiences (which is the creation of a juxtaposition experience repeated a few times) successfully dissolves the target learning maintaining the symptom. (For a case example illustrating this process, see Ecker et al., 2012, pp. 77–86.)

Nonimplementation of the required sequence of experiences is the other situation that needs to be examined here. Nonimplementation may be the actual situation though the therapist believes mistakenly that the sequence has been fulfilled. Such cases can involve misperceptions of various kinds. One mistake of this kind consists of assuming that a particular *procedure or technique* necessarily creates a particular subjective *experience* had by the client. The brain's requirement for deconsolidating and erasing a target learning is a certain sequence of internal experiences, not external procedures or techniques. In other words, there is an important distinction between the *procedure* that is carried out visibly in the room, and the *internal phenomenology* occurring in the therapy client's subjective experience. A particular procedure intended to create the necessary experience may or may not be successful at inducing that internal experience (be it reactivation of the target learning in explicit awareness, or a disconfirming mismatch of the target learning, or the juxtaposition of the two). If the therapist does not verify the quality of the client's inner experience, he or she might assume the experience was properly created when actually it was not created by the procedure used. In that case it will appear that memory reconsolidation has failed to be effective, when in fact it was not properly induced in the first place.

The first step of the erasure sequence is the reactivation in conscious awareness of the target schema that underlies and generates the client's problem or symptom. This requires the target schema to be not only retriggered by a suitable cue, but also *present in the foreground of conscious awareness*, so that the specific set of meanings and expectations that make up the schema are lucidly and explicitly in awareness. This explicit awareness is facilitated through specifically verbalizing this material while feeling it emotionally and somatically. Such conscious reactivation requires the implicit, nonverbal target schema to be integrated into conscious awareness. Typically, however, symptom-generating schemas are fully and deeply implicit and nonconscious, and in the course of decades they are retriggered hundreds or thousands of times without becoming conscious in the least. A therapist might guide a retriggering by guiding the client to revisit imaginally a recent situation that did retrigger the schema and the symptom. The therapist might believe that this retriggering procedure has fulfilled the reactivation step, though it has not done so because the emotional reactivation of the schema is not accompanied by integrated, cognitive awareness of the specific contents of the schema. The inner experience of reactivation required for reconsolidation has not occurred, so transformational change will not result when the remaining steps are carried out. The therapist, believing all the steps to have been fulfilled, comes to the false conclusion that sometimes the reconsolidation process fails to work.

Similarly, a procedure that the therapist believes has created a disconfirming experience or vivid contradictory knowledge—the next step in the key sequence of experiences—might not have actually created the inner experience of juxtaposition (mismatch or prediction error) that the brain requires for unlocking synapses, deconsolidating the target learning. There are various ways in which a mistaken belief that a juxtaposition experience has occurred may arise. To begin with, both sides of the juxtaposition need to be richly experiential. That is, the client must be having her or his own lucid experience of the felt realness of both (a) the target schema and (b) some other personal knowledge that absolutely contradicts what the target schema "knows" or expects. Therapists may believe they are guiding a sufficiently experientially vivid state of mismatch, engaging the client's limbic system in the disconfirmation experience as is necessary, when actually the work is too cognitive and not sufficiently experiential to create a true juxtaposition experience. This too can give the impression that the process has been ineffective, when actually it has not been properly guided and the brain's requirements have not been fulfilled. The therapist, believing that the necessary conditions have been fulfilled, may conclude that the reconsolidation process has failed to work.

This was the case of a therapist who wrote to me that in his experience, he "can offer reframes, tell Ericksonian stories, etc.; [but] simply offering and juxtaposing a mismatch does not guarantee transformation." He was assuming that those techniques were creating juxtaposition experiences as required. He was defining juxtaposition by the procedure rather than by the quality of the client's inner experience. In reply I pointed out that the contradictory knowledge that creates the mismatch must be *the client's own living experience of contradictory knowledge*, not just something the client is hearing about informationally from the therapist. I mentioned also that a procedure that has successfully created an effective juxtaposition experience for one client may fail to do so for another.

Another aspect that can be misjudged by the therapist is the matter of *what* is being mismatched and disconfirmed. The target of disconfirmation needs to be a core symptom-necessitating construct, or symptom production will be unaffected by the disconfirmation. Identifying suitable target constructs requires doing a thorough job in the preparation steps of finding, making explicit, and guiding integrated awareness of the implicit learning or schema driving symptom production (the methodology for which is described in detail by Ecker et al., 2012, and Ecker & Hulley, 2011). Symptom-generating schemas often have several layers. Therapists sometimes do an incomplete job of retrieving this material into integrated awareness, and then target a relatively superficial or even tangential construct. A transformational shift will not result from a mis-targeted juxtaposition experience, but that is not a failure of the reconsolidation process to effect change. When all four of the situations described in this section are navigated skillfully, the therapeutic reconsolidation process is consistently effective in producing the distinct and verifiable markers of transformational change.

Conclusion

The profound unlearning and cessation of acquired behaviors and states of mind occurs through the process of memory reconsolidation, according to the best available scientific knowledge and as extensive clinical experience bears out. A sound understanding of memory reconsolidation is therefore a vital guide for facilitating lasting, liberating change in psychotherapy and counseling with maximum regularity. The study, practice, and effort required to arrive at a sound understanding and use of memory reconsolidation and avoid the various possible misconceptions are a price well worth paying for the clinical effectiveness gained. It is my hope that the accounts and clarifications provided in this article will help to communicate this invaluable body of knowledge to mental health practitioners everywhere.

Appendix

Understanding the Results of Schiller Et Al. (2010) in Terms of the Memory Mismatch (Prediction Error) Requirement

In neuroscience research on memory reconsolidation, the erasure of a learned fear in human subjects was first accomplished through an endogenous behavioral process by Schiller, Monfils, Raio, Johnson, LeDoux, and Phelps (2010). Previously there were at least six published studies reporting behavioral methods of memory erasure or modification in human subjects (Forcato et al., 2007, 2009; Galluccio, 2005; Hupbach et al., 2007, 2009; Walker et al., 2003). By doing the same for a learned fear—a human response of clinical importance—Schiller et al. made the relevance of memory reconsolidation to psychotherapy very clear to science journalists and the lay public, generating much interest.

Various aspects of the reconsolidation process elegantly demonstrated by Schiller et al. (2010) are of fundamental importance, as described below. However, the authors' discussion and interpretation of results did not take into account major findings that were already well documented by other researchers regarding the brain's requirement of a mismatch or prediction error experience for inducing the reconsolidation process (discussed above in the sections on Misconceptions 1 and 3). As a result, Schiller et al. discussed their successful procedure without identifying the causes of its effectiveness. In what follows, this procedure is examined and understood in terms of the broader research findings. The main purpose of this reinterpretation of the results of Schiller et al. is to promote an accurate understanding of how the reconsolidation process functions. The utilization of reconsolidation in psychotherapy can yield major advances of several different kinds (Ecker et al., 2012, 2013a), but the realization of these benefits depends on accurate understanding. The reinterpretation below also illustrates the application of the mismatch relativity principle discussed in this article's main text, as well as the necessity of "minding the findings" (Ecker, Hulley, & Ticic, in press) for understanding reconsolidation research procedures and the results of those procedures.

In the Schiller et al. (2010) study, the fear response to be erased was created by a training experience on Day 1 of the procedure. Each of the adult subjects viewed an electronic screen and saw a colored square appear for 4 s, about every 15 s, for a total of 26 times. The square was yellow 16 times, a random six of which were accompanied by a mild electric shock to the wrist. Thus the conditioned stimulus (CS) was a yellow square and the unconditioned stimulus (US) was a wrist shock. The shock occurred at the very end of the 4-s display of the square. The other 10 squares in the series were blue, were not accompanied by any shocks, and were randomly intermixed with the yellow squares. Subsequent responses to the blue squares served as the control condition in this study.

Through that training experience—a classical conditioning procedure—each subject learned, subcortically, the CS-US association of the yellow square and the unpleasant shock. As the 26 presentations progressed, by using standard electrical sensors of skin conductance the researchers detected the increasing development of an anticipatory fear response with each successive presentation of a yellow square. In this way a subcortical learned fear of yellow squares was established.

In addition to the CS-US association, the training experience contained other features that were also learned subcortically by the subjects, but were not discussed by Schiller et al. as learnings: A yellow square is not always accompanied by a shock; and whenever any colored square disappears, it is followed by a blank screen for 11 s, and then by another colored square, many times in succession.

All of those features made up the learned schema or expectation of what happened on the screen, so it was those three features that were predicted and expected by each subject's implicit emotional memory. Analyzing the results with awareness of all features of the implicit learning proves essential for understanding the erasure process and seeing the critical importance of the neglected research findings.

Each subject returned 24 hr later, on Day 2, and underwent one of three different procedures, creating three groups of subjects.

First group. For the main experimental test group, each subject viewed the electronic screen and experienced the following sequence:

1. a yellow square appearing just once, for 4 s as on Day 1, with no shock (unreinforced CS presentation); followed by

2. the images and sounds of a television show episode, lasting 10 min; then

3. a random sequence of yellow and blue squares appearing, with no shocks: 10 yellow and 11 blue squares in random order, each for 4 s every 15 s as on Day 1.

On Day 3 (24 hr later), in order to determine whether the CS (yellow square) still elicited a fear response, subjects again viewed a series of shock-free yellow and blue squares. For all subjects in this group, fear responses no longer occurred, as indicated by the skin conductance monitor. At a 1-year follow-up test, again there was no fear in response to the CS. This complete and lasting absence of responsiveness of the target learning is what is meant by saying that it had been erased by the procedure on Day 2.

Without Experience 2, the procedure on Day 2 would have been a standard multitrial extinction procedure, and the result would have been only temporary suppression of the learned fear response, not its complete and long-lasting erasure.

With Experience 2, the procedure instead induced reconsolidation and erasure, which is a qualitative difference. Schiller et al. attribute their procedure's successful erasure to the 10-min "break," as they term it, but they provide no analysis of how that time interval caused the qualitative difference. However, if the procedure is examined in terms of the mismatch requirement and mismatch relativity (MRMR) defined in the main text, the primary cause of reconsolidation and erasure that becomes apparent is not the 10-min break. The MRMR analysis is as follows.

Experience 1. Seeing the CS appear induced reactivation of the learned fear (the target learning) in the standard manner of presenting a conditioned stimulus to reactivate a conditioned response. The absence of the US was consistent with the target learning's expectation that a shock may or may not accompany a yellow square. Therefore, Experience 1 was not a mismatch (prediction error) experience, so it did not trigger destabilization and reconsolidation of the target learning (as was demonstrated by Sevenster et al., 2014, and discussed in the main text). Thus the target learning was still stable following Experience 1.

Experience 2. Seeing and hearing the TV show was immediately a mismatch experience, because the TV show was sharply discrepant with the learned expectation that what follows any square is a blank, silent screen for 11 s and then another colored square, and then more of the same in a long series. The initial training consisted of partial reinforcement of the US (shock), but it had continuous (100%) reinforcement of the blank and silent screen occurring between colored square presentations. The striking mismatch with those expected features in Experience 2 would have caused rapid destabilization (deconsolidation). This illustrates the use of a surprising novelty to create mismatch. In addition, the continuation of the TV show for 10 min would have driven updating of the destabilized target learning to expect a TV show after any subsequent CS presentation.

The TV show played for 10 min. If the screen had instead been left blank for 10 min, a timing mismatch (Díaz-Mataix et al., 2013) would have been created because the target learning expected only 11 s of blank screen before the next colored square appeared. (With the screen left blank for 10 min, the procedure would have been structurally very similar to that used with rats by Monfils et al., 2009, who reported successful erasure of a fear learning. MRMR analysis of that study is in the main text of this article.) However, the perception of TV show images and sounds would have created a mismatch experience immediately. A timing mismatch would not have developed until the next colored square appeared 10 min later, creating a recognizable interval significantly longer than the expected 3 min. This experience of a 10-min interval coming 10 min after destabilization would likely have updated the target learning to expect a 10-min interval between colored squares henceforward.

By the MRMR account, then, the mismatch experience that triggered destabilization and allowed erasure to ensue was that of the visual and audio content of the TV show, not its time duration of 10 min. MRMR predicts that a TV show duration of 11 s (no extra time) instead of 10 min would also have resulted in erasure. This MRMR analysis challenges the conclusion drawn by Schiller et al. (2010) that the time duration was responsible (p. 52): "The current results also suggest that timing may have a more important role in the control of fear than previously appreciated. . . . Our findings indicate that the timing of extinction relative to the reactivation of the memory can capitalize on reconsolidation mechanisms." (Here the labeling of Experience 3 as "extinction" seems a misnomer, since it did not produce extinction.) These considerations illustrate the utility of MRMR principles for identifying cause and effect in procedures that induce reconsolidation or extinction.

Experience 3. The series of shock-free squares, each followed by 11 s of blank screen, began with the target learning in a destabilized condition due to Experience 2. However, as discussed in the main text in examining standard multitrial extinction, initial destabilization at the start of a series of unreinforced CS presentations does not guarantee that destabilization will persist or that erasure will take place. Therefore it is necessary to examine specifically why Experience 3 did erase the learned fear in this case. The examination consists of tracing out the effects of every step of the procedure according to MRMR principles and building an account of the accumulating effects.

Here that account begins with the first unreinforced CS presentation (CS1) in Experience 1, in response to which the target learning became reactivated while remaining stable, as noted. Following this, Experience 2 destabilized the target learning by mismatching the expected blank, silent screen with a TV show. Experience 3 then began for some subjects with an unreinforced CS (CS2, yellow square with no shock) or with a blue (non-CS) square for other subjects. CS2 by itself did not constitute a mismatch of US-expectancy and did not begin to erase the target learning, for the same reason as in Experience 1, namely that from the partial reinforcement schedule during initial acquisition of the target learning, subjects learned to expect that the US might or might not occur with any given CS.

Consequently, counterlearning and erasure of the target learning would require a series of unreinforced CSs that were unmistakably more numerous than the largest number of contiguous unreinforced CSs in the original training. In the latter, a random six of the 16 yellow squares were accompanied by shock, so the largest possible number of contiguous unreinforced CSs was five. (In this first group of eight subjects, statistically the likelihood of three, four, or five contiguous unreinforced CSs occurring among them was 66%, 40%, and 22%, respectively.) Therefore, since erasure did take place, the target learning must have been in a destabilized and erasable condition after significantly more than five unreinforced CSs had occurred. The MRMR model has to account for that if it is to be consistent with the results of this study.

The absence of a US mismatch in the experience of CS2 also occurs in the standard multitrial extinction procedure and there has the effect of terminating both the subject's ongoing experience of mismatch and the state of destabilization (as described in the main text). Here, however, such termination of mismatch and destabilization would not have occurred, for this reason: Whereas in standard extinction the target learning's initial destabilization is due to a mismatch of US-expectancy by CS1, in this case the initial destabilization was due not to a mismatch of US-expectancy, but rather to a mismatch of the blank, silent screen expected between CS presentations in Experience 2. That specific experience of mismatch was not canceled or terminated when CS2 brought no new US mismatch at the start of Experience 3, so the target learning remained destabilized. Furthermore, the appearance of CS2 created a timing mismatch, as noted above. These considerations are unchanged if it was a blue square that the subject saw first in Experience 3.

Following CS2 or non-CS blue square, the appearance of a blank, silent screen would have been a mismatch experience because the target learning had been updated in Experience 2 to expect a TV show. The target learning was updated by this to expect either a blank screen or a TV show between colored squares. This mismatch maintained the destabilized state of the target learning until the third appearance of a colored square after an interval of 3 min. That 3-min interval was a mismatch of the previously updated expectation of a 10-min interval, and this timing mismatch both updated the target learning and maintained its destabilization until the fourth colored square. After the fourth colored square, however, no more mismatches would have occurred, and there would be no lingering or fresh experience of mismatch for the rest of Experience 3. If destabilization were maintained solely by mismatch experiences, destabilization would have terminated too soon for a sufficient number of CS-without-US presentations to cause erasure to occur in this procedure.

This implies that destabilization was maintained in the other possible way in the MRMR model, namely MDU (maintenance of destabilization by updating), as hypothesized in the main text. MDU would occur through a molecular signaling pathway by which the updating process maintains destabilization independently of the mismatch requirement, so that updating has sufficient time to be accomplished once it begins. The MRMR account above identifies four distinct triggers of updating prior to the fourth colored square, and that updating would have triggered MDU and maintained destabilization presumably throughout Experience 3, allowing all 10 CSs to erase the target learning with the new learning that a yellow square is always harmless. The necessity of invoking MDU in order for the MRMR framework to account for erasure in this study puts a priority on testing the MDU hypothesis empirically. That would probably require detection of the separate molecular markers of destabilization and updating after each colored square throughout Experiences 1, 2, and 3.

Second group. For a second group of subjects, Schiller et al. (2010) carried out the same procedure with one difference: On Day 2, a 6-hr delay was added after the 10-min TV show, between Experiences 2 and 3. On Day 3 the researchers then found that for these subjects, the target learning's fear response was reevocable and had not been erased. The 6-hr delay was slightly longer than the approximately five-hour duration of the reconsolidation window (Pedreira, Pérez-Cuesta, & Maldonado, 2002; Pedreira & Maldonado, 2003; Walker et al., 2003). In other words, for this group of subjects, Experience 3 was conducted after the reconsolidation window had closed. The target learning, which was destabilized in Experience 2, had reconsolidated or restabilized and was no longer susceptible to being updated and erased by the series of no-shock squares in Experience 3, so the latter now functioned as a conventional extinction training, not as an erasure learning, and created a separate learning that competed with the target learning.

Third group. For a third group of subjects, on Day 2 Experiences 1 and 2 were omitted and only Experience 3 was implemented, which was a conventional extinction training. Tests on Day 3 again showed that the target memory's fear response was reevocable and had not been erased, though it had been suppressed temporarily by extinction. This demonstrates once again the well-established fact that extinction does not yield erasure.

Experience 3 of the procedure had the familiar structure of repetitive counterlearning that has long been termed "extinction training," but when applied during the reconsolidation window for the first group of subjects, its behavioral and neurological effects differed qualitatively and radically from those of extinction, as described above. It is worth repeating here the conclusion of a study by Duvarci and Nader (2004), "Reconsolidation cannot be reduced down to facilitated extinction" (p. 9269). Yet Schiller et al. (2010) refer to Experience 3 of their procedure as an "extinction training" even for the first group of subjects, and they describe the entire 1–2–3 procedure as the "interference of reconsolidation using extinction" (p. 50), "extinction conducted during the reconsolidation window of an old fear memory" (p. 52), and "extinction training during reconsolidation" (p. 52). Using "extinction" terminology to refer to a learning experience created during the reconsolidation window to erase and replace a target learning invites much confusion and misunderstanding of the reconsolidation process. In light of the fundamental differences between reconsolidation and extinction (discussed in the section above on Misconception 3), and with a view to facilitating widespread, accurate understanding of that difference, it seems desirable to use terms that clarify rather than obscure the functional role of the learning experience in the case under consideration. Terms such as "nullification learning," "update learning" or "erasure learning" seem more appropriate for functionally labeling Experience 3 in the first group of subjects, whose learned fear was erased. (For the other two groups of subjects, the series of no-shock yellow squares in Experience 3 was true extinction training, as noted above, because it was conducted outside the reconsolidation window and was not part of a reconsolidation process. In these cases, therefore, Step 3 is appropriately termed an extinction training.)

However, the results of this study by Schiller et al. (2010) are so striking and significant that a growing number of other researchers have adopted their procedure and have retained the "extinction" misnomer (e.g., Baker et al., 2013; Clem & Huganir, 2010; Liu et al., 2014; Quirk et al., 2010; Steinfurth et al., 2014; Xue et al., 2012). With the persistence of that terminology, it is especially important to recognize that there is no inherent necessity for the erasure learning during the reconsolidation window to have the same procedural structure as conventional extinction (a series of many identical countertraining experiences). The form of erasure learnings is limited only by the creativity of researchers and clinicians (and many examples from the latter are detailed by Ecker et al., 2012; see also Högberg et al., 2011; Gray & Liotta, 2012; Xue et al., 2012).

Yet another important and elegant demonstration described by Schiller et al. (2010) concerns the memory specificity of reconsolidation and erasure. Any long-standing piece of emotional learning typically has linkages to many other learnings and memories. If the erasure process is to be clinically useful and safe in humans, it must affect only the target learning and not its network of linkages. Destabilization of a target learning without destabilizing closely associated learnings was first reported in an animal study by Debiec, Doyère, Nader, and LeDoux (2006). Schiller et al. then demonstrated with human subjects that reconsolidation can eliminate a specific implicit learning with surgical accuracy, leaving intact an adjacent learned fear that was formed in the same original experience.

This was done with a separate group of subjects who, on Day 1, underwent essentially the same initial training experience as described above except for the addition of squares of a third color I will call brown (Schiller et al. did not indicate the actual third color), 37.5% of which, as with the yellow squares, were accompanied by a shock. In that way, subjects learned to expect a shock in response to squares of two colors, yellow and brown.

On Day 2, Experience 1 of the procedure described above—memory reactivation by a single presentation of a square with no shock—was carried out with a yellow square but not with a brown square. Experience 2, the 10-min TV viewing, and Experience 3 were then implemented as described above, with Experience 3 now including no-shock presentations of squares of all three colors, for new learning that yellow and brown squares are harmless.

On Day 3, another series of no-shock presentations of squares of all three colors revealed that the fear response to yellow squares no longer occurred and had been erased, but the fear response to brown squares was reevoked and had not been erased. In other words, only the fear learning that had received a reactivation-and-mismatch prior to the new learning in Experience 3 had been erased by that new learning (though as noted, no mention of mismatch is made by Schiller et al.). The series of shock-free squares in Experience 3 served as erasure learning for the yellow squares and as an extinction training for the brown squares. The erasure of fearful expectation of a shock for squares of one color had not spread associatively to the other color, showing that the subcortical emotional memory system is capable of great selectivity and accuracy in destabilizing and revising learnings. Closely adjacent implicit memories are handled independently, as is necessary for safe clinical use of reconsolidation.

References

Agren, T. (2014). Human reconsolidation: A reactivation and update. *Brain Research Bulletin, 105*, 70–82. doi:10.1016/j.brainresbull.2013.12.010

Alexander, F., & French, T. M. (1946). *Psychoanalytic therapy: Principles and application*. New York, NY: Ronald Press.

Baker, K. D., McNally, G. P., & Richardson, R. (2013). Memory retrieval before or after extinction reduces recovery of fear in adolescent rats. *Learning & Memory, 20*, 467–473. doi:10.1101/lm.031989.113

Balderas, I., Rodriguez-Ortiz, C. J., & Bermudez-Rattoni, F. (2013). Retrieval and reconsolidation of object recognition memory are independent processes in the perirhinal cortex. *Neuroscience, 253*, 398–405. doi:10.1016/j.neuroscience.2013.09.001.

Barreiro, K. A, Suárez, L. D., Lynch, V. M., Molina, V. A., & Delorenzi, A. (2013). Memory expression is independent of memory labilization/reconsolidation. *Neurobiology of Learning & Memory, 106*, 283–291. doi:10.1016/j.nlm.2013.10.006

Boccia, M. M., Blake, M. G., Acosta, G. B., & Baratti, C. M. (2006). Post-retrieval effects of ICV infusions of hemicholinium in mice are dependent on the age of the original memory. *Learning & Memory, 13*, 376–381. doi:10.1101/lm.150306

Bos, M. G. N., Beckers, T., & Kindt, M. (2014). Noradrenergic blockade of memory reconsolidation: A failure to reduce conditioned fear responding. *Frontiers of Behavioral Neuroscience, 8*, 1–8. doi:10.3389/fnbeh.2014.00412

Bouton, M. E. (2004). Context and behavioral processes in extinction. *Learning & Memory, 11*, 485–494.

Brunet, A., Poundja, J., Tremblay, J., Bui, E., Thomas, E., Orr, S. P., . . . Pitman, R. K. (2011). Trauma reactivation under the influence of propranolol decreases posttraumatic stress symptoms and disorder: Three open-label trials. *Journal of Clinical Psychopharmacology, 31*, 547–550. doi:10.1097/JCP.0b013e318222f360

Caffaro, P. A., Suarez, L. D., Blake, M. G., & Delorenzi, A. (2012). Dissociation between memory reactivation and its behavioral expression: Scopolamine interferes with memory expression without disrupting long-term storage. *Neurobiology of Learning & Memory, 98*, 235–245. doi:10.1016/j.nlm.2012.08.003

Cammarota, M., Bevilaqua, L. R. M., Medina, J. H., & Izquierdo, I. (2004). Retrieval does not induce reconsolidation of inhibitory avoidance memory. *Learning & Memory, 11*, 572–578. doi:10.1101/lm.76804

Clark, A. (2013). Whatever next? Predictive brains, situated agents, and the future of cognitive science. *Behavioral and Brain Sciences, 36*, 181–204. doi:10.1017/S0140525X12000477

Clem, R. L., & Huganir, R. L. (2010). Calcium-permeable AMPA receptor dynamics mediate fear memory erasure. *Science, 330*, 1108–1112. doi:10.1126/science.1195298

Coccoz, V., Maldonado, H., & Delorenzi, A. (2011). The enhancement of reconsolidation with a naturalistic mild stressor improves the expression of a declarative memory in humans. *Neuroscience, 185*, 61–72. doi:10.1016/j.neuroscience.2011.04.023

de-Wit, L., Machilsen, B., & Putzeys, T. (2010). Predictive coding and the neural response to predictable stimuli. *The Journal of Neuroscience, 30*, 8702–8703. doi:10.1523/jneurosci.2248-10.2010

Debiec, J., Díaz-Mataix, L., Bush, D. E. A., Doyère, V., & LeDoux, J. E. (2010). The amygdala encodes specific sensory features of an aversive reinforcer. *Nature Neuroscience, 13*, 536–537. doi:10.1038/nn.2520

Debiec, J., Díaz-Mataix, L., Bush, D. E. A., Doyère, V., & LeDoux, J. E. (2013). The selectivity of aversive memory reconsolidation and extinction processes depends on the initial encoding of the Pavlovian association. *Learning & Memory, 20*, 695–699. doi:10.1101/lm.031609.113

Debiec, J., Doyère, V., Nader, K., & LeDoux, J. E. (2006). Directly reactivated, but not indirectly reactivated, memories undergo reconsolidation in the amygdala. *Proceedings of the National Academy of Sciences, 103*, 3428–3433. doi:10.1073/pnas.0507168103

Debiec, J., LeDoux, J. E., & Nader, K. (2002). Cellular and systems reconsolidation in the hippocampus. *Neuron, 36*, 527–538. doi:10.1016/S0896-6273(02)01001-2

Delorenzi, A., Maza, F. J., Suárez, L. D., Barreiro, K., Molina, V. A., & Stehberg, J. (2014). Memory beyond expression. *Journal of Physiology (Paris), 108*, 307–322. doi:10.1016/j.jphysparis.2014.07.002

Díaz-Mataix, L., Debiec, J., LeDoux, J. E., & Doyère, V. (2011). Sensory specific associations stored in the lateral amygdala allow for selective alteration of fear memories. *The Journal of Neuroscience, 31*, 9538–9543. doi:10.1523/jneurosci.5808-10.2011

Díaz-Mataix, L., Ruiz Martinez, R. C., Schafe, G. E., LeDoux, J. E., & Doyère, V. (2013). Detection of a temporal error triggers reconsolidation of amygdala-dependent memories. *Current Biology, 23*, 1–6. doi:10.1016/j.cub.2013.01.053

Duvarci, S., Mamou, C. S., & Nader, K. (2006). Extinction is not a sufficient condition to prevent fear memories from undergoing reconsolidation in the basolateral amygdala. *European Journal of Neuroscience, 24*, 249–260. doi:10.1111/j.1460-9568.2006.04907.x

Duvarci, S., & Nader, K. (2004). Characterization of fear memory reconsolidation. *The Journal of Neuroscience, 24*, 9269–9275. doi:10.1523/jneurosci.2971-04.2004

Ecker, B. (2003, November). The hidden logic of anxiety: Look for the emotional truth behind the symptom. *Psychotherapy Networker, 27*(6), 38–43, 58.

Ecker, B. (2006, July). *The effectiveness of psychotherapy.* Keynote address, 12th Biennial Conference of the Constructivist Psychology Network, University of California, San Marcos. Transcript: www.coherencetherapy.org/files/ecker-2006cpnkeynote.pdf

Ecker, B. (2008, September). Unlocking the emotional brain: Finding the neural key to transformation. *Psychotherapy Networker, 32*(5), 42–47, 60.

Ecker, B. (2010, January). The brain's rules for change: Translating cutting-edge neuroscience into practice. *Psychotherapy Networker, 34*(1), 43–45, 60.

Ecker, B. (2011, January 13). Reconsolidation: A universal, integrative framework for highly effective psychotherapy [Web log post]. Retrieved November 15, 2014, from http://bit.ly/1zjKtMr

Ecker, B. (2013, May). Unlocking the emotional brain: Memory reconsolidation, therapeutic effectiveness and the further evolution of psychotherapy. Keynote address, 49th Annual Conference of the California Association of Marriage and Family Therapists, Sacramento, California.

Ecker, B. (2014, July 14). Annals of memory reconsolidation: Lagging accounts cause confusion [Web log post]. Retrieved from http://www.neuropsychotherapist.com/annals-of-memory-reconsolidation-lagging-accounts-cause-confusion/

Ecker, B. (2015). Using NLP for memory reconsolidation: A glimpse of integrating the panoply of psychotherapies. *The Neuropsychotherapist, 10*, 50–56. doi:10.12744/tnpt(10)050-056

Ecker, B., & Hulley, L. (1996). *Depth oriented brief therapy: How to be brief when you were trained to be deep, and vice versa.* San Francisco, CA: Jossey-Bass.

Ecker, B., & Hulley, L. (2000). The order in clinical "disorder": Symptom coherence in depth oriented brief therapy. In R. A. Neimeyer & J. D. Raskin (Eds.), *Constructions of disorder: Meaning-making frameworks for psychotherapy* (pp. 63–89). Washington, DC: American Psychological Association Press.

Ecker, B., & Hulley, L. (2011). Coherence therapy practice manual and training guide. Oakland, CA: Coherence Psychology Institute. Online: www.coherencetherapy.org/ resources/manual.htm

Ecker, B., Hulley, L., & Ticic, R. (in press). Minding the findings: Let's not miss the message of memory reconsolidation research for psychotherapy. *Behavioral and Brain Sciences.*

Ecker, B., Ticic, R., & Hulley, L. (2012). *Unlocking the emotional brain: Eliminating symptoms at their roots using memory reconsolidation.* New York, NY: Routledge.

Ecker, B., Ticic, R., & Hulley, L. (2013a, April). A primer on memory reconsolidation and its psychotherapeutic use as a core process of profound change. *The Neuropsychotherapist, 1*, 82–99. doi:10.12744/tnpt(1)082-099

Ecker, B., Ticic, R., & Hulley, L. (2013b, July). Unlocking the emotional brain: Is memory reconsolidation the key to transformation? *Psychotherapy Networker, 37*(4), 18–25, 46–47.

Ecker, B., & Toomey, B. (2008). Depotentiation of symptom-producing implicit memory in coherence therapy. *Journal of Constructivist Psychology, 21*, 87–150. doi:10.1080/10720530701853685

Eisenberg, M., & Dudai, Y. (2004). Reconsolidation of fresh, remote, and extinguished fear memory in Medaka: Old fears don't die. *European Journal of Neuroscience, 20*, 3397–3403. doi:10.1111/j.1460-9568.2004.03818.x

Eisenberg, M., Kobilo, T., Berman, D. E., & Dudai, Y. (2003). Stability of retrieved memory: Inverse correlation with trace dominance. *Science, 301*, 1102–1104. doi:10.1126/science.1086881

Exton-McGuinness, M. T. J., Lee, J. L. C., & Reichelt, A. C. (2015). Updating memories: The role of prediction errors in memory reconsolidation. *Behavioural Brain Research, 278*, 375–384. doi:10.1016/j.bbr.2014.10.011

Exton-McGuinness, M. T. J., Patton, R. C., Sacco, L. B., & Lee, J. L. C. (2014). Reconsolidation of a well-learned instrumental memory. *Learning & Memory, 21*, 468–477. doi:10.1101/lm.035543.114

Flavell, C. R., & Lee, J. L. C. (2013). Reconsolidation and extinction of an appetitive pavlovian memory. *Neurobiology of Learning and Memory,104*, 25–31. doi:10.1016/j.nlm.2013.04.009

Foa, E. B., & McNally, R. J. (1996). Mechanisms of change in exposure therapy. In R. M. Rapee (Ed.), *Current controversies in the anxiety disorders* (pp. 329–343). New York, NY: Guilford Press.

Forcato, C., Argibay, P. F., Pedreira, M. E., & Maldonado, H. (2009). Human reconsolidation does not always occur when a memory is retrieved: The relevance of the reminder structure. *Neurobiology of Learning and Memory, 91*, 50–57. doi:10.1016/j.nlm.2008.09.011

Forcato, C., Burgos, V. L., Argibay, P. F., Molina, V. A., Pedreira, M. E., & Maldonado, H. (2007). Reconsolidation of declarative memory in humans. *Learning & Memory, 14*, 295–303. doi:10.1101/lm.486107

Forcato, C., Fernandeza, R. S., & Pedreira, M. E. (2014). Strengthening a consolidated memory: The key role of the reconsolidation process. *Journal of Physiology (Paris), 108*, 323–333. doi:10.1016/j.jphysparis.2014.09.001

Forcato, C., Rodríguez, M. L. C., Pedreira, M. E., & Maldonado, H. (2010). Reconsolidation in humans opens up declarative memory to the entrance of new information. *Neurobiology of Learning and Memory, 93*, 77–84. doi:10.1016/j.nlm.2009.08.006

Frankland, P. W., Ding, H. K., Takahashi, E., Suzuki, A., Kida, S., & Silva, A. J. (2006). Stability of recent and remote contextual fear memory. *Learning & Memory, 13*, 451–457. doi:10.1101/lm.183406

Frenkel, L., Maldonado, H., & Delorenzi, A. (2005). Memory strengthening by a real-life episode during reconsolidation: An outcome of water deprivation via brain angiotensin II. *European Journal of Neuroscience, 22*, 1757–1766. doi:10.1111/j.1460-9568.2005.04373.x

Friston, K. (2010). The free-energy principle: A unified brain theory? *Nature Reviews Neuroscience, 11*, 127–138. doi:10.1038/nrn2787

Galluccio, L. (2005). Updating reactivated memories in infancy: I. Passive- and active-exposure effects. *Developmental Psychobiology, 47*, 1–17. doi:10.1002/dev.20073

Gray, R. M., & Liotta, R. F. (2012). PTSD: Extinction, reconsolidation, and the visual-kinesthetic dissociation protocol. *Traumatology, 18*, 3–16.

doi:10.1177/1534765611431835

Hernandez. P. J., & Kelley, A. E. (2004). Long-term memory for instrumental responses does not undergo protein synthesis-dependent reconsolidation upon retrieval. *Learning & Memory, 11,* 748–754. doi:10.1101/lm.84904

Högberg, G., Nardo, D., Hällström, T., & Pagani, M. (2011). Affective psychotherapy in post-traumatic reactions guided by affective neuroscience: Memory reconsolidation and play. *Psychology Research and Behavior Management, 4,* 87–96. doi:10.2147/PRBM.S10380

Hupbach, A., Gomez, R., Hardt, O., & Nadel, L. (2007). Reconsolidation of episodic memories: A subtle reminder triggers integration of new information. *Learning & Memory, 14,* 47–53. doi:10.1101/lm.365707

Hupbach, A., Gomez, R., & Nadel, L. (2009). Episodic memory reconsolidation: Updating or source confusion? *Memory, 17,* 502–510. doi:10.1080/09658210902882399

Inda, M. C., Muravieva, E. V., & Alberini, C. M. (2011). Memory retrieval and the passage of time: From reconsolidation and strengthening to extinction. *The Journal of Neuroscience, 31,* 1635–1643. doi:10.1523/jneurosci.4736-10.2011

Jacobs, N. S., Allen, T. A., Nguyen, N., & Fortin, N. J. (2013). Critical role of the hippocampus in memory for elapsed time. *The Journal of Neuroscience, 33,* 13888–13893. doi:10.1523/jneurosci.1733-13.2013

Jarome, T. J., Kwapis, J. L., Werner, C. T., Parsons, R. G., Gafford, G. M., & Helmstetter, F. J. (2012). The timing of multiple retrieval events can alter GluR1 phosphorylation and the requirement for protein synthesis in fear memory reconsolidation. *Learning & Memory, 19,* 300–306. doi:10.1101/lm.024901.111

Judge, M. E., & Quartermain D. (1982). Alleviation of anisomycin-induced amnesia by pre-test treatment with lysine-vasopressin. *Pharmacology Biochemistry & Behavior, 16,* 463–466. doi:10.1016/0091-3057(82)90453-1

Kindt, M., Soeter, M., & Vervliet, B. (2009). Beyond extinction: Erasing human fear responses and preventing the return of fear. *Nature Neuroscience, 12,* 256–258. doi:10.1038/nn.2271

Kirtley, A., & Thomas, K. L. (2010). The exclusive induction of extinction is gated by BDNF. *Learning & Memory, 17,* 612–619. doi:10.1101/lm.1877010

Lane, R. D., Ryan, L., Nadel, L., & Greenberg, L. (in press). Memory reconsolidation, emotional arousal and the process of change in psychotherapy: New insights from brain science. *Behavioral and Brain Sciences.* doi:10.1017/S0140525X14000041.

LeDoux, J. E., Romanski, L., & Xagoraris, A. (1989). Indelibility of subcortical emotional memories. *Journal of Cognitive Neuroscience, 1,* 238–243. doi:10.1162/jocn.1989.1.3.238

Lee, C. W., Taylor, G., & Drummond, P. D. (2006). The active ingredient in EMDR: Is it traditional exposure or dual focus of attention? *Clinical Psychology and Psychotherapy, 13,* 97–107. doi:10.1002/cpp.479

Lee, J. L. (2009). Reconsolidation: Maintaining memory relevance. *Trends in Neuroscience, 32,* 413–420. doi:10.1016/j.tins.2009.05.002

Lee, J. L., Milton, A. L., & Everitt, B. J. (2006). Reconsolidation and extinction of conditioned fear: Inhibition and potentiation. *The Journal of Neuroscience, 26,* 10051–10056. *doi:10.1523/jneurosci.2466-06.2006*

Lee, S. H., Choi, J. H., Lee, N., Lee, H. R., Kim, J. I., Yu, N. K., . . . Kaang, B. K. (2008). Synaptic protein degradation underlies destabilization of retrieved fear memory. *Science, 319,* 1253–1256. doi:10.1126/science.1150541

Lewis, D. J. (1979). Psychobiology of active and inactive memory. *Psychological Bulletin, 86,* 1054–1083.

Lewis, D., Bregman, N. J., & Mahan, J. (1972). Cue-dependent amnesia in rats. *Journal of Comparative and Physiological Psychology, 81,* 243–247. doi:10.1037/h0033524

Lewis, D. J., & Bregman, N. J. (1973). Source of cues for cue-dependent amnesia in rats. *Journal of Comparative and Physiological Psychology, 85,* 421–426. doi:10.1037/h0035020

Liu, J., Zhao, L., Xue, Y., Shi, J., Suo, L., Luo, Y., . . . Lu, L. (2014). An unconditioned stimulus retrieval extinction procedure to prevent the return of fear memory. *Biological Psychiatry, 76,* 895–901. doi:10.1016/j.biopsych.2014.03.027

MacDonald, C. J., Lepage, K. Q., Eden, U. T., & Eichenbaum, H. (2011). Hippocampal "time cells" bridge the gap in memory for discontiguous events. *Neuron, 71,* 737–749. doi: 10.1016/j.neuron.2011.07.012

Mactutus, C. F., Riccio, D. C., & Ferek, J. M. (1979). Retrograde amnesia for old (reactivated) memory: Some anomalous characteristics. *Science, 204,* 1319–1320. doi:10.1126/science.572083

Mamiya, N., Fukushima, H., Suzuki, A., Matsuyama, Z., Homma, S., Frankland, P. W., & Kida, S. (2009). Brain region-specific gene expression activation required for reconsolidation and extinction of contextual fear memory. *The Journal of Neuroscience, 29,* 402–413. doi:10.1523/jneurosci.4639-08.2009

McGaugh, J. L. (1989). Involvement of hormonal and neuromodulatory systems in the regulation of memory storage. *Annual Review of Neuroscience, 2,* 255–287. doi:10.1146/annurev.ne.12.030189.001351

McGaugh, J. L. (2000). Memory: A century of consolidation. *Science, 287*, 248–251. doi:10.1126/science.287.5451.248

McGaugh, J. L., & Roozendaal, B. (2002). Role of adrenal stress hormones in forming lasting memories in the brain. *Current Opinions in Neurobiology, 12*, 205–210. doi:10.1016/s0959-4388(02)00306-9

Merlo, E., Milton, A. L., Goozée, Z. Y., Theobald, D. E., & Everitt, B. J. (2014). Reconsolidation and extinction are dissociable and mutually exclusive processes: Behavioral and molecular evidence. *The Journal of Neuroscience, 34*, 2422–2431. doi:10.1523/jneurosci.4001-13.2014

Milad, M. R., & Quirk, J. G. (2002). Neurons in medial prefrontal cortex signal memory for fear extinction. *Nature, 420*, 70–74. doi:10.1038/nature01138

Milekic, M. H., & Alberini, C. M. (2002). Temporally graded requirement for protein synthesis following memory reactivation. *Neuron, 36*, 521–525. doi:10.1016/S0896-6273(02)00976-5

Mileusnic, R., Lancashire, C. L., & Rose, S. P. R. (2005). Recalling an aversive experience by day-old chicks is not dependent on somatic protein synthesis. *Learning & Memory, 12*, 615–619. doi:10.1101/lm.38005

Milner, B., Squire, L. R., & Kandel, E. R. (1998). Cognitive neuroscience and the study of memory. *Neuron, 20*, 445–468. doi:10.1016/s0896-6273(00)80987-3

Misanin, J. R., Miller, R. R., & Lewis, D. J. (1968). Retrograde amnesia produced by electroconvulsive shock following reactivation of a consolidated memory trace. *Science, 16*, 554–555. doi:10.1126/science.160.3827.554

Monfils, M.-H., Cowansage, K. K., Klann, E., & LeDoux, J. E. (2009). Extinction-reconsolidation boundaries: Key to persistent attenuation of fear memories. *Science, 324*, 951–955. doi:10.1126/science.1167975

Morris, R. G., Inglis, J., Ainge, J. A., Olverman, H. J., Tulloch, J., Dudai, Y., & Kelly, P. A. (2006). Memory reconsolidation: Sensitivity of spatial memory to inhibition of protein synthesis in dorsal hippocampus during encoding and retrieval. *Neuron, 50*, 479–489. doi:10.1016/j.neuron.2006.04.012

Myers, K. M., & Davis, M. (2002). Behavioral and neural analysis of extinction. *Neuron, 36*, 567–584.

Nader, K. (2003). Memory traces unbound. *Trends in Neurosciences, 26*, 65–72. doi:10.1016/s0166-2236(02)00042-5

Nader, K., Schafe, G. E., & LeDoux, J. E. (2000). Fear memories require protein synthesis in the amygdala for reconsolidation after retrieval. *Nature, 406*, 722–726. doi:10.1038/35021052

Naya, Y., & Suzuki, W. A. (2011). Integrating what and when across the primate medial temporal lobe. *Science, 333,* 773–776. doi:10.1126/science.1206773

Paz, R., Gelbard-Sagiv, H., Mukamel, R., Harel, M., Malach, R., & Fried, I. (2010). A neural substrate in the human hippocampus for linking successive events. *Proceedings of the National Academy of Sciences, 107,* 6046–6051. doi:10.1073/pnas.0910834107

Pedreira, M. E., & Maldonado, H. (2003). Protein synthesis subserves reconsolidation or extinction depending on reminder duration. *Neuron, 38,* 863–869. doi:10.1016/S0896-6273(03)00352-0

Pedreira, M. E., Pérez-Cuesta, L. M., & Maldonado, H. (2002). Reactivation and reconsolidation of long-term memory in the crab *Chasmagnathus*: Protein synthesis requirement and mediation by NMDA-type glutamatergic receptors. *The Journal of Neuroscience, 22,* 8305–8311.

Pedreira, M. E., Pérez-Cuesta, L. M., & Maldonado, H. (2004). Mismatch between what is expected and what actually occurs triggers memory reconsolidation or extinction. *Learning & Memory, 11,* 579–585. doi:10.1101/lm.76904

Pérez-Cuesta, L. M., & Maldonado, H. (2009). Memory reconsolidation and extinction in the crab: Mutual exclusion or coexistence? *Learning & Memory, 16,* 714–721. doi:10.1101/lm.1544609

Phelps, E. A., Delgado, M. R., Nearing, K. I., & LeDoux, J. E. (2004). Extinction learning in humans: Role of the amygdala and vmPFC. *Neuron, 43,* 897–905. doi:10.1016/j.neuron.2004.08.042

Piaget, J. (1955). *The child's construction of reality.* London: Routledge and Kegan Paul.

Pine, A., Mendelsohn, A., & Dudai, Y. (2014). Unconscious learning of likes and dislikes is persistent, resilient, and reconsolidates. *Frontiers in Psychology, 5*(1051), 1–13. doi:10.3389/ fpsyg.2014.01051

Pittenger, D. J., & Pavlik, W. B. (1988). Analysis of the partial reinforcement extinction effect in humans using absolute and relative comparisons of schedules. *American Journal of Psychology, 101,* 1–14.

Przybyslawski, J., Roullet, P., & Sara, S. J. (1999). Attenuation of emotional and nonemotional memories after their reactivation: Role of beta adrenergic receptors. *The Journal of Neuroscience, 19,* 6623–6628.

Przybyslawski, J., & Sara, S. J. (1997). Reconsolidation of memory after its reactivation. *Behavioural Brain Research, 84,* 241–246. doi:10.1016/S0166-4328(96)00153-2

Quirk, G. J., Likhtik, E., Pelletier, J. G., & Pare, D. (2003). Stimulation of medial prefrontal cortex decreases the responsiveness of central amygdala output neurons. *The Journal of Neuroscience, 23*, 8800–8807.

Quirk, G. J., Paré, D., Richardson, R., Herry, C., Monfils, M. H., Schiller, D., & Vicentic, A. (2010). Erasing fear memories with extinction training. *The Journal of Neuroscience, 30*, 14993–14997. doi:10.1523/jneurosci.4268-10.2010

Reichelt, A. C., & Lee, J. L. C. (2013). Memory reconsolidation in aversive and appetitive settings. *Frontiers of Behavioral Neuroscience, 7*, 1–18. doi:10.3389/fnbeh.2013.00118

Reichelt, A. C., Exton-McGuinness, M. T., & Lee, J. L. (2013). Ventral tegmental dopamine dysregulation prevents appetitive memory destabilisation. *The Journal of Neuroscience, 33*, 14205–14210. doi:10.1523/ jneurosci.1614-13.2013

Rescorla, R. A., & Wagner, A. R. (1972). A theory of Pavlovian conditioning: Variations in the effectiveness of reinforcement and nonreinforcement. In A. H. Prokasy (Ed.), *Classical conditioning II: Current research and theory* (pp. 64–99). New York, NY: Appleton-Century-Crofts.

Richardson, R., Riccio, D. C., & Mowrey, H. (1982). Retrograde amnesia for previously acquired Pavlovian conditioning: UCS exposure as a reactivation treatment. *Physiology of Psychology, 10*, 384–390.

Rodriguez-Ortiz, C. J., De la Cruz, V., Gutierrez, R., & Bermidez-Rattoni, F. (2005). Protein synthesis underlies post-retrieval memory consolidation to a restricted degree only when updated information is obtained. *Learning & Memory, 12*, 533–537. doi:10.1101/lm.94505

Rodriguez-Ortiz, C. J., Garcia-DeLaTorre, P., Benavidez, E., Ballesteros, M. A., & Bermudez-Rattoni, F. (2008). Intrahippocampal anisomycin infusions disrupt previously consolidated spatial memory only when memory is updated. *Neurobiology of Learning and Memory, 89*, 352–359. doi:10.1016/j.nlm.2007.10.004

Roozendaal, B., McEwen, B. S., & Chattarji, S. (2009). Stress, memory and the amygdala. *Nature Reviews Neuroscience, 10*, 423–433. doi:10.1038/nrn2651

Rossato, J. I., Bevilaqua, L. R. M., Medina, J. H., Izquierdo, I., & Cammarota, M. (2006). Retrieval induces hippocampal-dependent reconsolidation of spatial memory. *Learning & Memory, 13*, 431–440. doi:10.1101/lm.315206

Rossato, J. I., Bevilaqua, L. R. M., Myskiw, J. C., Medina, J. H., Izquierdo, I., & Cammarota, M. (2007). On the role of hippocampal protein synthesis in the consolidation and reconsolidation of object recognition memory. *Learning & Memory, 14*, 36–46. doi:10.1101/lm.422607

Roullet, P., & Sara, S. J. (1998). Consolidation of memory after its reactivation: Involvement of ß noradrenergic receptors in the late phase. *Neural Plasticity, 6*,

63–68. doi:10.1155/np.1998.63

Rubin, R. D. (1976). Clinical use of retrograde amnesia produced by electroconvulsive shock: A conditioning hypothesis. *Canadian Journal of Psychiatry, 21,* 87–90.

Rubin, R. D., Fried, R., & Franks, C. M. (1969). New application of ECT. In R. D. Rubin & C. Franks (Eds.), *Advances in behavior therapy, 1968* (pp. 37–44). New York, NY: Academic Press.

Santini, E., Ge, H., Ren, K., de Ortiz, S. P., & Quirk, G. J. (2004). Consolidation of fear extinction requires protein synthesis in the medial prefrontal cortex. *The Journal of Neuroscience, 24,* 5704–5710. doi:10.1523/jneurosci.0786-04.2004

Santoyo-Zedillo, M., Rodriguez-Ortiz, C. J., Chavez-Marchetta, G., Bermudez-Rattoni, F., & Balderas, I. (2014). Retrieval is not necessary to trigger reconsolidation of object recognition memory in the perirhinal cortex. *Learning & Memory, 21,* 452–456. doi:10.1101/lm.035428.114

Sara, S. J. (2000). Retrieval and reconsolidation: Toward a neurobiology of remembering. *Learning & Memory, 7,* 73–84. doi:10.1101/lm.7.2.73

Schiller, D., Monfils, M.-H., Raio, C. M., Johnson, D. C., LeDoux, J. E., & Phelps, E. A. (2010). Preventing the return of fear in humans using reconsolidation update mechanisms. *Nature, 463,* 49–53. doi:10.1038/nature08637

Schiller, D., & Phelps, E. A. (2011). Does reconsolidation occur in humans? *Frontiers of Behavioral Neuroscience, 5,* 1–18. doi:10.3389/fnbeh.2011.00024

Schore, A. N. (2003). *Affect dysregulation and disorders of the self.* New York, NY: W.W. Norton.

Sekiguchi, T., Yamada, A., & Suzuki, H. (1997). Reactivation-dependent changes in memory states in the terrestrial slug *Limax flavus. Learning & Memory, 4,* 356–364. doi:10.1101/lm.4.4.356

Sevenster, D., Beckers, T., & Kindt, M. (2012). Retrieval per se is not sufficient to trigger reconsolidation of human fear memory. *Neurobiology of Learning and Memory, 97,* 338–345. doi:10.1016/j.nlm.2012.01.009

Sevenster, D., Beckers, T., & Kindt, M. (2013). Prediction error governs pharmacologically induced amnesia for learned fear. *Science, 339,* 830–833. doi:10.1126/science.1231357

Sevenster, D., Beckers, T., & Kindt, M. (2014). Prediction error demarcates the transition from retrieval, to reconsolidation, to new learning. *Learning & Memory, 21,* 580–584. doi:10.1101/lm.035493.114

Sibson, P. & Ticic, R. (2014, March). Remembering in order to forget. *Therapy To-*

day, 25(2), 26–29.

Siegel, D. J. (2006). An interpersonal neurobiology approach to psychotherapy. *Psychiatric Annals, 36,* 248–258.

Soeter, M., & Kindt, M. (2011). Disrupting reconsolidation: Pharmacological and behavioral manipulations. *Learning & Memory, 18,* 357–366. doi:10.1101/lm.2148511

Steinfurth, E. C. K., Kanen, J. W., Raio, C. M., Clem, R. L., Huganir, R. L., & Phelps, E. A. (2014). Young and old Pavlovian fear memories can be modified with extinction training during reconsolidation in humans. *Learning & Memory, 21,* 338–341. doi:10.1101/lm.033589.113

Stollhoff, N., Menzel, R., & Eisenhardt, D. (2005). Spontaneous recovery from extinction depends on the reconsolidation of the acquisition memory in an appetitive learning paradigm in the honeybee (*Apis mellifera*). *The Journal of Neuroscience, 25,* 4485–4492. doi:10.1523/jneurosci.0117-05.2005

Suzuki, A., Josselyn, S. A., Frankland, P. W., Masushige, S., Silva, A. J., & Kida, S. (2004). Memory reconsolidation and extinction have distinct temporal and biochemical signatures. *The Journal of Neuroscience, 24,* 4787–4795. doi:10.1523/jneurosci.5491-03.2004

Toomey, B., & Ecker, B. (2007). Of neurons and knowings: Constructivism, coherence psychology and their neurodynamic substrates. *Journal of Constructivist Psychology, 20,* 201–245. doi:10.1080/10720530701347860

Toomey, B., & Ecker, B. (2009). Competing visions of the implications of neuroscience for psychotherapy. *Journal of Constructivist Psychology, 22,* 95–140. doi:10.1080/10720530802675748

Tronson, N. C., & Taylor, J. R. (2007). Molecular mechanisms of memory reconsolidation. *Nature Neuroscience, 8,* 262–275. doi:10.1038/nrn2090

van der Kolk, B. (1994). The body keeps the score: Memory and the evolving psychobiology of posttraumatic stress. *Harvard Review of Psychiatry, 1,* 253–265. doi:10.3109/10673229409017088

Walker, M. P., Brakefield, T., Hobson, J. A., & Stickgold, R. (2003). Dissociable stages of human memory consolidation and reconsolidation. *Nature, 425,* 616–620. doi:10.1038/nature01930

Winters, B. D., Tucci, M. C., & DaCosta-Furtado, M. (2009). Older and stronger object memories are selectively destabilized by reactivation in the presence of new information. *Learning & Memory, 16,* 545–553. doi:10.1101/lm.1509909

Wood, N. E., Rosasco, M. L., Suris, A. M., Spring, J. D., Marin, M.-F., Lasko, N. B., . . . Pitman, R. K. (2015). Pharmacological blockade of memory reconsolidation in posttraumatic stress disorder: Three negative psychophysiological studies. *Psychiatry Research, 225,* 31–39. doi:10.1016/j.psychres.2014.09.005

Xue, Y.-X., Luo, Y.-X., Wu, P., Shi, H.-S., Xue, L.-F., Chen, C., . . . Lu, L. (2012). A memory retrieval-extinction procedure to prevent drug craving and relapse. *Science, 336,* 241–245. doi:10.1126/science.1215070

Bruce Ecker, MA, LMFT, is co-originator of Coherence Therapy, co-director of the Coherence Psychology Institute, and coauthor of *Unlocking the Emotional Brain: Eliminating Symptoms at Their Roots Using Memory Reconsolidation*; the *Coherence Therapy Practice Manual and Training Guide*; and *Depth Oriented Brief Therapy.* He is in private practice in Oakland, California, gives clinical trainings internationally, and has taught graduate courses for many years. Clarifying how lasting, transformational change takes place has been the theme of Bruce Ecker's clinical career. He has contributed extensive innovations in concepts and methods of experiential psychotherapy, and has driven the clinical field's recognition of memory reconsolidation research and how it translates into new capabilities of consistent therapeutic effectiveness and psychotherapy integration. For more information, visit www.CoherenceInstitute.org.

INDEX

Topics & Researchers

The Neuropsychotherapist

We are your online source for news and information about the emerging field of Neuropsychotherapy and its community of professionals.

We aim to bring together researchers and practitioners in this multi-disciplinary field to share their latest findings and experiences.

Subscribe for exclusive access to the heart of our project: our monthly eMagazine. Feature articles from leading experts, news, reviews, and department columns on a wide range of subjects relevant to the progressive psychotherapist and integrative health care professional. While a member you have access to the complete archive of Members Only material including all of our magazine issues.

The Neuropsychotherapist eMagazine is presented as a digital online version and a downloadable PDF. These are interactive PDFs, so you can turn off the "image" layers to print just the text if you are reading the magazine in Adobe Reader. All feature articles are also presented as separate PDFs in A4 format for you to download and print.

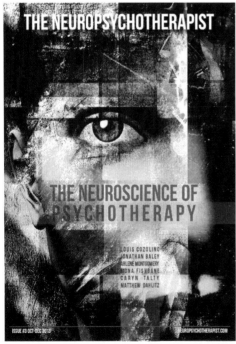

Access to additional stand-alone articles(monographs) that are not visible to the general public. Also blog articles, news, reviews, opinion pieces, and more that are invisible to non-members. When you log in to the site, all of the hidden material will be available to you for as long as you have an active membership. For more details on membership benefits, see the comparison tables below.

When you consider all these features for as low as $8/quarter*, we believe it's amazing value for money!

NEUROPSYCHOTHERAPIST.COM

182

Bruce Ecker, Robin Ticic, & Laurel Hulley

Unlocking the Emotional Brain

Eliminating Symptoms at Their Roots
Using Memory Reconsolidation

"Ecker's, Ticic's, and Hulley's Unlocking the Emotional Brain, like some earlier classics, draws from, adapts, and integrates the very best of the best currently available concepts and techniques into a powerful and accessible psychotherapeutic method. What sets this book apart is how these elements are mixed, matched, and delivered to each individual client. Packaged in a highly engaging read, psychotherapists of all sorts will find many resources which will enhance as well as ease their work."

—**Babette Rothschild**, MSW, LCSW, author of The Body Remembers: The Psychophysiology of Trauma and Trauma Treatment

Unlocking the Emotional Brain
Eliminating Symptoms at Their Roots
Using Memory Reconsolidation

Psychotherapy that regularly yields liberating, lasting change was, in the last century, a futuristic vision, but it has now become reality, thanks to a convergence of remarkable advances in clinical knowledge and brain science. In Unlocking the Emotional Brain, authors Ecker, Ticic and Hulley equip readers to carry out focused, empathic therapy using the process found by researchers to induce memory reconsolidation, the recently discovered and only known process for actually unlocking emotional memory at the synaptic level. Emotional memory's tenacity is the familiar bane of therapists, and researchers have long believed that emotional memory forms indelible learning. Reconsolidation has overturned these views. It allows new learning to erase, not just suppress, the deep, unconscious, intensely problematic emotional learnings that form during childhood or in later tribulations and generate most of the symptoms that bring people to therapy. Readers will learn methods that precisely eliminate unwanted, ingrained emotional responses—whether moods, behaviors, or thought patterns—causing no loss of ordinary narrative memory, while restoring clients' well-being. Numerous case examples show the versatile use of this process in AEDP, Coherence Therapy, EFT, EMDR, and IPNB.

INTERNATIONAL JOURNAL OF
NEUROPSYCHOTHERAPY

IJNPT

The International Journal of Neuropsychotherapy (IJNPT) is an open-access, online journal that considers manuscripts on all aspects of integrative biopsychosocial issues related to psychotherapy. IJNPT aims to explore the neurological and other biological underpinnings of mental states and disorders to advance the therapeutic practice of psychotherapy.

Visit www.neuropsychotherapist.com/submissionscall/

for more information on submitting articles, letters and research notes.

www.neuropsychotherapist.com/journal/